ARGENTINA: ECONOMIC, POLITICAL AND SOCIAL ISSUES

ARGENTINA: ECONOMIC, POLITICAL AND SOCIAL ISSUES

JEANNE B. HAVERLAND
EDITOR

Nova Science Publishers, Inc.
New York

For permission to use material from this book please contact us:
Telephone 631-231-7269; Fax 631-231-8175
Web Site: http://www.novapublishers.com

LIBRARY OF CONGRESS CATALOGING-IN-PUBLICATION DATA

Argentina: economic, political, and social issues / Jeanne B. Haverland, editor.
p. cm.
Includes bibliographical references and index.
ISBN 978-1-60456-469-3 (hardcover)
1. Argentina--Social conditions--1983- 2. Argentina--Economic conditions--1983- 3. Argentina--Politics and government--2002- I. Haverland, Jeanne B.
HN263.5.A7557 2008
982.07--dc22

2008009221

Published by Nova Science Publishers, Inc. ; New York

CONTENTS

PREFACE

Argentina, officially the Argentine Republic is a South American country, constituted as a federation of twenty-three provinces and an autonomous city. It is second in size on the continent to Brazil and eighth in the world. Argentina occupies a continental surface area of 2,766,890 km^2 (1,068,302 sq mi) between the Andes mountain range in the west and the southern Atlantic Ocean in the east and south. It is bordered by Paraguay and Bolivia in the north, Brazil and Uruguay in the northeast, and Chile in the west and south. The country claims the British controlled territories of the Falkland Islands (Spanish: Islas Malvinas) and South Georgia and the South Sandwich Islands. Argentina also claims 969,464 km^2 (374,312 sq mi) of Antarctica, known as Argentine Antarctica, overlapping other claims made by Chile and the United Kingdom.

Argentina has the highest Human Development Index level and Gross Domestic Product (GDP) per capita in purchasing power parity in Latin America. The country is currently classified as an Upper-Middle Income Country by the World Bank, or as a secondary emerging market. Argentina's nominal GDP is the 31st largest economy in the world.

This new book concentrates on the latest economic, political and social issues of Argentina.

Chapter 1 - Although the *globalizing* dynamics has had more or less close historical precedents, and even remote, at the end of the twentieth century achieved a new meaning. Beyond its significance in the intercommunications, and with regard to cultural factors that induced to the vision of a “world society”, the dissolution of the Soviet Union gave it a specific direction. By the nineties, the previous belief in the emergence of a *global village*, in spite of assuming polysemic aspects (legal, political, technical), was strongly impacted by the "fall of the Berlin Wall". The neoliberal strategies, started in the previous decade by the governments of the United States and Great Britain, were thrown to numerous countries from different continents. The power world centres tried to impose, in the whole world, a political-institutional model based on the figure of the representative democracy, together with a mercantile economic conformation *freed* of the state regulations. The extreme ideological framework, in conformity with that conjuncture, consisted of the theories diffusion about the hypothetical "end of the history", based on the apparent extinction of those doctrines that did not accept, unconditionally, the primacy of the mentioned model, looking for the validity of a realistic, pragmatic and unquestionable *only thought*. In this sense, the globalization means, in fact, the purpose of globalizing the neoconservative proposals, applied to the sociopolitical and economic restructuring.

The fundamental features that characterize this new expansive stage of capitalism are referred to the indiscriminate opening of the economic systems and national markets, as long as such arrangement does not affect to the interest of the most powerful countries. This results in the dismantlement of the protectionist and regulatory state policies, what has favored a huge increase in the international trade. Together with the expansion of the financial markets, a territorial reorganization of the productive activities and the interpenetration of the industrial processes are developed, systematically avoiding the frontiers among States and continental limits. Also the mobility of the capitals and production factors on a world-wide scale is encouraged for the sake of the unconditional achievement of comparative advantages, based on continuous technological innovations and on the labor costs reduction, that increase the levels of entrepreneurial competitiveness.

The constitution of the companies in *network* systems, under the technical aegis of the flexible specialization in the industrial manufacture procedures, goes with an inclination to the unemployment increase in most of nations, while decreases the average remuneration of the labor force, according to its historical parameters. Furthermore, we are witnessing a gradual interdependence among productive locations with heterogeneous socio-economic structures, sometimes geographical and culturally very separated mutually, and some inclination to the creation of regional "development" poles, sometimes temporary or relating to the moment. Otherwise, a trend to the markets formation unified through sub-continental *blocks* exists, whose efficiency is in correspondence with the evolution level of their own economies. Finally, in different areas of the planet, and even in the "first world" countries, proliferate situations of labor force overexploitation, especially the migrated active population from their indigenous places, in different sectors of the production.

Chapter 2 - The objective of this study is to reach an understanding of the problems that confront families burdened by the care of an elderly person with health problems. To this end, the authors approached key participants in "Caring for Those Who Care," a Buenos Aires City Government program. Basing our study on this organization, we interviewed family caregivers who have participated in the program. We worked with a sample of caregivers composed of spouses, sons and daughters, sons- and daughters-in-law, and grandchildren. The group of caregivers as well as the group of dependents includes participants of both genders; this permitted us to obtain a spread of cases ranging widely with regards to generation, to gender, and to familiar relationship; from these cases emerged the key issues in the caregiver´s situation to which we refer in this chapter.

The study focused on the City of Buenos Aires. The demographic structure of this capital city of the Republic of Argentina marks it as the country's most aged city, given that 22% (609,466) of its population is made up of people of 60 or more years of age.

Previous research conducted by this team (Oddone, 2001) indicates that 5% of the elderly population receives special care in a family setting. The Caring for Those Who Care data, which permits a general characterization of its attendees, indicate the following: that 88% of the caregivers are women, that 80% are over 50 years of age, that 60% spend more than 5 hours per day with the person in need of care, and that 72% carry out the caregiving duties on a daily basis.

In Argentina, and in particular in the city of Buenos Aires, various programs designed to help family caregivers have been implemented. These programs range from the formation of gerontological assistance to a program that proposes care for the family caregivers themselves. In between are found domestic internment, 24-hour attention centers, and retirement homes, among others. But the reach of these programs′ efficacy remains quite far from meeting demands, just as our interview subjects – who have been left alone in responding to the needs of their sick elderly and without hope of finding any help other than their own personal and family recourses -- prove. It seems to the authors that it is not the creation of new programs that is needed but rather their universality, seeing as the existing programs have had little chance to be assessed, given their limited reach. The problems of family caregivers will become solvable when the protective function of the state is reexamined, and the fact taken into account that the aging process is a phenomenon that modifies a society in its needs and demands.

Chapter 3 - Since the early 1990s, many developing countries have experienced economic crises following the liberalization of their capital accounts. These crises, often caused by the volatility of short term capital movements have had far-reaching effects, spreading from the financial sector to the real sector and then to socioeconomic indicators. The crises in individual countries have also had adverse effects in other countries, threatening the stability of the whole international financial system. 1994 Mexican, 1997 East Asian, 1998 Russian, 1994 and 2000-2001 Turkish and 2002 Argentinean crises have attracted the most attention in this respect.

The vast literature on economic crises has mainly concentrated on their causes and impact on the financial and the real sectors. The effects of crisis on income distribution, poverty, and the labor market, public expenditure on social sectors such as health and education, and indeed the whole social fabric of society which can be referred collectively as the socioeconomic effects have remained largely unexplored. The main objective of this study is to redress this imbalance in the context of three countries, Indonesia, Argentina, and Turkey, worst hit by economic crises in recent years.

Socioeconomic effects arise from a combination of many factors beyond those directly traceable to economic crises. Among these other factors the most noteworthy are the reaction of the public to the crisis and the attitude of domestic governments and key Bretton Woods institutions (BWI) like the World Bank and the IMF. These institutions which have played a major role in the neoliberal transition of a large number of developing countries during the past quarter century have often been in the forefront in the design of post-crisis economic programs. The fact that both Turkey and Argentina were caught in crisis in the midst of an IMF program makes it all the more important to examine the reaction of BWI.

Against this background, the study attempts to answer the following questions. What are the major socioeconomic effects of economic crises? What determines the magnitude of these effects and their pattern in different countries? Why is a comprehensive and active social policy package often missing from the post-crisis structural adjustment and stabilization programs? Which factors are likely to bring about a change in the attitude of domestic governments and the BWI toward more active social policies in the post-crisis setting?

Several factors have bedeviled our efforts to present a full account of the socioeconomic effects. Effects such as the deterioration of social relations, the rise in corruption and violence, despair and helplessness of individuals and society at large in the face of increasing dependency on external resources and institutions are not easy to quantify and document. The effects that are quantifiable, on the other hand, pertain to indicators for which available data is the most deficient. Finally, there is an acute lack of information about the relations between the countries in crisis and the BWI.

The study consists of five sections. In the following three sections, socioeconomic effects of the crises in Indonesia, Argentina and Turkey are analyzed in that order. The last section concludes.

Chapter 4 - This chapter has been planned and structured on the basis of common ideas present in definitions of lifelong learning. In it, the main aspects and characteristics of Argentina's situation will be exemplified. The context will be the hardships that the democratic process has gone through - and is still going through - in the search for its consolidation. Such a context will help to understand the social movements called upon to contribute to a more participative democracy. Non-governmental organisations have perceived education as the driving force that will contribute to solving the existing deficiencies.

The educational system, in its formal and non-formal modalities, and with its particular contents, plays an influential role so that lifelong learning may become gradually consolidated and may be regarded by the citizens as a satisfier fulfilling various needs.

The main topics upon which this chapter will pivot are: the background to Argentina's situation; Argentina's educational system; education as satisfier; the role of NGO's: a case study; and leisure time and lifelong learning.

Chapter 5 - Rural development begins in Argentina together with the restoration of democracy in the 1980s, but the first actions only started to be developed in the 1990s. Since then, different programs have followed and overlapped. These programs are precisely the purpose of our study.

This paper discusses the resultant rural strategies of the main rural development programs of Argentina in the context of the neoliberal macroeconomic adjustment. It identifies its institutions and analyses whether the actions that are being carried out are suitable or not, and if the assistance to help the rural poor (promoted by international financing organisms) is feasible in face of the negative impact of the neoliberal policy over the small and medium farmers. Besides, this paper looks into and develops questions about the suitability of local and provincial institutional structures for satisfying the institutional demands of rural development programs.

The author's starting point is the macroeconomic transformation of the 1990s, which affected the agricultural activity and brought about permanent processes of re-structuring and de-structuring of the public and private institutions linked with rural development management.

Chapter 6 - This work considers the importance of ethics in the practice of psychology. Within this general framework, this paper takes into account the central role that human rights take in the main professional ethic codes of psychology in Argentina, like in many other ethic codes from other countries. The particular inclusion of these topics in Argentinean ethic codes of psychology is analyzed in this case not only as the inclusion of general ethical principles that guarantee personal and community welfare. It is specially considered that the permanent direct or indirect reference to human rights in those Codes is related to the '70 dictatorial government that, as in many other Latin-American countries, established a terror system, in which personal and social rights were seriously damaged, causing a deep wound in society.

Chapter 7 - In the fragile environment of Southern Patagonian with limited opportunities for economic diversification, the predominant socioeconomic activities have focused on stock breeding in rural areas, and public services in urban ones. This particular investigation seeks to study specific actions, which relate to the agricultural conditions of the province of Santa Cruz.

Some of the processes that can contribute to this province's economic growth are: the public organizations and intervening communities' actions, and the producers' capability for innovation, decision-making and regulation. Thus, this investigation seeks to reflect on the positive and negative aspects that influenced both public and private organizations' activity, level of commitment and identity. It focuses on the organizations orientated to promoting local development and considerations of an environmental and cultural nature.

Chapter 8 - Since 1991, Argentina has had a rigid meontary system bazsed on as currency board. Althought this policy tamed the country's hyperinflation, a prolonged recession, external economic shocks, and growing fiscal deficit have exposed its limitations as a policy tool, leading to a seemingly intractable debt problem. Argentina has rescheduled its financial obligation and reportedly sought assistance from the International Monetary Fund (IMF), including the $21.5 billion stand-by agreement of March 10, 2000. Speculation in the world markets over Argentina's now limited and painful options further undermines its credibility to orchestrate a smooth outcome, increasing fears of another round of regional or global financial turmoil that could adversely affect a variety of U.S. trade and financial interests.

Because of prolonged economic problems, Argentina's President Fernanado de la Rua called for his country to begin a "voluntary debt swap" in November 2001, exchanging $60 billion of government bonds for lower interest rate debt to free up some $4 billion in interest payments. To encourage bondholders to participate, new debt payments are to be guaranteed by future tax revenues. Argentina argues that this will reduce risk levels sufficiently to warrant the lower interest rate and to consider the exchange voluntary. Bondholders, however, argue that, between the lower value of the new debt and the implication that failure to restructure will result in nonpayment, the swap is a "distressed exchange" and hence, effectively a default; The IMF, after augmenting Argentina's standby credit twice during 2001, has remained silent this time. Argentina is straggling to maintain its currency board, enact some type of economic stimulus plan, achieve a zero deficit, and make payments on debt. The debt restructuring is the latest, and perhaps last, attempt to strike this difficult balance.

In: Argentina: Economic, Political and Social Issues
Editor: Jeanne B. Haverland
ISBN 978-1-60456-469-3

Chapter 1

SOCIAL CONSEQUENCES OF THE GLOBALIZATION PROCESS IN ARGENTINA: ANALYSIS OF THE SPECIFIC SITUATION IN THE GRAN BUENOS AIRES

Juan Labiaguerre

INTRODUCTION

Although the *globalizing* dynamics has had more or less close historical precedents, and even remote, at the end of the twentieth century achieved a new meaning. Beyond its significance in the intercommunications, and with regard to cultural factors that induced to the vision of a "world society", the dissolution of the Soviet Union gave it a specific direction. By the nineties, the previous belief in the emergence of a *global village*, in spite of assuming polysemic aspects (legal, political, technical)[1], was strongly impacted by the "fall of the Berlin Wall". The neoliberal strategies, started in the previous decade by the governments of the United States and Great Britain, were thrown to numerous countries from different continents. The power world centres tried to impose, in the whole world, a political-institutional model based on the figure of the representative democracy, together with a mercantile economic conformation *freed* of the state regulations. The extreme ideological framework, in conformity with that conjuncture, consisted of the theories diffusion about the hypothetical "end of the history", based on the apparent extinction of those doctrines that did not accept, unconditionally, the primacy of the mentioned model, looking for the validity of a realistic, pragmatic and unquestionable *only thought*. In this sense, the globalization means, in fact, the purpose of globalizing the neoconservative proposals, applied to the sociopolitical and economic restructuring[2].

---

[1] Whereas in the sphere of the international law it has been attempted to eliminate the frontiers delimiting the sovereign spaces, corresponding to the different States, trying to implant a "universal jurisprudence", the huge progress of the cybernetics has led to some theoretical trends to suggest the advent of an *information era*.

[2] In view of this dogmatism, any minimal questioning of the supposed *inevitability* of that unidirectional development used to be qualified as "utopian or anti-system". On the other hand, the growing protests of the

The fundamental features that characterize this new expansive stage of capitalism are referred to the indiscriminate opening of the economic systems and national markets, as long as such arrangement does not affect to the interest of the most powerful countries. This results in the dismantlement of the protectionist and regulatory state policies, what has favored a huge increase in the international trade. Together with the expansion of the financial markets, a territorial reorganization of the productive activities and the interpenetration of the industrial processes are developed, systematically avoiding the frontiers among States and continental limits. Also the mobility of the capitals and production factors on a world-wide scale is encouraged for the sake of the unconditional achievement of comparative advantages, based on continuous technological innovations and on the labor costs reduction, that increase the levels of entrepreneurial competitiveness.

The constitution of the companies in *network* systems, under the technical aegis of the flexible specialization in the industrial manufacture procedures, goes with an inclination to the unemployment increase in most of nations, while decreases the average remuneration of the labor force, according to its historical parameters. Furthermore, we are witnessing a gradual interdependence among productive locations with heterogeneous socio-economic structures, sometimes geographical and culturally very separated mutually, and some inclination to the creation of regional "development" poles, sometimes temporary or relating to the moment. Otherwise, a trend to the markets formation unified through sub-continental *blocks* exists, whose efficiency is in correspondence with the evolution level of their own economies. Finally, in different areas of the planet, and even in the "first world" countries, proliferate situations of labor force overexploitation, especially the migrated active population from their indigenous places, in different sectors of the production.

1. Analysis of Argentina Particular Case

From the mentioned international scene, the *employment issue* in this country shows a peculiar situation, due to its previous evolution until the sixties, in contrast with the backwardness of a large part of Latin America. Having reached a high social integration of the working masses, and a remarkable expansion of its middle classes, in an increasing mobility context, it experiences in the beginning of the new millennium a deep economic crisis, reflected in the socio-occupational sphere. This circumstance gave rise to the gradual polarization of its social strata, generated by the permanent regression in the distribution of the national wealth.

Argentina shared the occupational mutation, in an intercontinental scale, due to the declivity of the Fordist model of productive relationships and Welfare States. This combined process, from the seventies, was functional for the globalization of the neoliberalism that, with regard to the *labor universe*, meant a deterioration of the socioeconomic conditions of massive groups in the world-wide population. That is, the progressive formation of a "global" productive and commercial space, maintained with the creation of consumption and

different protest movements, facing to the new order, with dissimilar levels of radicalism and opposed to the rigid implementation of "global" institutions and procedures, lately are having the support of the most diverse sectors and groups from the programmatic point of view.

occupational markets increasingly connected mutually, led to the degradation of the integral quality of life of a large proportion of the societies, in most of the nations.

This situation generates an omnipresent threat of employment loss, because of the continuous remodeling of the labor demand, or salary decreases, derivatives from the *turbulent* monetary contingencies in the change and financial world markets. Therefore, the country was not indifferent to the imposition of new flexible types of employment[3]. In that sense, it can be said that the "late modernity" *appears as the temporary threshold in which an expansion of the endless options and other one correlative of risks is produced* (Beriain: 1996, 8-9)

The national decadence was rushed from coup d'état in March 1976, that established a violating of human rights dictatorship, which repressed any critique or opposition attempt to the new military regime[4]. This favored the restructuring of the labor market, determinant of a growing inequity in the income perception, beginning also to dismantle the social security system. The government *de facto* implemented a series of economic mechanisms in advance of the strategy carried out during the neoliberal peak in the eighties: the promulgation of the "law of financial entities", that introduced the deregulation principles of this activity, already incipiently expressed in the advanced economies; putting into practice the privatisation premise in areas of the public-state sector; the monetary and change policies implementation in order to control the inflationary process, that derived in a strong overvaluation of Argentina currency; the external indebtedness as a means of diminishing the fiscal deficit and constituting stocks to support the struggle against the inflation; the reduction of the customs protection, in order to supply of cheaper capital goods, increase the range of consumption goods and increase the competitiveness in the inner market; and neutralization of union demands to avoid the nominal ascent of the remunerations to the inflationary pace, though this lessened in certain phases, reducing consequently the real salaries of the workers.

The economic plan of the unconstitutional regime contained the seeds of the program that would be implemented, under the democracy life and having an explicit and firm consensus of the "new international order", through the presidential management of Carlos Menem, in the last decade of the century. The prevailing model during the twenty-five years passed from the political-institutional breaking of dictatorship, beyond certain partial rectifications that maintained -in essence- its operation, applied a *dual* plan by transferring resources to the minority "modern sector" of the productive structure, through their subtraction from the rest of the economic agents, marginalized of the new hegemonic market, rigorously selective. About this, it can be asserted that "the social exclusion leads to the societal dualization, not only in function of enjoying or not the citizen condition [...], but also in the deep transformation of work as determinant of the social situation and position of an individual [...] The work no longer guarantees the integration in the social structure, providing a level and life style appropriate to its location in the social scale, induces to insecurity and alienation.

---

[3] In this aspect, the relaxation of the time devoted to the labor activity, and the spaces where it is carried out, *modify the limits between work and non-work*. Furthermore, the advance of the microelectronic, currently, let link the companies with the consumers through renewed methods, in a framework where unemployment on a large scale is a new social form of underutilization of labor force, factor *integrated* to the labor spectrum (Beriain: 1996, 14).

[4] The measures taken by it are the prelude of the systematically applied economic policies, already in the height of the "neoliberal globalization", since nineties. That precedent meant the reorganization of the productive body, favoring the interests of the agro-exporting landowner sector, the financial circles and the importing companies of industrial inputs and all kind of consumption items.

The dualization is produced not only in terms of social class, but also generational, spatial..." (Solé: 1998, 264).

As a result of the mentioned process, the country fell in a recurrent productive recession, accompanied of parallel deficits in the fiscal tributary collection, and cyclical imbalances in the commercial balance. The reduction of the macroeconomic growth indices, or G.D.P. (Gross Domestic Product), although in some stages that indicator had positive rates, affected the different segments of the society in a diverse way[5].

Simultaneously to the generalized decadence of the income and investment, privileged economic groups, benefited by the validity of the new redistribution strategy, concentrated fast power and capital, due to the indicated wealth transfer. We can indicate that the mentioned change was based on a deep question of the previous state action, intensely *active and participant*, becoming the absolute back of that policy, through the assignment of the main responsibility, in the productive organization of the society, to the own values of the arrangements, agreements and managements of the private institutions.

The whole nation, meanwhile, was losing on the sphere of the comparative advantages of its local production, within readjustment imposed by the parameter of the "global" competitiveness. On this matter, it is clear that *the world society is neither unitary nor homogeneous: on the contrary, it is crossed by huge varieties, practically in all its regions and activity fields*. Its emergence "also means an interpretation of different populations [...] There are no varieties without inequalities. What the *globalization* process has specially emphasized is the land division among affluent countries [...] and poor countries, or in process of progressive impoverishment -peripheral to the first ones-, and so the tensions among the different regions in the world have increased..." (Giner: 1999, 256-257)

The inequity increase in the socioeconomic conditions in Argentina can be verified through the officially carried out measurements, that allow to compare the changing proportion in the income perception, by the 10% richest of the country and the 10% with a deeper poverty level, through the Table I, that demonstrates the relative quantity of times of that indicator among the mentioned polarized groups, during the last fourth of the century[6]. In that sense, data of years separated by more than two decades have been considered in order to try to prove an outstanding trend in the middle term.

The growing distributive inequality process obeys, to a great extent, to the modification of the occupational situation, whose crucial expression is based on the occupational precariousness, being its clearest proof the unemployment increase[7]. For example, the variation of the unemployment rate can be verified, in the urban area, during most of the eighties and nineties, through the indices shown in Table II[8]. This period coincides with a decisive crossroads in the mutation of the socio-political world order, which meant an

[5] It is necessary to emphasize that, even in those years when the GDP increased, unemployment also did so and the existing gap among different groups was broadened, in the allotment of the general goods produced in a national scale.

[6] Data taken from the successive searches carried out by the INDEC (National Statistics and Censuses Institute), Economy Ministry, Buenos Aires, Argentina, 1974-2001

[7] The unemployment is not only due to technological changes, but a heap of complex factors, mutually involved, and its continuation allows to have a panoramic vision of the dimension of the transformations in the whole labor spectrum.

[8] The exposed data are partially from the period 1983-1998, a time featured by the return -and gradual consolidation- of democratic institutions. The measurement includes the government of Raúl Alfonsín, of the Radical Civic Union, and most of the two consecutive managements of the president Carlos Menem, of the Justicialista Party.

inflection point in the international economy, when numerous governments, as it has been referred previously, applied neoliberal programs[9].

Table I: Proportional Quantity of Income Among the Richest Tenth Part and the Poorest Same Percentage in Argentina Population[10]

Year	
1974	8.0
1975	12.3
1997	22.0
2001	26.4

Source: National Statistics Institute and Censuses (INDEC), Economy Ministry of the Nation (Argentina)

Table II: Unemployment Rates by Activity Sphere in the Metropolitan Area[11] (Units: percentages)

	1983 Apr/Oct	1984 Oct/Apr	1985 May/Oct	1986 May/Oct	1987 Apr/Oct	1988 May/Oct	1989 May/Oct	1990 May/Oct
Industry (a)	4.0/1.6	3.0/3.4	6.0/5.2	.../4.4	5.2/5.5	6.2/5.8	8.5/6.1	9.2/5.8
Construction	10.1/8.4	12.1/8.0	13.2/13.7	.../11.1	10.9/10.8	12.0/13.1	12.5/18.4	20.6/13.6
Trade	3.7/3.6	4.2/3.5	4.4/3.8	.../4.5	5.1/5.2	5.6/4.5	6.8/5.6	6.4/5.8
Services (b)	4.0/2.7	2.6/2.4	3.5/3.7	.../3.6	4.5/4.1	4.7/3.9	4.6/4.3	5.4/3.2

	1991 Jul/Oct	1992 Oct/Apr	1993 May/Oct	1994 May/Oct	1995 May/Oct	1996 May/Oct	1997 May/Oct	1998 May
Industry (a)	5.2/5.2	6.5/6.7	9.7/9.0	10.1/13.5	19.5/15.6	17.8/17.0	13.3/13.5	11.4
Construction	13.9/6.2	12.7/14.7	18.9/16.2	20.5/22.2	37.0/32.9	34.4/32.1	31.5/26.9	28.0
Trade	4.7/3.5	4.4/3.5	8.5/6.9	8.4/12.2	18.9/16.1	15.1/14.8	14.5/14.0	12.1
Services (b)	3.4/3.3	4.1/5.3	7.1/6.8	8.1/8.2	13.3/12.6	13.0/14.3	12.9/10.9	9.3

Source: National Statistics and Censuses Institute (INDEC), Economy Ministry of the Nation (Argentina), and Economic Commission for Latin America (CEPAL), based on data of the first one.

---

[9] In the beginning of the eighties, the "crisis of the debt" had a great impact on the economy of the country. In particular, due to the high level of indebtedness, the disintegration of its industrial productive body and the generation of certain trend to the commercial deficit. Furthermore, international demand of primary products showed a strong weakening, being reflected in a considerable fall of their prices; this helped to a narrowing of the dimension of the inner market. In that way, the national capacity to generate currencies was notably reduced; meanwhile, as a consequence of the growing increase in the purchases of elaborated products from abroad, the output of currencies had been substantially increased. The external restriction meant, therefore, a conditioning key factor of the economic policy.

[10] The two first indicators reflect the instance preceding the mentioned military coup, showing the abrupt beginning of the increase in the "gap" polarizing the mentioned distributive plan. On the other hand, the final numbers pair testifies the results, in the same direction, near the end of the millennium.

[11] Percentage of unemployed people, in the urban spaces, belonging to the economically active sector population. Notes: [a] manufacturing branch of the industrial sector; [b] communal, social and personal items of the service sector.

In the mentioned table the evolution of the unemployment rate is observed in different sectors of Argentina economic-productive structure in its urban areas. If the total lapse of sixteen years is divided, in an arbitrational way, by the average percentage of four consecutive four-year sub-stages, the rising development of this index can be verified. This occurs instead of some interruptions, partial and/or short, of that constant and sustained inclination. The increase in the mentioned average figure reached superior levels in the industrial sector, scaling up from 3.9% (1983-1986), to 6.5% (1987-1990), 8.2% (1991-1994) and 15.4% (1995-1998), that is, the unemployment, in the whole manufacturing spheres, practically was quadrupled, taking into account the total period considered by this measurement.

With regard to the building industry sector, featured itself by a high level of occupational instability and social security vulnerability, the signs of a larger relative deterioration of its situation are evident, since from the beginning of the analyzed stage existed a high level of unemployment, lightly over 10%. In this item, the average percentages of unemployment reached 11.0%, 14.0%, 15.7% and 27.9%, successively, according to the indicated partial periods. In relation to the commercial activity, the average of the unemployment rate is 4.0%, 5.6%, 6.5% and 13.2%, respectively. Finally, about the services sector, the indices show a peculiar behavior, due to the oscillatory, and considerable, variations, in certain years included in the general period. In the whole area, with various and heterogeneous types of benefits, the data indicate an unemployment of 3.2%, 4.3%, 5.8% and 10.8%, successively. Because of the complex composition of this last sector, the mentioned indexes have to be analyzed in the context of the widespread dynamics of *tertiarization* of the economic activities. In short, the sector increases of the unemployment are verified in Table III, through approximate percentages, considering the extreme years of 1983 and 1998.

Table III: Sectorial Increase of Unemployment in Argentina (1983-1998)

Sectors and branches of Argentina economy	Percentage increase of unemployment rate
Industry	395%
Construction	253%
Trade	330%
Services	337.5%

Source: elaborated by the author, from published data by the National Statistics and Censuses Institute (INDEC), Economy Ministry of the Nation (Argentina)

The broad adoption, in the nineties, of a neoconservative policy, by the *Menemist* government, had as origin the economic and socio-political transformations occurred in the country during the military dictatorship (1976/1983), and the failure of the democratic government of the Radical Civic Union (1983-1989). This last public management was unable to control the advance of the related sectors to the direction of the previous regime de facto, in the wide framework of the current conditions in the world sphere. In this planetary and national scene, considering "the wide consensus that was emanating from the traumatic hyperinflationary experience of 1989 and 1990, in 1991 started a new liberalizing experience with the Convertibility Plan" (Cimillo: 1999, 178). This economic program favored a deepening of the commercial and financial liberalization, the free conversion of Argentina monetary unit (peso) at a fixed and reduced exchange rate (equivalent to an American dollar), agreements for the payment of the external debt and the privatization of the public companies. These economic policies constituted crucial instruments directed to reach the anti-inflationary goals in a short term, but they also sustained a macroeconomic reorganization with a longer temporary extent.

That new stage meant the application of a strategy that modified several basic aspects of the socio-productive structure of the country. The deepest transformation was about the role of the State, changing its influence on the power relationships, being modified the relative pre-existing balance between the public and private sectors in the operation of the goods markets. This determined that the privatizations process became a key element of the emerging model, being abandoned one of the distinctive features of Argentina conventional economic, that is, its mixed condition.

The privatization policy derived in a huge enrichment of the economic groups taking part in it, due to the low price paid by them for the liquidated assets and, sometimes, to the subsequent resale of the bought companies. These obtained more profitability than when they were in operation, due to the prices rules established for the produced goods. That circumstance would mean, later, the extraction of an important part of profits from Argentina, caused by the growing penetration of foreign transnational companies, which, as is well-known, usually take out most of benefits provided by their activities from the countries where they operate.

We can state that most of the public companies were sold to transnational entities to reduced values and without any legal conditions that protected from normative regulation mechanisms of their action, which was finally discretionary, and even abusive. On the other hand, the currencies obtained through these liquidations were partially devoted to the amortization of the external debt, although its total amount continued increasing. In fact, the result was the transition from the implementation of policies based on a meaningful intervention of the State, to other ones guided by the slogan of *laissez faire*, with a neoliberal direction[12].

The outlined economic evolution showed deep social repercussions: in relation to the distribution of the national wealth, the fall of the real salaries and the occupational precariousness gave rise to the increase in the gross profits in the labor force exploitation, favoring clearly to the capital factors. The indirect tributary imposition with regressive character, transferred to the final prices of the products offered in the consumption market of goods and services, generated a remarkable reduction of the income received by a great part of the active population, favoring the power imbalance in the relationships between entrepreneurs and workers. These showed, furthermore, the decrease in the employed people, due to the productive restructuring, and a generalized backward of the negotiation capacity of the trade unionism[13]. Furthermore, the change generated by the restructured macroeconomic

---

[12] The reasons mentioned to justify the change, from the economic point of view, were: 1) to increase the average labor productivity; 2) to achieve the prices stability and a sustained growth of the *per capita* production of goods and services; 3) to overcome the chronicle difficulties of the balance of payments; 4) to constitute a capitals market and to allow the free access of Argentina companies to the international markets of goods as well as financial; 5) to reestablish the full operation of the prices system, so that this could carry out the efficient assignment of the productive resources and the maximization of the usefulness in the consumption sphere.

[13] The mutation of the productive body in a national scale answered, among other reasons, to the decrease of manufacturing establishments, the certain activities disappearance, the procedures adoption that reduced jobs through the increase in the working day, and the extension of the hidden employment.

scene, in the composition of the informal labor force, is an essential datum that explains the *flexible* adaptation of the employment informality to the successive production and commercial cycles. The intolerance of the "open economy" toward the jobs with a low productivity meant an obstacle for the redundant workers absorption by the independent activities. In that way, the economic viability of the autonomous work was also diluted (Cimillo: 1999, 179).

To reach a conclusion, we must add that the overvaluation of the national currency allowed the appropriation of a considerable proportion of the inner market by the cheapest foreign commodities offer, together with a smaller share of the national production in the foreign markets. Since the internal gross investment was less than required in order to achieve the increase in the labor productivity and to balance in this way the disparities typical of an overvalued exchange rate, that contributed to maintain a weak occupational demand and salary levels in continuous decrease.

2. The Deterioration of the Occupational State and the Growing Impoverishment Process

The decline of Argentina socio-economic situation is due to a series of reasons of internal order, overlapped to international determining factors, typical of the fin-de-siècle stage of "globalization". Among the first ones, we can mention the characteristic institutional instability of the last two and a half decades, together with the high levels of corruption in the common intrigues, in the public administration as well as in the private entrepreneurial activity. In the matter, it can be mentioned, as representative examples, the nationalization of the voluminous external debt contracted by a concentrated circle of private sectors and the subsidies allowed to certain spheres of industry arbitrarily selected.

In the first half of the nineties, some growth of the industrial gross product was shown, narrowly linked to an increase in the average occupational productivity in that sector[14]. This last factor was based on the labor force expulsion of the companies, while the evolution did not give rise to salary increases of the employed staff but, on the contrary, during this stage a fall in the average workers' income is verified. The increase in the productivity of the labor force, as well as the salary decrease, helped to emphasize the backwardness in the inner income distribution, mechanism that –at the same time- allowed to finance a concentration and centralization process of the economic power.

In the *informational capitalism* era is possible to distinguish several juxtaposed mechanisms of progressive social fragmentation. On the one hand, the increase in the inequality, polarization, poverty and misery processes answer to the own dominance of the "relationships of distribution-consumption", which mean a growing differential appropriation of the collectively generated wealth. At the same time, it is favored a dynamics that tends to the labor individuation, the occupational overexploitation, the social exclusion and the

[14] Facing that enclosed and situational industrial growth, the figures about proportional growth of the tertiary sector of Argentina economy are eloquent: while in 1980 meant 53% of the GDP, in the year 2000 that index reached 63%. The tertiarization and desindustrialization processes, in that aspect, contrast with the differential features of the most advanced economies.

perverse integration[15], series of elements referred to the "socio-productive relationships" sphere. Both fields must be discriminated, in empirical-analytical terms, in order to establish their causal interconnection, with the goal –at the same time- of understanding the unbalanced and inequitable operation of the so-called *global society* (Castells : 1998, 96-97)

One of the determinant items in which the economic policy of Argentina government was focused during the last decade of the last century consisted of the successive legal reforms of the labor market. The effects of these measures, together with the increase of the non-salaried occupations, as compelled exit of the active population in order to face unemployment, favored the fact that the national labor situation adopted some of the typical features of some historically underdeveloped Latin American countries. The increasingly inequitable mechanisms are referred to a double source: on the one hand, the marked distancing in the income levels obtained according to the different occupational categories; on the other hand, the growing disparity in the payments received by the wage-earners who carry out related activities, even in the same productive sphere, but who are employed in different companies. Toward the end of the recently concluded millennium, the phenomenon called as "reflexive modernization" *disintegrates and substitutes the cultural assumptions of the social classes by individualized forms of the distributive inequity*[16]. This circumstance involves that "the dimness of the perception of the social classes is going together with a deepening in social inequality, which is not permanently fixed in clearly identified social strata, but it is temporary, spatial and socially disseminated" (Beck: 1996, 242).

When the configuration of the different socio-labor strata is observed according to income levels, it is verified that the changes in the occupational spectrum of Argentina are the basic originators of the own alterations of the general structure in the society. Likewise, the *technical* changes of the labor universe, during the last fourth of the twentieth century, show a reciprocal interdependence with a set of parallel sociopolitical transformations. During the nineties the degradation in the situation of most of Argentina workers was stressed: the unemployment reached very high indices, increasing furthermore the underemployment and, in an apparently paradoxical contrast, also the over-employment of the decreasing employed labor force. Meanwhile, the precariousness and vulnerability of the occupational insertions tend to become chronic, even taking into account the future in a middle term, due to the accentuation perspective of the legal-juridical reforms of the labor market. Furthermore, the effects of the re-distributive dynamics are favored, featured by a deep regression polarizing life conditions extremely, due to the fact that the social groups with lower occupational qualifications have blocked the access to a stable employment and/or enough salary for their elemental sustenance, even on successive generational levels. Consequently, those people who still maintain a relatively steady occupation, whether salaried or self-employed, are threatened with its loss. That forces them to multiply the occupational efforts for preserving their income.

---

[15] This term refers to a typical labor mechanism of the globalized criminal economy, in the context of the "network society", and to its growing interdependence with the political institutions and the commercial and productive circuits characteristic of the *informal spaces*.

[16] The process of "labor individualization" implies that the contribution to the productive work is defined, specifically, for each worker, and taking into account only their individual contributions, being salaried or autonomous activities, governing the figure of the particular contract, deregulated to a great extent. That practice becomes gradually customary, in an emblematic way, in the urban informal sectors of the peripheral societies, although it also has force *in fact* in certain labor markets corresponding to developed economies.

Among the complex variables determining the evolution of the occupational area, the incorporation of renewed technologies of industrial production is outstanding, what involves massive staff dismissals, with their consequent socioeconomic impacts. In Argentina case, this gives rise to a question of the commitments that, traditionally, had achieved an institutionalization of the right to work and, specifically, the codification of the socio-juridical statute of the labor force[17]. This dynamics means a regression of the salary relationship - formal and regular- as well as the state *interventionism*, considered as complementary factors, as a result of the crisis in the preexist capitalistic regulation plan in the national sphere. These mentioned changes gave rise to the employment instability, originated in new occupational insertion ways for a definite time, in order to reduce the labor costs, avoiding the employers' organizations some contributions to the social security system, the holidays with pay acknowledgment, the compensation payment by activity suspension and the responsibility in case of contingent accidents of the workers.

The described scene shows a world situation in which "the social State loses some action possibilities facing the commercial State since, very often, has to limit its social actions in order to balance the monetary unbalances carried out by the price –and speculation- game of the foreign exchange in an international level (...) The tyranny of the finance markets, chaotic and destructive, imposes public policies essentially monetarist, but for (most) of the countries is not an autonomous or sovereign monetarism, but (another kind) subordinate and remedying –usually at the expense of cutback of any chance of expansion or social redistribution- of the most uncontrollable effects of the international monetary movements and storms" (Alonso: 1999: 113-114).

In those Argentine urban agglomerations in which in May 1995 was carried out the Permanent Households Survey (INDEC), the unemployment rate reached in that date 18.6%, at the same time that the total of labor segments with *employment problems*, what includes furthermore hidden unemployment situations, underemployment -visible or hidden- and activities in the "underground" economy, was evaluated in figures over the half of the workers, only in metropolitan zones[18]. The persistence of a high unemployment rate is just a side of the whole labor issue. The official indicators demonstrate that the unemployment and underemployment, as a whole, were affecting (in the second half of the nineties) to about three million and a half workers, that were the fourth part of the active population in urban areas, calculated in approximately 13 million people. On the other hand, the segment of the labor force working more than 45 hours per week surpasses 40% of the whole employed people[19]. The overexploitation of the labor force is shown by those "labor agreements that allow capital to retain systematically the payments/resources distribution, or to impose to

[17] That process blocks, or prevents directly, the access of large masses of population to the protection of the social security institutions, worsening the social experiences of vulnerability and impoverishment, situations that in our days includes furthermore to large middle class and qualified workers segments, conventionally protected under the coverage of the Welfare State. Most of these two last sectors are also affected by the insufficiency of their income and the progressive decay of their purchasing power.

[18] INDEC (National Statistics and Censuses Institute), Economy Ministry, Buenos Aires, Argentina, 1974-2001

[19] INDEC (National Statistics and Censuses Institute), Economy Ministry, Buenos Aires, Argentina, 1974-2001. With regard to the last mentioned segment, the effects of the market deregulation and the lack of state controls help to the jobs existence whose working time are over twelve hours a day, allowing that the supplementary time will be remunerated as simple and, in some cases through inferior amounts, due to changes in the calculation method corresponding to the "extra" time worked.

certain types of workers harder conditions than those in the norm/regulation in a labor market determined in a concrete time and space" (Castells: 1998, 97-98)

The course of the contemporary political and macro-social problematic explains the transformations of the rejection or social exclusion mechanisms, in the current Argentine reality, showed by the emergence of new sectors of population with scarce perspectives of incorporation to the "modern" and extremely selective labor market. These people are located in the periphery of the prevailing economic system, controlled by the meshes of the power which is supported on the commercial, financial, technological and occupational globalization process. In that sense, the social exclusion can be understood as the *process through which the access to positions allowing an autonomous subsistence is systematically hindered to some individuals and groups within the social levels determined by values and institutions in a certain context.* Specifically this stage, "in the network-society, affects to people as well as territories [so that] in some conditions, countries, regions, cities and entire neighborhoods remain excluded, including [...] most, or all their population" (Castells: 1998, 98-99)

The structural, and chronicle, impoverishment in the inner part of Argentina sends us to a far past; however, in our days, due to the destruction of the regional economies by the indiscriminate commercial opening and the lack of state regulation of the economic and social development, the degradation of the income of the poorest fifth part of the population in the provinces makes comparable it with similar figures, corresponding to the most backward nations of the planet, according to the data observed in table IV.

Table IV. Per Capita Income of the Poorest 20% of Population of Different Countries and of Argentine Regions or Provinces (Year 1998)

Income of the poorest 20% Countries and Argentine regions or provinces (*) Per capita income/Year (dollars)[20]	
Bangladesh	613
(*) Gran Catamarca/Mendoza	600
Brazil	564
India	537
(*) Santiago del Estero	516
(*) Gran S M Tucumán	468
Nepal	464
(*) Gran Resistencia (Chaco)	408
(*) Salta	396
Nigeria	357

(*) Countries and Argentine regions or provinces

Source: Economic Commission for Latin America (CEPAL): "Panorama Social de América Latina 1998"

[20] Economic Commission for Latin America (CEPAL): "Panorama Social de America Latina 1998", Introduction by Eduardo Gudynas.

On the other hand, in the country thousands of children are carrying out labor activities, so child work develops the role of a renewed "reservation army", devoted to certain activities that demand scarce or no qualification[21]. In reference to this issue, it is right mentioned that *the main labor issue in the information era is not the end of work, but the condition of the workers* (Castells: 1998, 176). Although the under-age workers proportion in rural areas overcomes the one in the urban areas, from the increase of the clandestine employment, that phenomenon has also meant a characteristic of the large cities. This is due to the easiness that implies for the employer the unlimited possibility of assigning them more exploitative work conditions, compared with those imposed to the adults[22]. The extreme poverty, or destitution, in the under-age population will derive in indelible expressions of social marginalization in the future: the early feeling of humiliation, together with the lack and multiple privations during the infancy and adolescence, lead to the reproduction of the general conditions of very poor existence in the adulthood, with few probabilities of obtaining decent labor insertions.

The indicated panorama is inserted in a world context in which, while the evolution of the social inequity inside each nation has changed, "what seems to be a global phenomenon is the increase in the poverty and, above all, the extreme poverty [at the same time that] the acceleration of the unequal development and the simultaneous incorporation and exclusion of the peoples in the growth process [...] is translated in a polarization and extension of the misery to an increasing number of people" (Castells: 1998, 106).

As well as the outlined labor stage helped to the expansion of the impoverishment to a national scale, and to the increase in its level, the society groups economically better placed tend to compensate the negative effects, caused by the productive recession, through a greater relative appropriation. That is, with regard to the repercussion of the successive crisis and respective adjustment programs, a process is fed back through which the so-called *economy modernization*, that implies the progress of certain privileged segments of the population, involves necessarily the massive marginalization[23].

In the framework of deterioration in the income levels, and the consequent quality of life of a large part of the society, it did not take place a "compact and organized" downward movement of some social strata, but worked an articulated dynamics formed by sharp changes, simultaneous and dissolving, inside various strata of the population. Two coexistent mechanisms acted in that direction, which transformed the social structure. On the one hand, a *polarization* was given rise due to the concentration of the highest economic power groups, facing the opposed increase of gradually impoverishment sectors. On the other hand, a stratified *heterogeneity* appeared, caused by the fall of the income of many groups of the

---

[21] "Informe Argentino sobre Desarrollo Humano", elaborated in the meetings carried out in the Senate of the Nation: Buenos Aires, National Congress, 1999.

[22] It is necessary to indicate that the thousands of children and teenagers "on the street" receive some kind of income through illegal and/or marginal tasks, taking into account the fact that almost the whole of them are -in different ways- exploited by informal organizations that transgress the current legislation in all its levels. That is, "a large number of children [participates] in activities generating income linked with the criminal economy, especially in the drug traffic, small thefts and the organized begging" (Castells: 1998, 177)

[23] Furthermore, instead of palliating the ominous consequences of those impacts on the general welfare, the social policies followed a coherent strategy with the essence of the imposed neoliberal model, determined by the regressive strategy, in terms of the distributive equity, inherent to the changes underway .

conventionally considerate as "middle class", making up in this way an extremely diversified scene of the impoverishment expressions[24].

Nowadays, more than half of Argentina employed workers perceives a salary lower to US$ 500 per month; furthermore, there are, in total, about four million people unemployed of underemployed. Since 1997 the unemployment rate remained *stabilized* around a "level" of 15% but, however, the percentage of population immersed in the poverty carried on increasing. This phenomenon is explained, to a great extent, by the emergence of "new poor", who integrate those *type-families* (couple with two children) whose members perceive, in total, less than US$ 480 per month for their general maintenance, when the cost of living meeting the set of expenses of these domestic groups reaches US$ 1,050[25]. The variation of this indicator obeys to the income fall, more than to the inactivity, and the extension of the groups placed under that *poverty line* is related to the deepening of the economic crisis at domestic level, emphasized by the productive recession started in the second half of the nineties.

In Argentina, toward the end of the last century, about 30% of its total population, about eleven million inhabitants, was living under the mentioned poverty line. These impoverished sectors belong, mostly, to "middle" social segments, which have their elemental needs (housing, town hall and urban infrastructure and essential public service) satisfied but, without having stopped their activity, they have suffered a remarkable degradation of their labor situation, beginning with a restriction in their remunerations. That is, the downward mobility process, carried out in these impoverished groups of the society, exceeds the unemployment problem, since numerous familiar groups whose *head* is in fact employed do not get to resolve the cost of the mentioned basic products basket, because of the loss in their labor remunerations. Taking into account the indicated changes, it can be stated that, "above all, since the economic aspect started to be essential, the globalization develops, creates or exasperates the oppositions between poor and rich or dominating. The impoverishment is an evil until now almost unavoidable of the globalizations. In fact, these have violated not only the cultures but also the history" (Le Goff: 2001). To sum up, the economic-financial globalization mechanisms tend to stress the heterogeneity of the social structures, giving rise to inequalities that distort the productive, labor and socio-cultural contexts previously in force, in occasions built throughout an extended historical period.

3. The Socioeconomic Transformations in the Gran Buenos Aires

The current labor situation in this urban agglomeration is characterized by an extended, and persistent, unemployment that affects to a large proportion of "family heads" and numerous groups of radically marginalized teenagers from the labor market, whose pitiful

[24] In other words, the whole impoverished groups have become multi-faceted, insofar as to the *structural poor*, that are those with unsatisfied basic needs, groups previously located in intermediate positions are added, although in economic and social decadence situation perceiving decreasing remunerations by their labor activity, estimate as "new poor", whose internal constitution also shows differentiations.

[25] *La situación económica: el golpe a la clase media,* in the newspaper "Clarín", November 23rd 2001 (Report of the consultant "Equis", submitted to the Second Industrial Conference, organized by the UIA - Argentine Industrial Union - in November 2001)

situation is closely related to the insufficiency in their qualification and/or educational levels. Those women who are forced to look for a job, because of they have to compensate the loss in the domestic income or due to the fact that they economically maintain their families, must be also added to these excluded groups. The massive and growing process of impoverishment, caused by the reduction of the income, temporarily coexisted with a relative moderation of the structural poverty, referred to the satisfaction level of the basic needs. However, recent reports have shown the expansion of malnutrition and endemic diseases situations, generated by the misery in many population settlements.

Inside Buenos Aires conurbation, apart from the total of people unemployed, who at the beginning of 2002 were over 20% of the active population, a similar percentage corresponds to underemployed labor force. With regard to the proportion of non-registered employment, or "hidden", it reached 40% of the employed workers in the second half of the nineties[26].

In order to exemplify the incidence of the *global* transformations in a specific territory of the Gran Buenos Aires, we can take the case of the classic automotive production, one of the bases of the previous national model of massive consumption during the conventional *Fordist-Keynesian* era. In this industrial branch, the current productive standards are "every time more dislocated and decentralized in the so-called emerging markets (Argentina, Brazil, Mexico, Asian Southeast, Eastern Europe), while the consumption of the top of the range, or luxury, models is standardized, through global advertising campaigns, among the elites of the most varied countries; at the same time a deepening process of the crisis and contraction of the medium and bottom of the range, [is developed], [what is a] clear example of the cited trend to globalization, on the one hand, and to the inner duality of the *national* societies, on the other hand" (Alonso: 1999, 114)

A representative case of the evolution of automotive industry is the German company, Volkswagen, which has branch offices in Pamplona (Navarra, Spain), Mexico (D.F.), San Pablo (Brazil) and in the district of La Matanza, next to the Federal Capital of Argentina. The derivations of the *globalizing* dynamics carried out by that transnational company, through its operative functioning "in networks", spread through various very far locations mutually, contributed to restructure the socio-labor ambit of the mentioned district, influenced at the same time by an exacerbation of the tensions coming from the commercial and financial disputes with Brazil, contiguous and partner country of the MERCOSUR regional block.

An own research has verified the effects of the application of *globalized* neoliberal strategies in the district of La Matanza, inside the Gran Buenos Aires, previously formed by urban centres put up around important industrial locations, among them huge automotive plants belonging to different companies[27]. This productive branch, as practically the whole industrial sector of Argentina economic structure, took part in the general transformations detailed in the previous paragraphs.

The percentage of active population that is in an unemployment situation in the investigated district, according to the results of the own surveys, was around the double of the

---

[26] INDEC (National Statistics and Censuses Institute), Economy Ministry of Argentina, Buenos Aires, 1974-2001

[27] Research carried out by the author of this chapter, called *Precarización laboral en el Gran Buenos Aires; un estudio de casos en el Partido de la Matanza,* Studies Center of Population, Employment and Development (Economic Researches Institute of the University of Buenos Aires), 2000. The analysis of the differentiated types of labor insertion, based on carried out studies of cases, allows an approximation to the fractional socio-labor universe, typical of that sub-conglomerate. The empirical corroboration of indicators corresponding to the district was carried out through semi-structured surveys, and subsequent interviews in-depth, selected in terms of the most representative cases, with regard to the investigated variables, during 1999 and 2000.

same average rate to a national scale, established according to data from INDEC. While this had an average "level" of 14-16% since middle of the nineties, the unemployment reached up to 30%, approximately, of the total of the interviewed people. In the district there is a less average proportion of formal employment, especially in the public sector, and capitalized self-employed workers, with regard to the Federal Capital, prevailing marginal labor situations and precarious independent activities. Furthermore, the highest indices of underemployment and work are registered in the "underground" or hidden economy within metropolitan area, together with other towns of the Buenos Aires peripheral belt.

From the information collected in the field work, it has been possible to discriminate a series of people doing some kind of rewarded job considered as "formal" and regularized. However, these regularly employed people are relatively scarce since the total amount is less than the half of men and women taken into account in the research. The activities typified in that research as "formal" and regularized are comprised in the following items: officially registered wage earners, that are with a relationship of *legal* dependency with regard to a company, legally protected by the social security system; self-employed workers of the commercial sector, with certain level of capitalization and contributors to the retirement social security regime; public workers, from the state and municipal spheres, a group integrated mostly by women (many of them underemployed) that, in spite of their reduced remunerations, is socially covered, due to its formal status.

In contrast with the previously mentioned labor force, more than 50% of the interviewed people, with some kind of job during the research, is part of various heterogeneous and amorphous groups but, nevertheless, they share a recurrent experience, chronicle since the beginnings of the last decade of the last century, of labor precariousness and consequent socioeconomic vulnerability. They are part of the categories of non-registered wage earners in middle companies or in *clandestine* micro-settlements; underemployed workers in the "underground" economy; independent non-capitalized workers, without neither retirement nor social assistance; temporary contracted through flexible labor insertions, partially ruled and registered in the social security, but with employment modalities that includes from three to six months of activity; ex industrial workmen that carry out intermittent and/or sporadic *odd jobs*; "swallow" workers[28] of the building industry, absolutely marginalized of the normative regulation that governs the work contracts; domestic service, predominantly women, in the same conditions of deprotection and lack of legal and /or institutional cover that the latter, and so on[29].

The trend to the proliferation of different modalities of *flexible* employment, the increasing fragility in the salaried relationship and the escalation of the self-employed sector –through different ways of expression- denote the meaningful weight of those tasks linked with the activities tertiarization, with regard to certain functions, externalized *by* the productive managers' job, or referred to the intermediation and/or to an activity corresponding to the service sector. The mentioned transformations imply "a huge change in the structure of the societies that, to a great extent, can be characterized by a general

---

[28] Labor force (or workers) that carry out temporary labor activities, especially depending on the seasonal nature of certain occupations, such as crops, according to the season of the year, national tourist services, according to the holiday periods, and so on.

[29] Changes in the labor market, especially since the nineties, impact on the multiplication of temporary employment or *odd jobs*, together with domestic production modalities for the street or home sale. Also, the presence of non-

phenomenon: *the fragmentation* [...] The punished groups are distributed in a very unequal way according to the regional diversities; in the obscure areas of the globalization, the precarious employment, the destructuralization of the biographical cycles of workers -as dramatic ways in and frequent exits of the regular employment world-, the perpetuation of the subsidized social sectors which are increasing more and more..." (Alonso: 1999, 115-116).

In the urban agglomeration of the Gran Buenos Aires, including the capital city, live almost four millions poor people (more than 30% of a population over 12 million), and among them, 60% are from middle-class. The families receiving less total income than US$ 200 per month are considered indigent people, condition in which are about 265.000 households; if it is taken into account that the more lacking domestic groups, generally, have a number of children over the ones by the *type-families*, it can be understood the real magnitude that this figure involves. Also, more than 40 % of children (under 14 years old) in the periphery of the Federal Capital belong to poor households. In Table V indicators are exposed that corroborate the growing impoverishment in the Buenos Aires conurbation, being estimated also the impoverishment levels according to their distance with the demarcation limit established by the "poverty line" (PL), mentioned previously, in percentages on the total of its population:

Table V: Percentage Evolution of Poverty in the Gran Buenos Aires, 1980-1996[30]

	OCT 1980	OCT 1986	OCT 1987	OCT 1988	OCT 1989	OCT 1990	OCT 1991	OCT 1992	OCT 1993	OCT 1994	MAY 1995	OCT 1996	MAY 1997
Poor	11.6	15.2	25.5	32.4	47.0	33.7	26.2	21.8	19.4	20.5	23.9	25.8	26.5
Indigent	1.0	1.6	6.7	8.4	12.3	4.2	2.1	1.8	2.8	2.0	3.2	3.6	3.8
Until 0.75PL	4.7	6.2	9.3	12.6	24.5	19.3	12.1	11.0	9.0	11.1	11.0	12.3	12.7
0.75 to 1 PL	5.9	7.4	9.5	11.4	10.2	10.2	12.0	9.0	7.6	7.4	9.7	9.9	10.0
No Poor	88.4	84.8	74.5	67.6	53.0	66.3	73.8	78.2	80.6	79.5	76.1	74.2	73.5
Until 1.25 PL	7.5	9.7	8.9	10.0	9.4	9.0	8.3	7.6	8.6	8.6	8.9	8.3	8.4
1.25 to 2 PL	22.5	20.6	20.6	19.6	19.1	21.9	20.8	22.3	20.4	21.4	22.0	21.7	20.7
Over 2 PL	58.4	54.5	45.0	38.0	24.5	35.4	44.7	48.3	51.6	49.5	45.2	44.2	44.4
TOTAL	100	100	100	100	100	100	100	100	100	100	100	100	100
Poverty Intensity (*)	0.28	0.30	0.37	0.39	0.45	0.38	0.32	0.31	0.35	0.34	0.34	0.36	0.35

(*) Average distance between poor household income and poverty line
Source: UNICEF, "Analysis of the Situation of the Infancy in Argentina ", 1997

Until mid-seventies the urban poverty was a marginal issue in Argentina, due mainly to historical structural factors, affecting around 5% of domestic groups in the country. That situation involved the *shanty-town* inhabitants or precarious population settlements, with serious lack in housings and services infrastructure. By 1980 that figure came near 12%, increased abruptly as consequence of the hyperinflation in 1989-1990, came down in the beginning of the application of the "convertibility plan" (1991-1994), from the restraint of the

remunerated *familiar help* are frequent, as well as occupations corresponding to diffuse, random, informal and indeterminate tasks, carried out in commercial places, workshops or neighbor, relatives or friends' houses.

30 UNICEF: "Análisis de la Situación de la Infancia en la Argentina", 1997

inflationary process and took up again since 1995[31], being maintained since then its increasing trend.

CONCLUSIONS

In the current world situation, featured by a new economic transnationalization process, the great power of markets obeys to the subordination of most of governments to the global financial aegis, which determines –in the last analysis- the unconditional control of capital over labor. This submission affects to the whole social relationships, typical of the so-called *post-industrial* capitalism, situation that implies the emergence of a "global" system that selects, discriminately, some specialized productive locations. That phenomenon is inclined to generate varied tensions and conflicts, that are reflected -according to the different regions of the world- in the population migrations among countries, and even inside them, in the problem of the peasants deprived of their lands and the continuous rural exodus, and so on. It can be stated, generally, that the neoliberalism globalization, in the "information era", leads to a worsening of the life conditions of large masses of planetary population.

Nowadays, the most important and dynamical markets work in an interrelated way because, although most of them operates in located spaces, a key element in the evolution of the multinational companies is the possibility of penetrating commercially in different territories, even in those very far away mutually. The production in the world order would be *globalized*, if we take into account strictly the significance acquired by certain corporations "without frontiers", together with their auxiliary productive networks, in diverse and disperse geographical areas. In spite of the fact that these companies employ to several tens of million workers in several continents, this figure –even though it can be considerable- is not too meaningful, in comparison with all the population on earth. Nevertheless, apart from that quantitative proportion, these huge companies, through their subsidiary *satellites*, are the vital center of the industrial activity and services creation, hegemonic in a supranational scale (Castells: 1999).

The basic premises of the supposed existence of a "world society" are adapted to the specific features of differentiated continental and regional contexts, which show trends and own behaviors of the directly involved social actors, locally having certain autonomy, opposite to heterogeneous circumstances, detectable –for instance- in terms of the socio-productive relationships (Pérez Sáinz: 1994).

We can mention the vulnerability imposed to several Latin America societies, due to the huge pressure of the accumulated external debt, therefore their governments are urged to access to the international loan. Some countries of the area were forced, then, to renegotiate their whole indebtedness, at the expense of restricting the government spending and obtain fiscal discipline and balance, under the strict control exercised by world credit organizations. In front of the described panorama, the public powers of the region carried out a deep

---

[31] INDEC (National Statistics and Censuses Institute), Economy Ministry of Argentina, Buenos Aires, 1974-2001. Also, the income loss frustrated the expectations of the middle social sectors: according to a survey carried out by the Graciela Römer research, 76% of Argentina people thinks that their parents had a better standard of living than nowadays. The most forceful figure is that 60% of the consulted people considered that in the future, their children will have more privations than they are suffering today; due to this, 35% of the polled people notes that if they had the possibility of leaving the country, they would do it.

economic-productive rationalization, at the same time that the States, previously *interventionist* and many-sided, had to be reoriented through a reduction of their dimensions and a sharp shift in their functions.

In Argentina, as example of dislocation of the pre-existing socio-labor structures, made up throughout several decades, in certain marginal neighborhoods of the Gran Buenos Aires young population suffer weak and pernicious social relationships. In the concrete sphere of work, the cyclical rotation among the unemployment experience, alternated with sporadic underemployment, hinder the youth to concrete, in general terms, a stable labor evolution. On the other hand, in this population segment, a loss of relational identity is shown, caused by the weakened transferable social capital through the own family nucleus, and the cultural externality of the formal educational system, phenomenon accentuated when immigrants are considered. In that sense, "the functional illiteracy unleashes unemployment, poverty and - finally- social exclusion mechanisms, in a society based increasingly on a minimal capacity of language decodification" (Castells: 1998, 189).

The previously mentioned set of problems is a crucial obstacle in order to get the integration in the formal labor market, in every level, and is closely connected with the expansion of the lowest remunerated employment and the consequent impoverishment process. In that sense, some territorial spaces of the peripheral belt of the Buenos Aires conurbation share, as well as many other areas of the current global village, the fact of being part of the "fourth world, made up of multiple black holes of social exclusion throughout the planet" (Castells: 1998, 191)

In the described situation, the framework of general sociality is progressively limited to ephemeral interpersonal contacts, featured in terms of simple "recreations", as antidotes opposite to a feeling of deep apathy, determined by the uncertainty of an empty future of projects, which frequently crystallize in criminal behaviors. We can emphasize the strong anomic component that characterizes to considerable parts of the urban society, insofar as an absolute alteration of the means and goals has reconverted the social coexistence, to such an extent that there are actions that formally are offenses, but that the social conscience does not reprove (De Soto: 1987). Also, the mentioned "pathological" expressions are carried out in a devalued context of political leadership, taking into account the inefficient and/or corrupt actions, executed in the governmental levels.

It is important to consider the undergone experience of those unemployed people that are still without any chance to be workably inserted, during vast temporary lapses, who usually fall in a customary state of "non-work" and the people absorbed by the *discouragement syndrome*. These last ones abandon the employment search because of hopelessness, due to the unsuccessfulness, and psychophysical wear of their task. This happens in the context of severe obstacles in order to get employment and/or alternative income sources, giving rise to a social configuration represented by the constitution and widening of these workers groups in long term and chronic unemployment. The urgency of finding an acceptable way out in the market from this critical labor scene, and taking as implicit reference the absence of the minimal State support, results in many cases in the intention of transforming the activity cessation into a training situation in which, due to the apparent non-viability of the conventional skills, the competence for selling in the labor market certain personal attributes or abilities is shown, attributes of abilities such as sociability, complete availability, initiative spirit and so on, which until now had been left aside due to they were seen as non-decisive factors for determining the level of labor preparation required for carrying out some jobs.

In the current labor situation panoramically considered, and specially in the marginal areas of the Gran Buenos Aires, individual and group experiences of stagnation, unemployment or underemployment are overlapped. This circumstance configures a questioning reality of the inherent elemental principle to the social function of labor, which is considered -by itself- in terms of a creative, productive and enriching task (not merely in the profitable aspect), inducing a relatively *harmonic* joint of the relationships among sectors, strata and classes making up society. So, a segment of the increasingly relevant labor force, in a proportional sense, excluded from the labor market, seeks the achievement of some kind of occupation, through the strategies deployment -external and parallel to the "formal" circuit of employment- tending to the obtainment of subsistence resources.

The permanent spread of this *exclusion logic* leads to a multiplicity of isolated and concrete transitory tasks, to the self-generation of futile and non-productive occupations, and to the resigned acceptance of extremely precarious employments due to the urgent pressure of surviving in the physical sense. This way of labor insertion, isolated and sporadic, showing a growing fragility as structural feature, gives rise to a sort of "informal occupational universe", in which the specific situation of the part-time, situational and discontinuous workers, as well as the circumstance of the *bunglers* carrying out limited and intermittent activities, may be integrated.

The above mentioned researches about the socio-labor level in the urban area of the Buenos Aires conurbation show the coexistence of extremely heterogeneous features. So, these researches prove the existence of diversified modalities of labor insertion, still irregular, uncommon and even fugacious, experienced during the last decade by different social groups, beyond their situation in the temporary situation of the carried out reports. It is obvious that if the information from unemployed workers, officially accounted or hidden, had been belittled, meaningful data might have been wasted, coming from the precedents of a considerable part of the society, data known on the base of the reconstruction of the past vital careers of these marginalized people in a middle term.

In short, focusing punctually on the consequences of globalization over the peripheral spaces, such as the Argentine case, diverse situations of socioeconomic degradation are produced with regard to the modern sector of the economy and to its respective "formal" market. These situations are mainly due to the fact that separate redoubts from the operation of the hegemonic center of the productive system tend to proliferate in these spaces. All this results in a growing utilization of "extra-commercial" mechanisms, that are devoted to the provision of use goods, many times provided by the political-administrative system now in phase of dismantling or in chaos. As a consequence of this we are witnessing a substantial broadening in the dimension of the *non-marketized* areas, moved away from the own dynamics of the commercialization of change values, including the use of the available labor demand. For example, the practice of bartering diverse social services and material goods became generalized in the Argentine situation of deep socioeconomic crisis, due to the notable scarcity of cash and possibilities of earning it for many people, what greatly increases the difficulties for selling or buying the labor force and many other basic goods.

BIBLIOGRAPHY

Abramo, Laís and others (1998) "La institucionalización de la sociología del trabajo en América Latina", in *Sociología del Trabajo review N° 32*, Madrid

Alonso, Luis Enrique (1999) "*Trabajo y ciudadanía. Estudios sobre la crisis de la sociedad salarial*", Trotta, Madrid

Barbeito, Alberto and Lo Vuolo, Rubén (1992) "*La modernización excluyente. Transformación económica y Estado de Bienestar en la Argentina*", Losada (UNICEF), Buenos Aires

Basualdo. Eduardo (2000) "*Concentración y centralización del capital en la Argentina durante la década del noventa*", Universidad Nacional de Quilmes, Buenos Aires

Beccaria Luis (1992) "Transformaciones en la estructura social argentina", in Minujin, A., comp., *Cuesta abajo. Los nuevos pobres: efectos de la crisis en la sociedad argentina*; Losada (UNICEF), Buenos Aires

Beccaria, Luis and Quintar, Aída (1995) "Reconversión productiva y mercado de trabajo. Reflexiones a partir de la experiencia de SOMISA", in *Desarrollo Económico review, N° 139* (pages 401 to 418), Buenos Aires

Beck, Ulrich (1996) "Teoría de la modernización reflexiva", in Beriain, J., comp., *Las consecuencias perversas de la modernidad.* Modernidad, contingencia y riesgo, Anthropos, Barcelona

Beriain, Josetxo (1996) "El doble sentido de las consecuencias perversas de la modernidad", in Beriain, *J., comp., ob. cit.* (Preface)

Brodersohn, Mario (1970) "*Estrategias de industrialización para la Argentina*", Editorial del Instituto, Buenos Aires

Canitrot, Alfredo (1980) "Teoría y práctica del liberalismo", *Publicaciones del CEDES*, Vol. N°10, Buenos Aires

Castel, Robert (1997) "*Metamorfosis de la cuestión social. Una crónica del salariado*", Paidós, Buenos Aires

Castells, Manuel (1998) "Fin de milenio", third volume of the text of *La era de la información*, Alianza, Madrid

Castells, Manuel (1999) "Globalización, tecnología, trabajo, empleo y empresa", in Castells, M. and Esping-Andersen, G., *La transformación del trabajo*; Factoría, Barcelona

Cimillo, Elsa (1999) "Empleo e ingresos en el sector informal en una economía abierta: el caso argentino", in J. Carpio, E. Klein and I. Novacovsky, eds., *Informalidad y exclusión social*, Fondo de Cultura Económica, SIEMPRO (Sistema de Información, Monitoreo y Evaluación de Programas Sociales, Ministerio de Desarrollo Social) – OIT (Organización Internacional del Trabajo), Buenos Aires

Comisión Económica para América Latina (1999) "La CEPAL y la teoría de la industrialización", in *Revista de la CEPAL*, special number, Valpy FitzGerald, St. Antony's College, Oxford

De Soto, Hernando (1987) "*El otro sendero*"; Sudamericana, Buenos Aires

Giner, Salvador (1999) "*Sociología*", Península, Barcelona

Guillén Romo, Héctor (1997) "Globalización financiera y riesgo sistémico", in *Comercio Exterior review, N° 11*, México D.F.

Guillén Romo, Héctor (1997) "*La contrarrevolución neoliberal en México*", Editorial ERA, México D.F.

Instituto Nacional de Estadísticas y Censos (INDEC) "*Índices de precios al consumidor*" (1975-2000), Ministerio de Economía de la Nación, Buenos Aires

Katz, Jorge (1997) "*Apertura y Desregulación de la actividad productiva, cambio tecnológico y comportamiento del sistema innovativo nacional*"; paper for the Tercer Taller Iberoamericano sobre Indicadores de Ciencia y Tecnología, Santiago de Chile

Kay, Cristóbal (1998) "Neoliberalismo y estructuralismo. Regreso al futuro"; *Memoria review (Centro de Estudios del Movimiento Obrero y Socialista), N° 117*, México, D.F.

Kessler, Gabriel (1996) "Algunas implicaciones de la experiencia de desocupación para el individuo y su familia", in Beccaria, L. and López, N., comps., *Sin trabajo. Las características del desempleo y sus efectos en la sociedad argentina*; Losada (UNICEF), Buenos Aires

Kliksberg, Bernardo (2000) "La inequidad. Mitos y realidades", *La Gaceta review*, Facultad de Ciencias Económicas, N° 1, Universidad de Buenos Aires

Le Goff, Jacques (2001) leading article of Le Monde newspaper (París), reproduced in "*Clarín" newspaper*, November 27th 2001, Buenos Aires

López, Ernesto (1999) "Globalización y democracia: esbozos" in *Revista de Ciencias Sociales, N° 7/8*, Buenos Aires

Lo Vuolo, Rubén (2001) "*Alternativas La economía como cuestión social*", Altamira, Buenos Aires

Minujin, Alberto (1992) "*Transformaciones en la estructura social argentina*"; in Minujin, A., comp., ob. cit.

Murmis, Miguel y Feldman, Silvio (1996) "*De seguir así*", in Beccaria, L. and López, N. [comps.], ob. cit.

Organización Internacional del Trabajo (1986) "*El sector informal urbano*", OIT, Ginebra

Peñalva, Susana (1999) "Condición salarial e intervención del Estado a la hora de la mundialización: la Argentina en el MERCOSUR", Gestión de las Transformaciones Sociales (MOST), *Documentos de debate N° 21*, Buenos Aires

Pérez Sáinz, Juan Pablo (1991) "*Informalidad urbana en América Latina*", FLACSO/Nueva Sociedad, Caracas

Pérez Sáinz, Juan Pablo (1994) "*El dilema del nahual. Globalización, exclusión y trabajo en Centroamérica*" [Conclusions], FLACSO, San José de Costa Rica

SIEMPRO (1997) "*Evolución de la pobreza en el Gran Buenos Aires*", Sistema de Información, Monitoreo y Evaluación de Programas Sociales, Ministerio de Desarrollo Social, Buenos Aires

Solé, Carlota (1998) "*Modernidad y modernización*", Anthropos, Barcelona

Villadeamigo, José (1999) "*El modelo en su laberinto. La situación económica en la Argentina*"; Fundación Illia, Buenos Aires

In: Argentina: Economic, Political and Social Issues
Editor: Jeanne B. Haverland
ISBN 978-1-60456-469-3

Chapter 2

A Pendular Movement between the Intergenerational Pact and the Exhaustion of Support Networks in Argentina

María Julieta Oddone[1] and Mónica Beatriz Aguirre[2]
CONICET- FLACSO, Ayacucho 551 – Capital Federal
Universidad de Buenos Aires, Argentina

Introduction

The objective of this study is to reach an understanding of the problems that confront families burdened by the care of an elderly person with health problems. To this end, we approached key participants in "Caring for Those Who Care," a Buenos Aires City Government program. Basing our study on this organization, we interviewed family caregivers who have participated in the program. We worked with a sample of caregivers composed of spouses, sons and daughters, sons- and daughters-in-law, and grandchildren. The group of caregivers as well as the group of dependents includes participants of both genders; this permitted us to obtain a spread of cases ranging widely with regards to generation, to gender, and to familiar relationship; from these cases emerged the key issues in the caregiver´s situation to which we refer in this chapter.

The study focused on the City of Buenos Aires. The demographic structure of this capital city of the Republic of Argentina marks it as the country's most aged city, given that 22% (609,466) of its population is made up of people of 60 or more years of age.

Previous research conducted by this team (Oddone, 2001) indicates that 5% of the elderly population receives special care in a family setting. The Caring for Those Who Care data, which permits a general characterization of its attendees, indicate the following: that 88% of the caregivers are women, that 80% are over 50 years of age, that 60% spend more than 5

---

[1] FLACSO, Facultad Latinoamericana de Ciencias Sociales y Consejo Nacional de Investigaciones Científicas y Técnicas (the Latin American Faculty of Social Sciences and the Nacional Council of Scientific and Technical Research). mjoddone@mail.retina.ar

[2] FLACSO, Facultad Latinoamericana de Ciencias Sociales. maguirre@mail.retina.ar

hours per day with the person in need of care, and that 72% carry out the caregiving duties on a daily basis[3].

In Argentina, and in particular in the city of Buenos Aires, various programs designed to help family caregivers have been implemented. These programs range from the formation of gerontological assistance to a program that proposes care for the family caregivers themselves. In between are found domestic internment, 24-hour attention centers, and retirement homes, among others. But the reach of these programs′ efficacy remains quite far from meeting demands, just as our interview subjects – who have been left alone in responding to the needs of their sick elderly and without hope of finding any help other than their own personal and family recourses -- prove. It seems to us that it is not the creation of new programs that is needed but rather their universality, seeing as the existing programs have had little chance to be assessed, given their limited reach. The problems of family caregivers will become solvable when the protective function of the state is reexamined, and the fact taken into account that the aging process is a phenomenon that modifies a society in its needs and demands.

The Exhaustion of Family Support Networks

In everyday life, family units, in order to meet their needs, maintain networks of reciprocity and mutual help which are expressed through the exchange of tasks associated with the maintenance of members' well-being (Lomnitz, 1977). Both love and moral obligation play a role in these networks. Obviously, reciprocity is not always achieved in every interaction. Actors can expect a returned benefit mostly in the long term, sometimes even on the scale of the life cycle itself, across generations. The temporal dimension of these exchanges (their timing) that leads us to understand them as either short- or long-term constitutes a fundamental focal point for understanding family relationships with regard to aging. Effectively, in the short-term exchanges correspond to everyday situations; a typical example is that in which grandparents care for their grandchildren while their daughter works, and the daughter in turn assists her parents economically.

In the long-term generational-scale exchanges in which the help that parents give in their children's growth and development is returned by the children in the form of protection in the parents' old age are found. These exchanges are reciprocal and include the variable of time and are thus marked by normative values. In each act, the services exchanged are considered favors and the emotional availability of each person is tested. The exchange is valued as a link in and of itself and the very relationship is based upon the rationale – be it conscious or not of everyday or material needs, or of social values/norms that have been internalized as obligatory. In this sense, these exchanges form a part of the social capital which the old possess in our society. This form of organization is valid for all social sectors, though it changes the content of the exchange.

In his research conducted in France, P. Pitaud (1999) stresses that a large portion of the dependent elderly is involved in these exchange networks, and receives care from

[3] Data provided by Susana Aguas, Director of the Municipal Office for the Elderly of the City of Buenos Aires, year 2003.

predetermined sources in compensation for past assistance. This fact brings to mind a sort of symbolic debt.

In today's Argentine society, impacted by the crisis of the 1990s and the large-scale privatizations and devaluation, this social capital constitutes, in most cases, the only security for the elderly. It does not, however, escape a certain level of conflict. Within the circle of family relationships (especially those which link ancestors and descendents) the weight of moral obligation, reinforced by social expectation on the one hand and affection on the other, constitutes the reciprocity relationship (the proportions of these components in the determination of behavior is not easy to evaluate even in concrete cases). Disequilibrium is produced when these feelings are put to the test by material conditions – incomes, housing, health – that generate tensions within the systems (Oddone, 2002).

It is not only the factor of economic conditions that casts doubt on families' capacity to assume responsibilities which may overwhelm them. Nowadays certain social changes are arising which are affecting this capacity and will certainly come to affect it even more. In the first place, demographic changes – particularly the drop in fertility rates – have significant effects on the number of potential support providers. The correlative rise in life expectancy produces families of up to five generations, increasing the possibility of a greater number of aged dependents and, in consequence, the possibility that elderly persons must take charge of the caregiving of even older relatives[4] (Monk, 1997). Finally, if we bear in mind that females generally provide the family-member support, the greater participation of the woman in the labor market and the trend towards their greater social independence casts doubt on the continuity of a caregiving model headed by housewives.

> I have long believed we have the global capacity to support all the earth's people, but to do so will require a revolution in economic and political action which re-establishes human solidarity and reciprocity as central features of our social order. As has been argued these transformations are essentially moral; but failure to address them puts at risk not only the contact between young and old, but society itself". (Johnson, 1995, 262)

Just as Johnson stated, we believe that families preserve their capacity to sustain their members and in this sense continue to be the principal source of these members' wellbeing. But the changes that constantly challenge this capacity to the point of provoking true crisis at the group and individual level cannot be forgotten. For this reason, we think it necessary that public policy consider both aspects: the existence of these networks and the resilience of the families' classes to sustain themselves as well as the tensions to which they are subjected. The Caring for Those Who Care Program was conceived within these lines and for that reason we have chosen it as the entryway to access the caregiving families. Before presenting the result of our study, we will briefly describe recent developments in the support services system to family caregivers in Argentina.

---

[4] One issue which ought to be highlighted is that concerning caregivers of more than 60 years of age: the elderly who care for the elderly. This is obviously generally the case for spouses, but many caregiving daughters are also over 60 years old. The majority of out interviewees actually are aged over 60: Jorge W., 76, cares for his wife, 78; Hebe M., 72, cares for her husband, 82; Esther C., 70, cares for her husband of 85, María Isabel F., 65, cares for her 90-year-old mother; Lidia R., 60, cares for her mother, 84, and Teresita S., 66, cares for her mother, 91, and her aunt, 89.

THE RETRACTION OF THE WELFARE STATE IN ARGENTINA

From the early 1940s to the late 1970s, a set of policies were developed, based on three legal principles: need, merit, and citizenship (Fraser, 1997). The aid policies – based on the first of these principles, need are meant for those who are unable to hold a job – above all, for the elderly and for children. Merit-based protection policies grant benefits according to the contributions of each person. Here we find employment policies, in which work takes on an important role as social integrator. Universal policies reach all people considered citizens, that is to say, any member of society. Through this set of public policies, the Welfare State fulfills its central role, guaranteeing protection.

In the last two decades, with the disappearance of this protective state, which has been the result of neoliberal adjustments, notable transformations have taken place in diverse dimensions (Vinocur and Halperín, 2004). Economically speaking, decentralization, privatization, greater concentration of wealth and inequity; socially speaking, impoverishment, vulnerability, and disaffiliation. All of these transformations restructure society, producing new characteristics in new configurations.

Confronted by the difficulties that the national state and its historical institutions have had in meeting the needs of the people, theorists have posited that various actors, by means of non-governmental organizations, will begin to re-knit the fabric of social networks. In this line of thought, belonging to such networks is a fundamental tool. It lends a sense of dignity to life because these networks suppose the existence of communicative processes carried out jointly with other actors, and give action a certain directionality. Things have not, however, turned out to work that way. Instead, what Wacquant (2001) calls organizational desertification has been observable.

In this new setting, the conditions for collective action are lost. Forms of participation are reduced to what is close at hand, given that, as has already been observed, institutions are shrinking. Close relationships are usually found in the family setting. The research of Bertaux (1996) demonstrates the importance of using the family as a unit of analysis and becoming acquainted with the transformations taking place within it. All family histories create a mirror wherein social history, great moments of change, and their various dimensions are reflected. Forging a family history makes people aware of the family unit importance in the formation and development of social activity and praxis. It is in this way that, gradually, generalized instability is reflected in family instability. The vulnerability of the family thus becomes evident in any emergency situation, in this case, the care of the oldest family members. As a counterpoint, the multiplication of cases of families with this type of need, reflects not only the aging of the population in general but also represents a situation of social risk to which institutions respond only very partially.

The exhaustion of family support networks is obvious in relation to the illness of the elderly. We must not continue burdening domestic groups with functions that are the general responsibility of society and the particular responsibility of institutions and state social programs. It is imminently important, then, that we find a position that will ensure that the planning of social policies will facilitate the complementation of informal family resources and more formal aid resources. To this end, it is necessary to rehabilitate and reconstruct the Welfare State, with the goal of having it guarantee universal, high-quality services that assure citizens´ rights. Today these services are almost non-existent in the context of an emerging economy burdened by foreign debt.

As Neena Chappell (1996) argues, the new recognition of informal caregivers has highlighted the need for a thorough understanding of caregiving. However, "...without the expansion of formal community services, the tightening and steamlining of medical and hospital care can easily result in a greater burden on informal caregivers. This fact is not being considered seriously within the new vision [*of the health care system*]" (p. 149). Our point of view is that family caregivers remain the dominant source of assistance for elders and that there is very little actual concern in regards to the burden this assistance represents for them. So much so that we could make ours the words of Pitaud (1999), who, as we do, recognizes and values family support for the elderly as well as highlighting the social risk implicated by the burden and responsibility of caregiving: "I only hope that our government will not wait until the situation takes a turn for the worse before taking measures to aid dependent persons and their families!" (p.29). In the next section we will describe the method of data collection. Then in the analysis, reporting transcripts from the interviews, we describe the presence and character of support networks involved in the caring for older disabled family members. Moreover we highlight the position of the main caregiver (spouse, son/daughter, grandchildren, etc.), the tensions within the family, the financial implication of caregiving (the weight on the family budget) and the role of community resources. We conclude providing a set of recommendations based on our findings.

The Study

Methodological Aspects

"Caring for Those Who Care," a Buenos Aires City Government program, included the organization of a course[5] for family caregivers to older disabled people. The course consisted of six weekly group meetings of two hours each.

The field work first centered on interviewing the key informants, professionals from the Center of Old Age of the Government of the City of Buenos Aires. These workers know the aged population and its central problems, and pointed us in the direction of individuals who would meet the definition of informal caregiver. The key informants enjoyed the trust of the group in question. Being assured of the seriousness, discretion, and utility of our work, they granted us the possibility of contacting the participant to the course.[6]

The material used in the field study was based on 15 freely-conducted in-depth interviews and on the information produced by the authors´ observations. This blend shows us the basics of the scenario in which the caregiver families go about their everyday lives. Of the 15 interview subjects, two were a married couple that cared for three elderly family

5 The course coordinating team included a nurse, a social worker, and a psychologist. The course was divided into three sections:
I- General Information about gerontology.
II- Practices of the caregiver.
III- The connecting relationship. Responsibilities and limitations. The personal projects of the caregiver.

6 We especially thank the help offered by key informants Mariana Kesselman and Fabian Oliveira from the Buenos Aires City Government.

members; another two were a mother and son that cared for two elderly family members. Two subjects were dropped from the analysis, in one case because the dependent was not a family member and in the other because the interviewee's answers did not correspond with the study´s objective. (his wife had begun to manifest some cognitive disorders but did not need special care yet) The sample ended up comprised of ten women and five men, each representing a different family relations to the dependent they cared for.

The main objective of the interviews was to distinguish the strategies that families have created to meet the needs of the elderly dependent as well as to detect the economic, emotional, and health costs which these strategies imply for the caregivers. We also evaluated the success or failure of these same strategies in terms of quality of life of both caregiver and dependent. To this end, we analyze the presence and character of support networks, family tensions, financial aspects, and the role of community resources.

The semi-structured in-depth interviews took place in the houses of the informants. Each interview covers a mixture of topics, according to the following list:

Family caregivers´ information: Sociodemographic and economic information (age, gender, etc.), Personal family situation (marriage, children, age of children, etc.), Work and earning situation. Family relation with the dependent person. Why did they take charge of the dependent? Does the dependent live with them?

Information about the dependent: Sociodemographic and economic information (age, gender, etc), Work and earning situation, Ownership of the living quarters, living quarters´ adequateness for the necessities of the dependent person, Sickness, Level of incapacity or dependency. Treatement, time, and attention required.

Composition and history of the family: Live-in and non live-in family members, family history and relationship networks.

Relationship of the dependent person: Quality of the caregiver-dependent relationship. Help of friends and family, help of institutions and economic questions.

- Free time.
- Changes in the quality of life of the caregiver (stress, depression, physical illness, etc.)
- Conflicts in family relationships (fatigue, tension, aggression, violence, abandonment, negligence, usurpation).
- Strategy implemented for the dependent person.
- Level of satisfaction with the implemented strategy.

Records of attitudes and expressions of the interviewees were reported in ethnographic notes, together with the descriptions of the physical space, the surroundings, and the quality of the caregiver-cared for relationship, according to what could be observed in the interviewees´ houses.

The duration of the interviews varied, according to the cases, between four and eight hours, divided among one or various sessions. They were done in the city of Buenos Aires during the months of October and November, 2003. With the consent of the subjects, the interviews were recorded on mini-cassette and transcribed. The topics were codified and categorized by the computer program Atlas Ti in a matrix of data obtained in the aforementioned manner making webs of thematic relationships. Analysis of the data was done by exemplifying characteristics (types) that arose from the interviewees′ narration, and these cases are those that appear in the text. In the next section we are going to illustrate the results of the analysis.

THE ANALYSIS

In the presentation of this study we have given priority to the actors' voices[7], though the richness of the face-to-face interviews is so great that it would be impossible to fully communicate its force. We have chosen to present interviewees' perspective articulated around thematic focuses. The most important elements of the testimonies are unfolded gradually in order to show the links between various themes. We cannot deny that in this method some of the interviews' substance is lost; however, we believe that this form of presentation transmits the lived experiences of the interviewees while at the same time permits us to treat in some depth the issues which we consider ought to be highlighted.

With regards to the various units into which we have grouped the content, we shall try to approach them separately so as to lend order to our presentation. These units, however, are so closely related that this separation sometimes becomes a bit artificial. Despite these provisos, we continue to believe that this is the best option and the most likely to promote a serious discussion of the cared for problems which in turn could yield the implementation of social policies targeted towards caregiving families. First, we address the ethics of care to prove the existence of the intergenerational pact. Second, we focus on the caregiving relation, its positive and negative aspects, regarded as punishments and rewards by the caregiver. Then we consider at length the costs of care. Here we take into account the consequences occasioned by caregiving such as lack of free time, health problems, economic costs, etc. We then describe the strategies that these families employed to cope with the situation and, finally, we examine the reasons for which the caregivers signed up for the class.

THE ETHICS OF CARE: WHAT SUSTAINS ITS FUNCTIONING?

We contacted our interview subjects during high-stress times for the networks to which they belong. The fact that they resorted to a support program to seek relief proves the existence of tension and stress.

One of the first issues we wanted to investigate is the reason for which the families took responsibility for the dependents. The moral values and feeling that sustain the commitment to care then began to appear:

> From a certain point of view, I feel fine. I feel that I'm finishing or fulfilling something that was done for me. One can only hope that the same thing happens with his own children. It's like a payback. That wouldn't be the exact word, because payback would be like giving

[7] We consider that the actors have an important weight in the authorship of the ethnographic text. (J. Clifford, 1998)

something that they… it's more that it has to come naturally. Without a doubt, the word would be… it's a way of showing your affection for them. (Jorge K.)[8]

Jorge K. cannot find the exact word to express what he feels he is doing. It is not a payback of something concrete that his parents have given him, but rather something more. It is the fulfillment of a tacit agreement which seals intergenerational solidarity. The existence of this intergenerational pact becomes clearer when he says:

At home we had my grandparents, my grandparents lived and died in our house. Because of that I feel like, for me, it´s familiar, the fact that it´s my turn now to care for them. (Jorge K.)

The same feeling of duty is reiterated in the words of María Isabel F. and Alicia B.:

I feel that it's my obligation, it's my duty. That she cared for me when I was little and that I… (María Isabel F.)[9]

It's what we're given in life. He (referring to her husband) is the son of Italians and he follows his duty 'til death. An only son… it's having a clean, clear conscience. To be able to say, well, that you looked after them while you could. (Alicia B.)[10]

Lidia R., in contrast, is less sure that she is complying with some duty. Her response show a process of elaborating the reasons that she feels she must stay by her mother's side.

I don't know. I was sort of angry with my brothers but I also know I have no right to be angry. I don't know, I'm probably being selfish. I don't really understand it all. I like to supervise everything. I do, I really do. And then it all weighs me down…and I don't know why it has to be me. Why I think I am… it's because I'm the only woman. My brothers haven't said so, but I get the impression that my brothers think that I'm already retired and so it's up to me to go take care of my mom. Because it's my house. The house where my mom lives is mine. When my dad made his will, I got that house. It's a house I really love, truly. And, well, it's mine. And it's like, I get the impression that it's an obligation. And, hey, I'm already retired and so I have to go to take care of my mom. But look, it's not a hassle, when I do for her. I get worn out because, logically, I'm a human being and I can overdo it. But it's

---

[8] Jorge K., 48, single. He lives with his parents and a brother. He cares for his 82-year-old father who suffers neurological disorders which cause mobility problems. Family of Japanese origin. Jorge has several married brothers and sisters and has organized family aid so that when he has to be away for work or to be with his girlfriend, they take his place. He believes that his task is to "be there" controlling the situation.

[9] María Isabel F., 65, married, one married son, two grandchildren. He took the course so as to be able to care for his widowed mother, 90, who suffers cognitive disorders. María Isabel has always lived with her parents, though she is married. Three years ago she cared for her sick father until he passed away. At that time she counted on the help of her only sister and her niece. Currently, her sister is showing signs of Alzheimer's and her niece must care for her, and therefore she no longer has them to help care for her mother.

[10] Couple B., made up of Alicia, 55, and Salvador, 53. They have a son, a student, 19. They care for Alicia's mother, a widow, 89, for Salvador's mother, 75, and for his father, 78. The father suffers paraplegia and aphasia as the consequence of a stroke, for the last four years. When they got married, Salvador and Alicia built their house behind that of Salvador's parents and they have always lived together. When Alicia's mother was widowed, they brought her to live with them. Currently they are charged with the care of all three. They took the course because the situation had become intolerable.

not a hassle. I have a good relationship with my mom. We've never had problems. I've never had problems with my mom. Thank God. (Lidia R.)[11]

As we can see, the reasons Lidia R. alludes to are multiple, as much about gender — being the only woman — as economic — her parents' having put the house in her name — and work-related — her being retired. However, it seems that she feels most burdened from the need of control: if she does not supervise everything she can't feel calm. This doubtless has to do with duty.

It is noteworthy that, coming from the notion of the intergenerational pact, this emotional commitment appears with force and clarity in the case of parent-child relationships. The same obligation, however, does not occur with regards to the care of a spouse. This is what Hebe M., 72 years old, who cares for her 82-year-old husband, expresses:

Because there's no choice, I have no alternative. (Hebe M.)[12]

In the same situation, Esther C. declares:

...and so, it's up to me now to take care of him and I have to be aware that I have to be there, at his side. (Esther C.)[13]

The sense of being compelled to care, and the complex array of reasons bound to it were pointed out in various chapters, in particular by Paoletti, in chapter 1 and Katila, in chapter 2. In the next section we are going to discuss the caregiving relationship.

THE CAREGIVING RELATIONSHIP

The Power Within the Couple

In the case of wife-caregivers gender issues appear clearly linked to wives' "taking power" in the relationship. Esther C. expresses this:

-...Positive, though he tells me I'm like his cane, and I don't like it. The handle of the cane, that I have to be always with... that he leans on me. But it's positive that I've made my own decisions, which before I couldn't do.

-Was he very dominating?

-No, he was just a man of his time. He decides, he decided, and he will decide. It's his character. No, I don't know if it's his character, the role he has to have. Let's give it a more

[11] Lidia R., 60, separated, one son. She cares for her widowed mother, 83, who lives alone. She is retired but continues to work. She spends all weekends with her mother. Initially she came to take the course thinking mistakenly that it was about learning to be with older people. She took it anyway and it has helped her feel less dependent on her mother. She regrets than in spite of there being four brothers and sisters in her family they are not close, and suffer family tensions.

[12] Hebe M., 72, married, one married daughter, two grandchildren. Currently retired, she lives with her 82-year-old husband, also retired, for whom she must care due to his cognitive disorders. She took the course because she realized that even if the illness of her husband limits her, she is also limiting herself.

[13] Esther C., 70, married, four children, several grandchildren. She took the course three years ago foreseeing the future, given the age difference between herself and her husband, who is currently 85. At the moment of the interview his cognitive disorders had worsened.

psychological image, then, the role. The role he has assigned himself. I'm more in the condescending role, and everything. (Esther C.)

Esther C's contradictions make clear that only in the interview itself does she begin to question what role each partner had in her marriage and probably also question if it was necessary to wait until her husband fell ill to begin to make decisions. In any case, her allusions to masculine and feminine roles refer to the traditional gender differentiation which, on the other hand, she seems to accept.

By contrast, Hebe M., who always worked and managed her money, experiences ambivalent feelings in terms of caring for her husband, but she nonetheless highlights as positive that he is now much more manageable. She says it this way:

> ...When he was still with it, he wasn't even remotely my companion, someone to go out with. He had his group, his friends, didn't give me the time of day. So now, of course, my payback is pretty big. Because sometimes he says to me, "Are you going to leave me alone?" And I go out to buy something at the store and come back. And sometimes I've just had it, and I say, "How many times did you leave me alone!" "Sure, but, you're being so mean!" And then afterwards it passes, but the anger is there. So sometimes it makes it harder for me. Because I remember certain things, when, well, I really needed him, when I got sick.(Hebe M.)[14]

And later on:

> The positive part is that he's much more manageable than before. More manageable for me is more comfortable. Because before he saw everything differently than me, thought of everything different. Then it was a lot more work. Now he's much more manageable. Dependent, because he depends on me. Not manageable because he likes to be, he has no choice. (Hebe M.)

It seems that in the marriage relationship the woman often takes her revenge, seizing the power in the relationship, and sees this as a benefit. This does not appear in other types of relationships; the intergenerational pact between parents and children differs from the marriage contract, the spousal duty is lived differently from the filial. This observation that arises from the data must be considered as a hypothesis to be tested in upcoming research.

As we have seen, the feelings that the function of caring awaken in the caregiver are multiple. But we shall focus first, as we have done so far, on those feelings which sustain the caregiving function in spite of how exhausting it generally proves. One of these feelings is related to the responsibility that constantly weighs on the caregiver as a result of the dependent´s vulnerability.

Constant Vigilance

Many caregivers manifest something similar to the "nursemaid's sleep"; they are never completely at ease but instead feel constantly vigilant, even in their sleep. But no one better

[14] See footnote number 10

than them to describe what they feel. Alejandro S., who along with his mother cares for his grandmother, tells us:

> It's lots of things together. I should spend more time looking for work, and I share this feeling with some friends of mine who take care of their loved ones. What they've found, just like what I'm finding, is that they're constantly in a state of vigilance. The first few nights my grandmother was in my house we all kept being jerked awake because of the constant cough she has which she can't stop. So it messes up your normal sleep. We just generally lived in a state of permanent vigilance. My mother more than I because she's more involved. But ít hits me too, transitively, because I see my mother, who's caring for my grandmother. The feeling we have is that no matter how much we do for her it isn't enough. Its because we lack means. She feels caregiver's fatigue. And I feel it, personally. (Alejandro S.) [15]

Salvador B. (husband of Alicia B.), who takes care of his paraplegic father, tells us that something similar happens with him:

> And uneasiness... as a psychologist said, about the bad nights, the hard nights… I don't sleep. I wake up a lot. He has these attacks. And he gets convulsions. My mom comes... I sleep in fits and starts. It's never sound sleep. My mom comes at night and when I hear anything, like if she calls me, Ah! … (Salvador B.)[16]

Another frequent consequence — whether made explicit by the caregivers or inferred from their behavior — of the anxiety provoked by the elderly person's vulnerability is an unnecessary and counterproductive overprotection which induces dependence. Lidia R., 60, who cares for her 84-year-old mother, clearly understands this when she tells us:

> Oh yeah, she moves fine. She does the shopping, everything. She even walks pretty fast. She can move great, thank God. Because of that the girls here always said: But if your mom is fine, why do you feel so obligated? Because I feel sort of … when, sometimes, I'm invited to do something on a Saturday and I still stay in. Until, the other day I was telling Mariana, until… generally, a little past one o'clock I leave and come back Sunday evening. All week we talk, every day we speak on the phone. If need be, two or three times a day, whatever. And I can't tell her until Saturday morning, at twelve o'clock noon, only then I tell her: Mom, you know I'm not going to be able to go… And Mom, happy in life, because my mom isn't irritating, at all. I don't know why. It's me who has some issue with my mom. I don't know why it's so hard for me. (Lidia R.)[17]

---

[15] Alejandro S., 38, single, and his mother, Teresita S., 66, widow. Alejandro lives with his mother and took the course so as to be able to help her care for his widowed grandmother, 91, and his great-aunt, also a widow, 89. Teresita has always lived close to her parents. In the last few years she has had to take charge of the care of her father and later of her own husband until they passed away. To cover costs she sold property. Seven months ago her only brother died. After this, the health of her mother, who suffered heart problems, worsened, and she became depressed. A sister of her mother, 89, a widow, has begun to manifest cognitive disorders which make it impossible for her to continue living alone. Teresita plans to bring this aunt to live with her so as to be able to care for her and sell her apartment to cover the costs, since the three women have very reduced pensions. Her strategy is, therefore, to sell property.

[16] See footnote number 8

[17] See footnote number 9.

A similar feeling, though certainly nuanced differently, tends to arise in the situation where the dependent—especially when it is a parent or loved one—is deteriorating (especially in cognitive function):

> I had a stage… because, well, there are a lot of things to it. One is seeing one's parents' deterioration which certainly isn't any fun. I don't think anyone would find it funny, the fact that… But you also take it as a part of that… that cycle we all go through. There comes a time when your mind raises those questions: what's going to happen here… and you sometimes try not to agonize over it, but… there is a sort of underlying anxiety there that, well, sometimes I can shake it off until later and sometimes it really hits me and, well, it's a matter of getting through it, and it passes. It passes because you have other distractions. If you didn't, you might get stuck on that, and that would be terrible. (Jorge K.)[18]

A similar sentiment appears in the words of Liliana P.:

> Emotionally, it takes me a long time. And I feel a lot of emotional pressure because my mother was always all-powerful. And suddenly she isn't all-powerful, she wants to keep being all-powerful. But there's also a fight. You have to fight to make her understand that there are things she can't do anymore and that you have to adapt to the way things are now. Apart from that it's as though the myth has fallen, the idol. Because all her life she was independent, she did everything according to her whim. She came and went. She raised all of us by herself. Without my dad's help, because he was fading. But she didn't ask anything of him, because she was all-powerful. (Liliana P.)[19]

Summarizing, we find that, among the feelings that sustain the caregiving function, the subjects note some that, in some way or another, cause anxiety for the caregiver. This anxiety generally derives from the precarious state of the dependent, who seems unprotected, weak, needy, and from the fact that a strong internal sense of duty mandates that the caregiver take the responsibility of ensuring the well-being of that sick dependent. As we stated before, this sense of duty can be conceptualized as the payment of a symbolic debt (P. Pitaud 1999) or as the fulfillment of an intergenerational pact (M. Johnson, 1995), but its existence is observed on all fronts.

We have also seen the distinctions in the relationships between parents and children and husband and wife. In respect to these differences, it must be said that while the former feel great anxiety as they witness the deterioration of their parents, the wives, in some cases, seem to experience a sort of revenge upon seeing their husbands undergo the process. This feeling results from the traditional gender roles that marked the man´s decision-making power in the couple, especially in this generation.

---

[18] See footnote number 6.

[19] . Liliana P., 37, married, one son. She took the course so as to collaborate with her sister who currently cares for her widowed mother, 77, who suffers cardiac problems and has begun to suffer cognitive disorders and depression. In the past the mother lived with one of their sisters, a drug addict, who made various attempts at suicide. All the brothers and sisters got together and decided to send the mother to live in another city with one of the daughters, since they considered that she needed a more tranquil environment.

The Lack of Gratitude

Especially when the dependent suffers from cognitive disorders, or is very dependent, the caregiver receives little or no sign of gratitude from the dependent person, which generates great resentment and makes the caregivers begin to question the reason for their sacrifice. Teresita S. dares to express this in all its harshness:

> I take care of her as if she were a queen, clean, impeccable. Now I have to buy her diapers. In her life, she has used diapers. Just think, she has no strength… and then: "Forget you have a mother," she tells me. How can I not… because my defenses are down. So then I leave and start to swear. Because I have this attitude of anger. Which I don't want. I can't help it… (Teresita S.)[20]

And then she later adds:

> Because she says: "Bring me the coffin so I can get inside…" all those things… you know what happens, I can't, I don't listen to her. Then yesterday I was furious because my friend asked me: "Teresita, why have you treated her badly?" And I said: "No, if I don't explode like that I'll have a heart attack." I have been taking two anxiety pills a day, that's how bad I felt. Because it overwhelms me. It overwhelmed me. This situation has overwhelmed me. No, at that moment it was too much, because I know I'm making an effort to give her a quality of life that she doesn't want to have. Sincerely, I'm speaking harshly. Excuse me for talking this way. Because, I tell you. I'd rather she closed her eyes and went peacefully. And I could say: "Dear, I owe you nothing, dear, we are at peace." (Teresita S.)

Teresita S. is, without a doubt, overwhelmed by her situation. Her anxiety is perceptible at every moment, throughout her story. As we can see, aside from the economic problems that caring for her mother have caused her, and to which we will refer later on, it is this lack of recognition on her mother's part that most upsets her. In this scenario, she tries to move her mother and, in doing so, becomes a torturer who wants to force her out of bed:

> Yesterday I take off her glasses and she says, "Ah! Why do you treat me this way?" I swear, that's what she does. And I tell her: "Because we've got to take your glasses off." But she has to see me like the bad guy in a movie. It's like that. Because I make her sit down… I may be a little hot-headed, but, yes, I'm always a disturbance, the one who forces her to sit. She yells like someone who's being… and besides, she does nothing to help me. She's a dead body… (Teresita S.)

Though without these dramatic extremes, María Isabel F. is going through similar situations with her 90-year-old mother, especially since the death of her father:

> Yes, 65 years of marriage. And she says that dad is calling her. That he sees her when she is alone. These are things that I have to get over, but it's hard. (María Isabel F.)[21]

In spite of her efforts to renew her mother's will to live, she cannot:

---

[20] See footnote number 13.
[21] See footnote 7.

> My family is very close. For Mother's Day, even, since my father was a person who likes to get the whole family together, we tried to get everyone to come and I was happy, and the response my mother gave me was: "Yes, but someone is missing." How do I solve that? There is no solution. My son was there, my niece, the great-grandchildren. She has four great-grandchildren, and they all came. We had a barbecue. Even my mother-in-law, from the geriatric home. We had a really nice get-together of 25 people. And I was happy because Dad would have wanted it and she says to me: "yes, but someone is missing." And, okay, well, I can't solve that. (María Isabel F.)

In the caregiver-dependent dyad, reciprocal victim-victimizer situations involving mutual mistreatment often arise. It is a vicious cycle in which relationship forms establishes in infancy are doubtless reproduced. As counterevidence, Lidia R. highlights the good relationship she has with her mother:

> As far as positive aspects go, it seems to me that the relationship is nicer. I can tell her I love you and before I couldn't. My son taught me to say I love you to someone. Because my son calls me on the phone: "I love you, Mom" ... and I learned to say it to my mom. And I like that. I've also probably grown up more, I'm older... the relationship is different. A good relationship with my mother. (Lidia R.) [22]

To summarize, the dependent frequently fails to recognize the caregivers′ efforts. This lack of recognition generates feelings that can range from sadness and powerlessness to anger and rage. In the caregiver-dependent relationship, reciprocal relationships of victimization are common, and this victimization, in turn, gives way to violent responses and possible somatic/pyschological illnesses in the caregivers (McDonald, L, 1996). In the next section, we refer more specifically to the burden — objective and subjective — that the dependents represent for the family members who have the primary responsibility of supporting them.

THE COSTS OF CARE

Throughout this chapter reference is made to the extremely high costs that all of these families are paying in order to care for an elderly relative; it seems opportune, then, to analyze this concept. Various studies have attempted to arrive at a definition. Montgomery, Gonyea and Hooyman (1985) introduce the term "burden," conceptualizing a subjective state associated with the grade of inconvenience or bother occasioned by caregiving. Their definition also includes objective consequences such as the restriction of free time or the health deterioration; in nothing these effects, the burden inherent in the act of caregiving ceases to be merely a concrete fact. Instead, it has a definite subjective effect, which is apparently related to the mishmash of negative feelings and perceptions that caregivers experience in regards to their function, that is to say, to the level of bother or inconvenience originated by the continual care of the dependent.

From the stories of our interviewees arose various significant topics related to the costs or the burden of the caregivers, such as the abandonment of projects that we are going to present in the next section.

[22] See footnote 9.

Abandonment of Projects

María Juliana T. and Jorge K. have given up their independence.

> I would have been able to do it easily and say, okay, all set… At the moment I had my home. Or, I left the house to live with my partner, everything. And just afterwards my mom lost her job and I went back. I went back because I was saying "I'll just invest some money in a rental, because I know my family has always helped me." It just didn't seem fair to me… But, well, we were talking about how I could have stopped and said, okay, all set, done. I don't know why I didn't. They're things that… I couldn't break that tie with my family, even though it's often hard for me, makes me groan. I can't break ties. (María Juliana T.)[23]

Jorge K. tells us something similar:

> Yes, maybe, at some point I've wanted to do certain things, which I needed some time to be able to do and it's been impossible to do them because I'm with my parents. That's an aspect which… I had the opportunity a few years ago to go and live with someone and I kept putting it off… I think that at the relationship level the subject was sort of off-limits. (Jorge K.)[24]

As it appear clear from those transcripts, there are no alternatives, different caring arrangement are not possible, not as much because they are not available, but they are not even thinkable. Another major cost of caregiving is having no time left for oneself, this is probably the most frequent complaint of caregivers.

Time Gone By

The costs to which all subjects without exception make reference are those which pertain to the lack of available time: with having life restricted and being unable to decide freely what they want to do. Hebe M., 72, who cares for her 82-year-old husband, with cognitive disorders, laments:

> Emotionally, I'm mad. My life is passing by. Am I going to end my life this way, caring for others, in this case for him? And I also see the deterioration. A really brutal kind. Sometimes he asks me, "what should I wear?" and I tell him "wear the same thing you wore yesterday, the pants and the polo shirt." And he comes in wearing pajamas. But not always. And I tell him, "No, that's to sleep in, Raúl, look closely." For example, sometimes I come home and tell him, briefly… "you didn't tell me where you went." And, a little while later,

[23] María Juliana T., 27 years old, single. She took the course so as to solve a very complex family problem caused by the illness of her widowed grandmother, 75. Together with her mother and grandmother she is part of a typical verticalized family group. They have always lived all three together, the mother has worked as a domestic employee who slept at the site of her employment while María Juliana lived with her grandmother. When the grandmother began to have heart troubles María Juliana took care of her. But currently she works and studies and her grandmother suffers cognitive disorders which make it impossible for her to stay home alone. After much suffering they decided to send her to a geriatric home close to the house so they could visit her regularly. This is an enormous economic burden for them, and the three women have all felt the reduction in their quality of life.

"why don't you tell me." I live on one floor... I either get mad myself or get mad at him. "I already told you a thousand times." "You didn't tell me anything!" My question is, how long will I be able to stand it? For example, I'd like to go on vacation. Alone, with my daughter, on an exchange with a group. And where would I leave him? He can't stay alone, there's no way. He wouldn't want to stay alone, either. It's a pretty heavy backpack, sometimes. (Hebe M.)[25]

Teresita S., to whose case we have dedicated much space, expresses it this way:

I'm doing as much as I can. Then, God will decide. But I, right now, no, it's like I've stopped living. Because I used to go out to walk. Simple things. I took my rosary, prayed the rosary. Now I haven't gone to mass in three or four weeks. I don't have time and when the moment comes I don't feel like it. I had a little Virgin in the house, I prayed. But now I don't have the strength. I don't know if it's physical strength or mental strength I lack. But it's too much for me. See, when you've been taken over, you do what you have to do like a robot... So the bad part is that I'd like to see the sun and say, "what a beautiful sun!" Go out walking. The other day I put my sneakers on, walked four blocks, and came back. It's like my energy is exhausted. (Teresita S.)[26]

The lack of time for relaxation, the stress connected to caregiving, often translate in actual sickness and health problems for the caregiver, as it will be discussed in the next section.

Costs for the Health of the Caregiver

The health costs, physical as well as mental, are also very high, especially for primary caregivers, that is to say, for those who are most involved in the task. Alicia B. tells us that she began psychological treatment:

And now I take psychological treatment. When he met me he said that I was bitter, but I used to be happy. I like to go out, but now I stay at home more and more. And I'm more and more exhausted. (Alicia B.)[27]

Liliana P. refers to the disorders suffered by her sister who cares for their mother in Córdoba:

The other day I was talking with my brother-in-law and he was telling me that when there's some kind of or whatever, immediately my sister's health seems affected. She has digestive problems, something like that. Nerves. Because she, when my mother gets really nervous or out of it... my sister starts feeling bad, and, yeah, she falls apart. She loses her voice. (Liliana P.) [28]

---

[24] See footnote 6.

[25] See footnote 10.

[26] See footnote 13.

[27] See footnote 8.

[28] See footnote 17

María Margarita B., 47, who cares for her mother, 78, also feels that her health has suffered:

> My health has been endangered, too. I've been getting checkups, because I feel something like exhaustion. But, no, luckily there's nothing. You can tell that it was tiredness, from coming and going. But no, it's under control now, for me, too. I realized in time that I needed to get under control, see someone... (María Margarita B.)[29]

Liliana P. also indicates having gone through spells of depression:

> Yes, even, when all of this had just recently come up and I began my class, two months, three months, it was really hard for me to go to class because it was hard to leave the house. I shut myself in... one of the symptoms that it said on the paper that they gave us the first day was about isolation and that sort of thing. And it was really hard for me to leave my house. I stayed shut in all day, in bed. I got up in the morning, gave the boy his breakfast. My husband took him to school, and I stayed there until three-thirty in the afternoon until I got off to run and pick him up from school and only then did I start doing anything at all. (Liliana P.)

Caregiving often represent an health hazard, it is also often a significant financial burden for the family involved. In the next section we are going to present some interviewees' accounts in relation to the effect of caregiving on the financial stability of the family.

Economic Costs

Without a doubt, under the category of "costs" experienced by the caregiver, the economic one is relevant. In effect, financial problems arise over and over in our interviewees' stories and are recurrently mentioned in this chapter:

> Yes, there have been economic problems. I've taken responsibility for that as well. Because, economically, there was nothing... like I couldn't give her money and I couldn't buy her medicine. It's not that she went without eating, but many of her needs could not be met... (Liliana P.)
>
> My father's medicines are expensive. We go without some things of our own to give them to them. (Salvador B.)[30]
>
> There are times when she needs to buy her medications, but her pension isn't enough. That's why I have economic problems, because I get paid by the hour, I don't have a salary. I may do some juggling, but my mom will not go without. (María Margarita B.)[31]
>
> We've had a lot of expenses, especially hiring people to be with her during the day and at night. (Alejandro S.)[32]

---

[29] María Margarita B., 47, has a married son and a grandson. She lives with her partner. She works cleaning family homes. She cares for her mother, 78, a widow, who lives alone even though she suffers problems with her legs which limit her ability to walk to the point that she does not leave the house. The family group is composed of nine brothers and sisters of which only four take responsibility for their mother's care. María Margarita is the principal caregiver but counts on her brother's and a niece's contributions.

[30] See footnote 8.

[31] See footnote 27.

32 See footnote 13.

The problem is money. I'm spending what I don't have. I take out loans and I have to pay them back. Money doesn't come into the house, it only goes out. The savings are gone. I don't know where to get money from. (Teresita S.)32

The economic cost of care passes the breaking point and frequently implies deterioration in the family economy which can be suffered by future generations of the involved families. Furthermore, when the caregivers are older people themselves, their savings may be negatively impacted, affecting their quality of life in their own old age. This is the case of Teresita S., to whom we refer in more detail upon discussing the topic of strategies implemented. Housing issues are often implicated in caring, they are mentioned in various chapters throughout the book and they are discussed in details by Watson, in chapter 8. In the next paragraph we present in particular the problems connected to different generations living in the same household.

Costs of Being a Verticalized Family

One couple among our interviewees constitutes a paradigmatic example of a verticalized family. Living in the same household seems to be a supplementary stressing factor. We will take the space here to tell their story because we believe that it shows a concentration of various key aspects of the family caregivers' problem.

Alicia B., 55, and Salvador B., 52, a married couple, are taking responsibility for the care of three of their respective parents, with whom they live, while at the same time supporting their only son, a 19-year-old student. This is a typical example of a verticalized family; Salvador is an only son and at the same time has had an only son; Alicia has only one brother. Between the two they care for the father of Salvador, who is 78, the mother of Salvador, 75, and Alicia's mother, 88. Furthermore, they are part of the so-called "sandwich generation," which must look after its parents while its children are themselves not yet independent. They are overcome by the weight of this responsibility and the demands of the people under their care. As we mentioned earlier in reference to the families with many elderly members who must be cared for and the few younger family members available to help, this couple has reached the limit of their possibilities.

In the unfolding of their story they have made decisions which now seem like mistakes, most importantly the decision to live with their parents. They explain it this way:

It's all theirs. It's all in my dad's name, the land. So when we got married, we built our place behind theirs...it's not that we want leave them alone, because to start off with we would have to have been apart. I didn't realize, because I lived there. The place is pretty, we did something nice, whatever, but... (Salvador B.)[33]

...my mother was widowed and she came to live with me. Since my parents-in-law already lived with us.... I don't know. And now that we've gotten started, we're not going to leave them. (Alicia B.)32

[33] See footnote 8.

Four years ago, when Salvador's father got sick and became paraplegic, the problems started. Salvador feels that he must be at his father's side and Alicia blames him for not being able to tear himself away.

> Because we were already going crazy. Because the situation got worse. When he got sick my father-in-law was terrible. And my mother-in-law doesn't really know how to stay uninvolved, more like not at all. So it was chaos. At that point I more or less took the wheel, but the time came when we were totally destroyed. We fought a lot because he, every little thing... he wanted to be on top of every little thing. And I didn't. We went through hell. (Alicia B.)

Throughout the entire interview Alicia does not stop explaining that it's not caring for her relatives that bothers her, but rather living with them. She would have rather had them live in another house and had to go there to care for them, to be able to enjoy some intimacy with her husband and son.

> For me, taking care of them doesn't bother me at all. Even helping them economically, if I have to buy their medications, because they aren't bad people, bad parents. The only thing that kills me is living all together. If we lived separately I'd go to them. Because, sometimes, I've taken his aunt to the doctor. You can tell that I'm inclined to do that. So what bothers me isn't the... what bothers me more than anything is the living together. (Alicia B.)

To summarize, the "costs" refer to the level of inconvenience produced by the caregivers′ efforts, as measured by objective indicators such as restriction of free time, deterioration of health, abandonment of personal projects, or economic pressure derived from caregiving costs. "Cost" implies the objective and subjective encumbrance that the caregivers′ task brings. In order to lighten the load of costs, the caregiver tries out various organizational strategies. Those strategies implemented by our subjects are discussed in the next section.

Strategies for the Organization of Care

One aspect of our research that has especially interested us is the strategy that these families employed to cope with this situation. And we encountered a wide variety of different solutions. In effect, in some cases the families were able to somehow organize themselves and this way kept the situation under control, while in others, the organization seemed chaotic and irresolute.

The Home Office

Jorge K., who is a real estate agent by profession, opted to work at home in order to "be there," as he puts it, and keep control over household events. He is single, and this permits him to be with his parents for the most time possible. On the weekends, as well as on days when he must travel for work, one of his brothers or sisters takes his place. He is confident that he can count on one of them whenever he might need to. He himself declares that the strategy that he has found is satisfactory, but also implies the sacrifice of some aspects of personal life.

> I'm usually around in the morning. My office is my house. I do everything by phone, and so... maybe I go by the office in the afternoon, or, like today, I'm doing things downtown because we're diversifying. Besides, I have to travel every once in a while, and at those times another family member steps in. (Jorge K.)[34]

As we can see, Jorge K. seems to be the organizer of a family support network in which members can trade places, sometimes being the primary, secondary, or tertiary caregiver, as becomes necessary.

Internment in a Retirement Home Close to the Family Home

María Juliana T., 27, tells us that she and her mother had to take the decision to intern her grandmother when the situation became unmanageable, given that both must work. She says:

> ...Before, it was under control, she made her own food, did some things, and lately she's stopped doing anything. If she doesn't have her food served to her she doesn't eat, or get hungry, or remember to eat. There were three people in our house taking care of her, and we couldn't manage. She wouldn't take her medicines, she wouldn't eat. And, well, given all that we had to opt to put her in a home one block from the house, so we're always over there visiting her... (María Juliana T.)[35]

This is another case of a verticalized family, of three generations of women, granddaughter, mother, and grandmother, who have always lived together. The internment decision had a very high cost for the family group, emotionally and economically. The grandmother´s retirement funds cover only half the cost of the geriatric ward and the rest must come out of the other two women's salaries.

> ...This home costs 470 pesos (160 US dollars) for a person like my grandmother who is mobile. My mother can't pay that amount, so she told them that what she can pay, with a lot of effort, is 400, and they left it at 400. But just now, today before coming here, we were doing all our bills, and we said, we won´t make it! (María Juliana T.)

This case also illustrates another of the aspects of the caregiving problematic which we initially mentioned: the changes in the situation of the woman. María Juliana T. works and does postgraduate studies and is not inclined to sacrifice these projects in order to stay at home and care for her grandmother.

> I´m trying to see things objectively because when I didn't, I suffered a lot. I cried a lot. And I said no. I think it was unfair for me. (María Juliana T.)

[34] See footnote 6.
[35] See footnote 21.

Though she thinks they made the right choice, she has not stopped suffering for having made it. Often, caregiving imply moving house for the cared for. This is a choice that is often difficult for both parts.

Move to Another City with a Daughter

Liliana P. has a large family: there are seven brothers and sisters. The difficulty that arose was reaching an agreement regarding what was best for their mother. But they did it, and decided that she would go to live with one of the daughters, in Córdoba, where the surroundings are calmer. The other children collaborate economically, when they can, from Buenos Aires. This way they took her out of an extreme situation linked to a suicidal drug-addict daughter who was negatively affecting the family network.

> ...somehow, we all got together. When we had to take her to Córdoba even the furthest gone of us was there. Since it was very difficult to take her, even the furthest gone... we used to take her to Córdoba, or send her on a bus, and it was tremendously traumatic because it was my sister Silvia and me and my brothers and sisters had taken themselves out of it. They gave us the money, but it was "you do it." Or, more like, you be the bad guy. The other one still used to come to my house to console my mother before she left. This time he didn't. This time we broke down and said: it's like this and it has to be like this and this is what we're going to do. And we all sort of took that stance. (Liliana P.)[36]

Family conflicts are often generated in relation to the allocation of caring responsibilities as in this case; in the next section we discuss as the property of one's house can be at risk because of the costs of caregiving.

Selling the House and Using up One's Personal Wealth

Teresita S.'s is another typical case. She is a widow of 62 years who takes care of her 91-year-old mother. In the past, she cared for her husband and father until they passed away. Her only brother passed away seven moths ago. She is now alone, and desperate. Little by little she has been using up her savings so as to be able to meet the costs of her mother's care and now she finds herself having to sell her possessions. She tells us:

> Here the problem is basically money. I am spending what I don't have. I've taken out loans, I have to repay that money... the problem is that there is no money coming into the house, it´s only going out. So all my savings are used up, everything has been used up and I find myself in a really tough situation at a time when I have to make any number of decisions... I'm killing myself. I'm giving... I don't want to be tragic, but I am sacrificing myself. And I don't want to sacrifice myself, sincerely... I've had to pawn jewels to be able to stay afloat. Because my economic situation is very bad... (Teresita S.)[37]

---

[36] See footnote 17.
[37] See footnote 13.

But Teresita S. does not only take care of her mother, but also of an 89-year-old aunt, who suffers early Alzheimer's symptoms which makes her unable to continue to live alone. This aunt has donated her apartment and Teresita plans to sell it and bring the aunt to live with her, to make ends meet. She explains this to us:

> Imagine now that I have to bring over my aunt, it's a mess. My aunt is in the early stages of Alzheimer's. I have to sell her apartment to be able to survive myself. Because she gave it to me. But until I sell it... I'm going through... I've had some terrible moments when my father, when my husband died I was left with debts, I sold the house, I paid it all... but now this is the worst moment of my life, emotionally and psychically speaking... the only thing I want is to lie in bed with the heating pad and not think. Because when I wake up in the morning my head is chaos. I don't know how to fix all this... (Teresita S.)

In Teresita S's story we observe a middle-class family with a good economic history whose wealth has shrunk during the last few years to afford the care of the oldest family members. The strategy has remained the same, to sell property in order to pay debts. This is another highlighted aspect of the caregiving problem: the possibility of inheriting wealth from the previous generation becomes less and less, since that wealth must be used for their care in old age.

In this section, we presented the strategies that the subjects implemented to resolve the problems of every day life. Some may be considered sucessful because they have allowed the caregiver to control the situation; others, on the other hand, have driven the families toward situations of even more vulnerability. Attending the course "Caring for Those Who Care" was considered by the participants an additional strategy, but we think it is worthwhile to examine the class in a separate section.

Why the Course?

In this section, we will reveal the interviewees´ opinions about the course—how they came across it and the impact it has made in their lives. We will point out how attending classes was a strategy that some caregivers adopted in the hope of alleviating the burden they felt in their caregiving role.

Different Kinds of Motivations

Among the myriad of interesting responses our subjects gave us during interviews, the reasons for which they approached Caring for Those Who Care and their success in the program surprised us. We found a wide variety of answers, from those who did it in the moment of maximum family tension to those who turned to the program anticipating future troubles and even those who sought to collaborate with a fellow family caregiver; there were even some who mistakenly approached the course thinking its subject matter was something different and who stayed because it interested them anyway. The following interviewees related these different motivations. At the most dramatic extreme, Salvador B. and Alicia B., as we saw before, say:

Because we were already going crazy... we went through hell. (Alicia B.) [38]

The course was greatly helpful to them:

It was very useful for us in the sense of getting away a little bit. Because we were all very close to the problem. What's more, we started leaving the house a little more. Because staying that way, with my father-in-law, paraplegic, it was like we were all paraplegic. We used to go out walking, the two of us, and we stopped. We started staying inside all the time. (Alicia B.)

Esther C., by contrast, began the course so as to prepare herself for possible future situations:

What's going on now is that at this moment I am taking charge. When I took the course for caregivers I was sort of foreseeing the future. He's (*referring to her husband*) 85 years old. It's a 15-year difference. I could already see that I would have to take care of him and of myself. Not just take care of him, but of me, too, keep myself up. (Esther C)[39]

Liliana P., for her part, saw in the course the possibility of supporting her sister, who cares for her mother in Córdoba:

I took the course because, at that time, I could not take charge of her myself, have her living with me and all that... She went to live at my sister's house in Córdoba and the situation is a little complicated. She started with cognitive problems, she still doesn't have a certain diagnosis of her illness... so it seemed to me to be a way to contribute something to my sister, who was there, to take the class and pass it along to her, because where she is this sort of course doesn't exist, and I'd pass along all the information. (Liliana P.)[40]

Alejandro S. also thought that participating in the course would permit him to help his mother care for his grandmother and great-aunt:

And why did I do the course, well, up until a year ago there was the possibility of her coming to live with us and now she is going to have to. So I wanted to be prepared. Because the course generates a structure, information and assistance from the social workers. There was a nurse in the course, and also psychological assistance. The course helped me a lot, and it keeps helping me. My worry was how to open my head up to be able to help these older people and, in case of not being able to assist them full-time, how to give ideas to my mother or whoever was right there, to tell them: look, we have people to turn to. (Alejandro S.)[41]

Others did the course because they felt bad for the people they cared for, as is the case for María Isabel F., 65, who cares for her 90-year-old mother. She tells us:

Because I felt bad. I felt like I was being aggressive with Mom. Because Mom has a problem which is like an arteriosclerosis of old age. So she says things that hurt me. And I respond badly and then make myself feel worse. So because of all that I took the course, and

[38] See footnote 8.
[39] See footnote 11.
[40] See footnote 17.
[41] See footnote 13 .

they told me that my mom's problem was first, and I had to understand that, but it was hard. She's medicated, they took her to another doctor and medicated her. For a month and a half she's doing well with the forgetting and all. But yesterday we started with the robberies. Because she keeps thinking she's being robbed. So since I'm the only one in the house it's hard for me to hear that. For example, we fought yesterday and today she's like a puppy and I feel bad. And now she's been saying that everything hurts, so they'll pamper her. Before I came I gave her some tea with aspirin and told her to go to sleep... but yes, it's hard for me. It's really hard on me, that's why I took the course. *(María Isabel F.)* [42]

Jorge K. also felt conflicted about his role as caregiver and wanted to receive help:

Strictly speaking, I did the course because my sister recommended it to me. The course's rationale is consistent with a certain unease one sometimes feels. It's that about caring for those who care, like the term says. We needed to take another look at what was happening to us. Sometimes one gets worked up over certain things. And sometimes the trigger is, of course, those we care for. And it's not their fault that they are the way they are. It's part of our life. *(Jorge K.)*[43]

In actual fact the course had a positive impact on the participants' life as it is illustrated in the next section.

How the Course Helped Caregivers

Regarding whether the course gave him skills which help him better carry out his duties, he has the following opinion:

To say that it wears me out... it would be a lie to say it didn't. But I think those are moments, and they pass later. I think that, exactly, after the course, the way I get made has changed a little bit. I think I started to take some time, started to delegate some things a little bit. I've got a ways to go yet, but... *(Jorge K.)*

We have observed that one of the principal aids that the course gives to the caregivers is something very simple: it gives them permission to take distance and delegate their duties to others, even temporarily. We believe that the "mandate" that in large part sustains the situation generates a sense of responsibility that make caregivers nervous when they are absent. Jorge K. again illustrates what "being there" means:

I believe that what I do, more than anything, is just be there. Sometimes that term seems a little passive, but the fact of being there implies that my mom is calmer. I tell you this because, sometimes, I find myself in situations like: we have to bathe him. Usually my mom goes with him when he bathes. But, my mom has some problems, so I ask her to bathe him when someone else is there, just in case. I might hand her a towel, or help with the chair... the fact is that, well, while someone else is there everything that could be dangerous has to be done. I think that's my job, the simplest one at least. There's also taking him to the hospital, of

[42] See footnote 7.
[43] See footnote 6.

course, staying with him, talking to the doctors, going to buy medicine. I do take charge of that, which no one else does. It's generally me. (Jorge K.)

This needs to ensure that nothing bad happen therefore generates a permanent nervousness, a sense of anxiety, sometimes produced by the overprotection of the dependent, which over time leads to exhaustion. The course enables the caregiver to take some distance and delegate his tasks to others, which brings relief. The sequence would be like this:

Anxiety
↓
Overprotection
↓
Exhaustion
↓
COURSE
↓
Permission to take distance
↓
Relief

María Juliana T., 27, who has her grandmother in a geriatric home, tells us that the course helped her to set limits, to know how far she had to take her dedication to the dependent.

-Because I wanted to be capable, to do my best. I wanted, well, there are things that I believe that because of my age I might not know, might not have enough experience. And also a little restraint. Maybe sometimes I said: okay, I'm young, I'm intolerant, and, well, how much do I have to put up with, and what things are really okay? To what extent I have to set limits. And, well, these days I'm the one who sets the limits.

-Did you learn that in the course or is that your character?

-Well, in the course it was like they told me: Okay, it's all right for you to set limits. Or at least that's the message I got. It's okay, setting limits. Even if she's like a kid, and all, because she isn't a baby. Sometimes you say: no, because she's older and she has severe cognitive disorders she's acting like a little kid. Yes, she might be acting like a little kid, but you have to set limits for little kids. And my mom can't. My mom can't set limits. So she suffers and now she's suffering, seeing her mother in the geriatric home: no, it shouldn't be like this. And, well, so that's the restraint that I have to have, on both counts. (María Juliana T.)[44]

To summarize, the interviewees′ responses indicate that one of the courses′ main effects was the possibility of establishing limits on their dedication, by coming up with alternative strategies for alleviating family and personal strain.

To take a distance from the caregiving situation physically, but above all psychologically, was the most important positive effect of the course.

[44] See footnote 21.

Conclusion

In this chapter, we have discussed the key themes that play roles in family care of the elderly with health problems. Using these as a basis, we examined the existence of networks of solidarity and the intergenerational pact as the fundamental basic ethic that forms and sustains the caregivers´ personal mandate. Families that take care of their elderly relatives and, consequently, experience stressful situations remain strong by invoking moral and ethical values. These values are maintained due to a strong psychological sense of duty in the caregiver. This sense of duty derives from the tacit pact that clinches solidarity between generations, which we call the intergenerational pact. There is a difference in the caregiving-ethic between the feeling of obligation that a parent-child relationship elicits (intergenerational pact) and the obligation that derives from a marriage contract. In the latter case, changes in the exercise of power are observed, given that women seem to take advantage of their spouses´ dependent situation. This observation should be taken up as a hypothesis in future research.

Of the multiple feelings – positive and negative – that arise in the caregiving situation, the responsibility that encumbers the caregiver due to the dependent person´s vulnerability generates a situation of permanent unease, even while sleeping the "nursemaid´s sleep." It has been observed that overprotection of the elderly person augments dependence, creating a vicious cycle. In the caregiver-dependent dyad, reciprocal relationships of victimization commonly arise that generate situations of mutual abuse and sickness. Family caregivers refer to the "high costs" incurred by supporting their sick elderly. Among the most important ones that arose in this project are: the abandonment of personal projects, lack of independence, lack of free time, lack of future personal time, the caregivers´ loss of physical and psychological health, and massive economic payments that endanger the future of the family caregivers.

Caregivers have come up with various strategies in an attempt to deal with the uncertainties of daily life. Some of these strategies we consider successful because they manage to control the situation; others, on the other hand, have not been able to resolve the crisis. Among the proposed strategies, attendance in the course "Caring for Those Who Care" has been found to offer caregivers information and facilitate a conscientious understanding of the situation. This knowledge helps the caregivers to distance themselves and set limits, and thus modifies the emotional burden of caregiving.

Recommendations

Be attentive to the demands for help that caregiving families and their elderly present, with the purpose of contributing to the job they are undertaking. These demands focus fundamentally in:

1. economic help (monthly subsidy, loans, etc);
2. complimentary services of domestic help (gerontolocial caregiver, nurse, domestic hospitalization, etc);
3. institutional care for the elderly during some period of time or season.

- Make known, through various means of communication, the different programs that exist to help family caregivers and end their isolation.
- Develop stable, uniform means and procedures of socio-healthcare coordination and complementation, given that a plan for caregivers integrates health questions as well as social ones.
- Develop and broaden a diversified aggregate of social services, with the idea of being able to furnish each case with adequate resources. Keep in mind that some families may need one or more services at the same time or in alternate form.
- Strengthen technical-professional services with the purpose of being able to guide the caregivers in utilizing and reaping their benefits of services at the level they require. Create the position of "Case Administrator." This could be a formal or voluntary job.
- Stimulate development of the complementation of social policies, given that currently, in practice, the informal caregiver is "punished" by the fact that in-home help services are not offered.
- Favor the possibility of making professional life compatible with the care of a dependent by means of legislation that would facilitate obtaining special licenses (remunerated or unremunerated).
- Encourage volunteering by facilitating a greater presence of such work in the field of the caring for the elderly and in helping the caregiving families. Technical and economic help should be given to them.
- Offer technical help in regards to adapting living quarters. This includes everything from the orientation to the execution of the modifications.
- Promote research in different regions whose results would permit the adjustment of policies and programs destined for caregiving families, keeping in mind their socio-cultural differences.

References

Bertaux, D. (1996) Historias de casos de familias como método para la investigación de la pobreza. *Revista de Sociedad, Cultura y Política,* 1, 10-21 Buenos Aires.

Chappell, N. (1996) The Sociological Meaning of Caregiving and Social Support: Issues for Older People, the Family and Community. In V. Minichiello, N. Chappell, H. Kendig and A. Walker (Eds.), *Sociology of Aging. International Perspectives.* (pp. 148-151) Melbourne: ISA, Research Committee on Aging.

Clifford, J. (1998) Sobre la autoridad etnográfica. En C. Reynoso (Comp.), *El surgimiento de la Antropología Posmoderna.* (pp. 141-170) Barcelona: Gedisa.

Fraser, N. (1997) *Iustitia Interrupta. Reflexiones críticas desde la posición postsocialista.* Bogotá: Universidad de los Andes-Siglo del Hombre Editores.

Instituto Nacional de Estadísticas y Censos (INDEC) (2003) La población argentina envejece. *Aquí se cuenta. Revista informativa del censo 2001,* 6, 1-4. En http://www.indec.mecon.gov.ar/webcenso/aquisecuenta/aquisecuenta.asp

Johnson, M. (1995) Interdependency and the Generational Compact. *Ageing and Society*, 15, 243-265.

Lomnitz, L. (1977) *Como sobreviven los marginados*. México: Editorial Siglo XXI.

McDonald, L. (1996) Abuse and Neglect of Elders. In J. Birren (ed.) *Encyclopedia of Gerontology*. (Vol.1, pp. 1-10). Los Angeles: Academic Press.

Monk, A. (1997) *Actualización en Gerontología*. Buenos Aires: Asociación Gerontológica Argentina.

Montgomery, R., Gonyea J. and Hooyman N. (1985). Caregiving and the experience of subjective and objective burden. *Family Relations. Journal of Applied Family and Child Studies, 34, 19-26.*

Oddone, M. J. (2001) Actitudes, percepciones y expectativas de las personas de mayor edad. Buenos Aires: FLACSO/STEAS. Versión electrónica en http://www.flacso.org.ar/posgrados/cursos/ig/publicaciones.jsp

Oddone, M. J. (2002) Ageing and Society. In S.D. Gorkhale and N. Pandit (Eds.), *Ageing in Search of its Identity.* (pp. 262-271). Pune: IFA, Community Aid and Sponsorship Programme and Aameyra Publishers.

Pitaud, P. (1999) La dependencia y su price en charge (responsabilidad) en Francia: Análisis crítico de un nuevo dispositivo. In R. Moragas Moragas (Ed.), *El reto de la dependencia al envejecer.* (pp. 17-30) Barcelona: Herder.

Vinocur, P. y Halperín, L. (2004) Pobreza y Políticas Sociales en Argentina de los años 90. Santiago de Chile: CEPAL. Versión *electrónica en http://www.eclac.org/*

Wacquant, L. (2001) *Parias Urbanos. Marginalidad en la ciudad a comienzos del milenio.* Buenos Aires: Manantial.

In: Argentina: Economic, Political and Social Issues
Editor: Jeanne B. Haverland
ISBN 978-1-60456-469-3

Chapter 3

SOCIOECONOMIC EFFECTS OF ECONOMIC CRISES: A COMPARATIVE ANALYSIS OF THE EXPERIENCES OF INDONESIA, ARGENTINA AND TURKEY[1]

Fikret Şenses [*] ***and Murat Koyuncu*** [†]
[*]Middle East Technical University, Turkey
[†]Department of Economics, University of Washington, Seattle, WA, USA

1. INTRODUCTION

Since the early 1990s, many developing countries have experienced economic crises following the liberalization of their capital accounts. These crises, often caused by the volatility of short term capital movements have had far-reaching effects, spreading from the financial sector to the real sector and then to socioeconomic indicators. The crises in individual countries have also had adverse effects in other countries, threatening the stability of the whole international financial system. 1994 Mexican, 1997 East Asian, 1998 Russian, 1994 and 2000-2001 Turkish and 2002 Argentinean crises have attracted the most attention in this respect.

The vast literature on economic crises has mainly concentrated on their causes and impact on the financial and the real sectors. The effects of crisis on income distribution, poverty, and the labor market, public expenditure on social sectors such as health and education, and indeed the whole social fabric of society which can be referred collectively as the socioeconomic effects have remained largely unexplored. The main objective of this study is to redress this imbalance in the context of three countries, Indonesia, Argentina, and Turkey, worst hit by economic crises in recent years.

Socioeconomic effects arise from a combination of many factors beyond those directly traceable to economic crises. Among these other factors the most noteworthy are the reaction of the public to the crisis and the attitude of domestic governments and key Bretton Woods institutions (BWI) like the World Bank and the IMF. These institutions which have played a major role in the neoliberal transition of a large number of developing countries during the past quarter century have often been in the forefront in the design of post-crisis economic programs. The fact that both Turkey and Argentina were caught in crisis in the midst of an IMF program makes it all the more important to examine the reaction of BWI.

Against this background, the study attempts to answer the following questions. What are the major socioeconomic effects of economic crises? What determines the magnitude of these effects and their pattern in different countries? Why is a comprehensive and active social policy package often missing from the post-crisis structural adjustment and stabilization programs? Which factors are likely to bring about a change in the attitude of domestic governments and the BWI toward more active social policies in the post-crisis setting?

Several factors have bedeviled our efforts to present a full account of the socioeconomic effects. Effects such as the deterioration of social relations, the rise in corruption and violence, despair and helplessness of individuals and society at large in the face of increasing dependency on external resources and institutions are not easy to quantify and document. The effects that are quantifiable, on the other hand, pertain to indicators for which available data is the most deficient. Finally, there is an acute lack of information about the relations between the countries in crisis and the BWI.

The study consists of five sections. In the following three sections, socioeconomic effects of the crises in Indonesia, Argentina and Turkey are analyzed in that order. The last section concludes.

2. Indonesia: From the Social Miracle to Social Explosion

Indonesia was regarded as one of the success stories of East Asia at the onset of the 1997 crisis. It had an uninterrupted growth record of 30 years, during which its GDP quadrupled. This was accompanied by a substantial improvement in socioeconomic indicators. Poverty rate fell from 70 percent in 1965 to 19 percent in 1996, and the illiteracy rate declined from 61 percent to 15 percent (Hill, 2000: 5, Table 1.2). The crisis in 1997 had a devastating effect on the economy and was responsible for the ensuing social explosion. Real GDP fell by 13 percent in 1998, manufacturing production declined by 34 percent and inflation rate jumped from six percent to almost 60 percent. Socioeconomic effects of the crisis were even more worrisome. As real wages plummeted, poverty rate doubled. There were riots, arson and looting all over the country, leading to the loss of more than one thousand lives.

This section first analyzes the socioeconomic effects of the 1997 crisis and then discusses the measures taken in response to it.

2.1. Socioeconomic Effects of the Crisis

2.1.1. Labor Market

The labor market has proven to be quite flexible in the face of the crisis with both wage employment and real wages declining drastically (Table 1). The flexibility of the labor market was attributed to the availability of considerable surplus labor and the absence of trade unions and protective labor legislation (Manning, 2000: 106). It seems that the labor market

---

[1] This is a revised version of Koyuncu and Şenses (2004), published in Turkish.

adjustment has taken the form of a rise in agricultural employment and non-wage employment rather than unemployment which increased only slightly from 4.7 percent in 1997 to 5.4 percent in 1998. In 1999, as the country started a fragile recovery, there was some improvement in employment and wage indicators.

Table 1. Labor Market Indicators, Indonesia, 1997-1999

	1997	1998	1999
Unemployment Rate (%)	4.7	5.4	6.3
*Real Wage Index**	100	68.0	75.2
Employment			
Agriculture	100	113.1	110.9
Industry	100	87.6	97.3
Wage Employment	100	94.5	96.4
Non-Wage Employment	100	106.8	107.8

*: For Manufacturing
Source: IMF (2002: 81, Table 2).

2.1.2 Income Distribution and Poverty

The crisis produced mixed results in this respect: While there was a sharp increase in poverty indicators, income distribution registered some improvement (Table 2). Tjiptoherijanto and Remi (2001: 11-12) suggest two factors to explain the improvement in income distribution. The first is that the crisis may have affected the modern-formal sectors in which the middle and high income groups are concentrated more than the traditional-informal sectors. The second factor is attributed to consumption smoothing by these very groups- an option not available to the poor already living at subsistence levels.

Table 2. Income Distribution and Poverty Indicators, Indonesia, 1996-1999

	Feb 96	Sep 98	Dec 98	Feb 99	Aug 99
Gini Coefficient	0.36	0.32			0.33
*Poverty (%)**	19.2	37.2	24.2	22.9	18.2
Poverty Severity Index (P2)					
Urban	0.85		1.27	0.93	0.74
Rural	1.06		1.48	1.18	1.17

*: Headcount ratio, using national poverty line
Source: Dhanani and Islam (2000: 12-13 and 19, Figure 3-4 and Table 6).

After rising sharply during the first year of the crisis, both the headcount poverty rate and the poverty severity index have returned to their pre-crisis levels by August 1999. Dhanani and Islam (2000: 15-16) underline the transient nature of poverty in this period and argue that the initial worsening was due to the 'inflation shock' in 1998. The reduction in inflation and the social protection measures introduced by the government have contributed to the rapid improvement in poverty indicators. The crisis seems to have had a more lasting effect on rural households with the depth of poverty as measured by Rural Poverty Severity Index (P2)[2] remaining above its pre-crisis level.

2.1.2. Education and Health Expenditures

The impact of the economic crisis on public health and education expenditure was mild with only slight changes in the share of education and health expenditures in GDP and in consolidated government budget (Table 3). The share of education expenditure in government expenditure declined from 15.7 percent in 1997 to 14.1 percent in 1998. As a share of GDP, educational expenditure actually increased from 2.8 percent in 1997 to 2.9 percent in the following year. There were, however, slight declines in national enrolment rates of primary and junior secondary schools (Lanjouw, *et al.*, 2001: 14, Table 4). During the same period, the share of health expenditure GDP went up from a mere 0.5 percent to 0.6 percent, while its budget share remained constant at 3.5 percent.

The effect of the crisis has not been uniform for different sections of the population. The percentage increase in dropout rates of the poorest quartile of children in primary school and upper levels were three to five times worse than the richest quartile's (Frankenberg, *et al.*, 1999: 21-22, Table 1 and Table 2). For health, there was no major deterioration in the overall service quality and health status of children, except a decline in the use of health services by children under 15.

Table 3. Education and Health Expenditures of Indonesian Government, 1996-1998

	1996	1997	1998
Education Expenditure/GDP (%)	2.8	2.8	2.9
Education Expenditure/Government Expenditure (%)	15.4	15.7	14.1
Health Expenditure/GDP (%)	0.6	0.5	0.6
Health Expenditure/Government Expenditure (%)	3.1	3.5	3.5

Source: Lanjouw, *et al.* (2001: 57-58, Table A1 and A2).

2.2. Social Safety Net Programs

A distinctive feature of the Indonesian experience was the introduction of the Social Safety Net (SSN) programs as part of the government's social policy response to the crisis. These programs which were aimed to mitigate the negative socioeconomic effects of the crisis can be summarized under four main headings: food security, employment creation, education and health (Table 4).

[2] Developed by Foster, Greer and Thorbecke (1984), also known as FGT (α=2) index. This index measures the depth of poverty by taking the square of the distance between the income levels of the poor households and the poverty line.

Table 4. Social Safety Net Programs in Indonesia

Safety Net Area	Programs
Food Security	Sale of subsidized rice to targeted households
Employment	Job opportunities through labor-intensive work programs
Education	Targeted scholarships, and block grants to the schools in poor regions
Health	Subsidy program for health services and nutritional support for pregnant women and their children

Source: Sumarto, Suryahadi and Widyanti (2002: 6, 26, Table I and VI).

The government attached a great deal of importance to the SSN programs which in 1998 accounted for 5.6 percent of total government expenditures. The major component of the SSN programs was the rice subsidy program covering a massive 40 percent of the total population. It reached more than one half of the households in the first quintile, thus enabling the poor to buy the main staple of Indonesian people for a quarter of the market price (Sumarto, Suryahadi and Widyanti, 2002: 16). Tabor and Sawit (2001: 279) have estimated that the average monthly per capita transfer through the rice subsidy program has been around 10 percent of the average income of the poor households in 1998. Dhanani and Islam (2000: 17) have argued that the transfers through this program may have prevented 7 to 12 percent of households from falling into poverty. Although the other components of the programs had a relatively limited coverage with smaller benefits for the poor, SSN programs are regarded as having contributed significantly to the alleviation of the burden of the economic crisis on the poor (Dhanani and Islam, 2000: 17-18).

Another aspect of the SSN package that deserves further attention is its timing and the motivation behind it. Safety net measures under the package were put in action in mid-1998, exactly one year after the eruption of the economic crisis (Dhanani and Islam, 2000: 16). The social upheaval during that one-year period as prompted by the economic crisis reached massive proportions, claiming more than 1000 lives and leading to the resignation of President Suharto, who had been in power for the past three decades. One of the first actions of the new government which took office in May 1998 was the introduction of the SSN package. Pritchett, Sumarto and Suryahadi (2002: 19-20) have summarized the situation clearly: "The SSN programs were being designed literally in the shadow of burned out buildings and with ongoing protests and hence there was a desire to design programs that could generate political support". Evidently, safety net programs were the direct result of the public reaction to the crisis and its effects.

Another point of concern in this respect is the attitude of the BWI which had a close relationship with the Indonesian government over the course of the crisis, especially in the design of post-crisis stabilization and structural adjustment programs. Official statements of the IMF[3] on Indonesia during the period from the beginning of the crisis to January 1998 do not include any comments on either the socioeconomic effects of the crisis or the policy measures designed to mitigate them. On January 15, at a time when public protests were gaining momentum, the IMF stated that if the government reallocated some of its budgetary expenditures of lesser importance to alleviation of the plight of the most vulnerable people in

[3] Official IMF statements ('News Brief's) on Indonesia are available at http://www.imf.org/external/country/idn/index.htm?type=9998#6.

the country, this would be approved by the Fund. Requiring the government to meet this spending on social safety nets without increasing its total expenditures already cut to the limit during a severe crisis, the IMF has made it clear that it was more committed to a balanced budget than to poverty alleviation. It was only when the new government introduced the safety net measures explicitly into the new Letter of Intent[4], IMF changed its attitude and approved the poverty alleviation package and the budget deficits that it would entail. The chronology of these events clearly shows that the change in IMF's attitude was prompted by the social explosion in the country and the new government's belated yet decisive approach to deal with it.

The World Bank's involvement in the SSN programs began only in mid-1999, a year after they were first introduced (World Bank, 1999: ii), and two years after the eruption of the crisis. Moreover, the amount of the loan, 600 million dollars, fell drastically short of coping with the gravity of the problem. For the 37.5 million Indonesians who were under the poverty line in 1999, this represented a meager 16 dollars per poor person. Its late response to the crisis and weak commitment to the poverty alleviation efforts of the government has shed considerable doubt over the World Bank's concern about the socioeconomic effects of the crisis in Indonesia.

3. Argentina: Marching into Social Chaos under the Supervision of the IMF

In December 2001, Argentina drew the attention of the world with its deep economic and political crisis amidst widespread demonstrations and riots. Some have blamed the IMF-supported stabilization and structural adjustment program for pushing the country into a vicious debt-crisis-debt cycle (Dinerstein, 2001). Others have put the blame squarely on the government for not fully complying with IMF's directions (Mussa, 2002). Leaving aside the debate on who is responsible for it, the crisis marked the economic and social collapse of a country that had implemented BWI-supported stabilization and structural adjustment programs during the last quarter of a century, at different periods and with different intensities.

The main thrust of Argentina's story is the neoliberal Convertibility Plan which was implemented for 10 years, between April 1991 and December 2001, with the continuous support of the BWI. It is for this reason that the socioeconomic effects of the Argentinean crisis should be examined in longer term perspective against the background of the Convertibility Plan.

3.1. Socioeconomic Effects

3.1.1. Labor Market

The most pronounced effect of neoliberal reforms on the labor market was a rise in the unemployment rate which increased steadily from 6.5 percent in 1991 to 17.5 percent in 1995

[4] Letter of Intent dated June 24, 1998 is available at http://www.imf.org/external/np/loi/062498.htm.

and remained around 14-15 percent in the second half of 1990's (Table 5). Moreover, underemployment rate has followed a similar path and reached 14.6 percent in 2000. As the Argentinean economy had recorded positive growth rates during the 1990s, except 1995 and 1999, worsening of unemployment can be linked with certain aspects of the neoliberal transformation of the economy. Two main channels in this transformation were of particular importance. First, 150,000 workers, corresponding to 10 percent of the number of unemployed were laid off during the privatization of state enterprises (Altimir, Beccaria and Rozada, 2002: 77). Second, the production of large firms as the real force behind Argentina's export success was biased towards capital-intensive methods as the fixed exchange regime was instrumental in artificially cheapening imported capital goods (Pastor and Wise, 1999: 486).

Between 1991 and 2001, real wages increased in the formal sector and exhibited a declining trend with some minor fluctuations in the informal sector (Table 5). The increase in real wages in the formal sector can in part be explained by the historical bonds of labor unions with Menem's Peronist Party, which remained in office between 1989 and 1999, and in part by economic factors such as the rise in productivity (Pastor and Wise, 1999: 489). However, as productivity increased faster than wages, workers' share in national income declined during this period.

The crisis in 2001 had an adverse effect on both wages and unemployment. While unemployment rate increased by 2.3 percentage points and reached 19.7 percent, underemployment rate rose by 3.7 percentage points and reached 19.3 percent, in 2002 (Table 5). Meanwhile, real wages declined by 21 percent in the formal sector and by 34 percent in the informal sector. This sharp worsening of labor market indicators points to the devastating impact of the crisis on the working population.

Table 5. Labor Market Indicators, Argentina, 1991-2002

	1991	1993	1995	1997	1999	2000	2001	2002
Employment Rate (%)	6.5	9.6	17.5	14.9	14.2	15.1	17.4	19.7
Underemployment Rate (%)	8.3	9.1	11.9	13.2	14.0	14.6	15.6	19.3
Average Real Wage-Formal Sector *	840**	957	939	944	976	979	970	769
Average Real Wage-Informal Sector *	634**	643	576	603	561	529	549	363

*: For Greater Buenos Aires region, in 2002 Pesos.

**: Data for 1992.

Source: Unemployment data from the Ministry of Economy and Production of Argentina website at http://www.mecon.gov.ar/peconomica/basehome/infoeco_ing.html; Real wage data from World Bank (2003: 12, Table 1.7).

3.1.2. Income Distribution and Poverty

The Convertibility Plan had a negative impact also on income distribution with the Gini coefficient increasing from 0.45 in 1990 to 0.53 in 2001 (Table 6). Top 10/Bottom 10 ratio, comparing the income of the richest 10 percent and poorest 10 percent of the population increased sharply from 21.6 in 1990 to 58.1 in 2001 and further to 85.5 in May 2002 in the immediate aftermath of the crisis. This was accompanied by a further increase in the Gini coefficient from 0.51 in 2001 to 0.53 in May of the following year. As the economy began to recover after that point, there was a slight improvement in both measures.

Table 6. Income Distribution and Poverty Indicators, Argentina, 1990-2002

	1990	1992	1994	1996	1998	1999	2000	2001	2002-May	2002-Oct
Gini Coefficient	0.45	0.46	0.47	0.49	0.50	0.49	0.51	0.53	0.55	0.53
Top 10/Bottom 10 Ratio	21.6	22.0	24.6	35.3	35.2	33.8	39.6	58.1	85.5	43.8
Poverty Rate (%)	40.4	23.0	21.3	30.8	29.5	31.0	33.1	37.1	55.3*	
Extreme Poverty Rate (%)	11.3	4.7	4.5	8.7	7.8	8.6	9.3	12.6	26.2*	

*: Average annual data for 2002.

Sources: World Bank (2000: 3, Table 1) and (2003: 57, Table A.4), and ECLAC Online Database at http://www.eclac.cl/badestat/.

Note: Poverty rates are based on the Argentinean government's official poverty lines, which are as follows. Poverty Rate (Row 4) is based on the poverty line of $160 per male adult per month in 1998. Extreme Poverty Rate or Indigence Rate (Row 5) is based on the food consumption portion of the poverty line and was equal to $69 per month in 1998 (World Bank, 2000: 4).

Poverty figures in Table 6 show that poverty incidence in Argentina has improved sharply during the 1990-1992 period. However, this improvement was more a result of the taming of hyperinflation of the 1980s than deliberate poverty alleviation efforts of the government. Moreover, after 1994, poverty rate rose continuously and reached 37.1 percent in 2001 while extreme poverty rate tripled during the same period.

The effect of the 2001 crisis, however, was much more dramatic. In 2002, both the poverty and the extreme poverty rates hit historical highs, even surpassing the very high levels of 1990, the last year of the hyperinflation period. While the poverty rate rose by 18.2 percentage points to 55.3 percent, extreme poverty rate more than doubled, from 12.6 percent in 2001 to 26.2 percent in 2002 (Table 6). The crisis brought the majority of the population, nearly 21 million people, face to face with poverty with nearly 10 million people classified as extremely poor.

3.1.3. Social Sector Spending-Education and Health

Social sector spending of the Argentine government as a percentage of GDP was quite high and increasing during the Convertibility Plan period (Table 7). But this result needs to be qualified on both counts. With regards to its level one should take note of the fact that public spending on social sectors in Argentina includes social insurance spending. As the latter is financed mainly by its beneficiaries and not by the government, this spending category, representing around 39 percent[5] of total public social spending (PSS), exaggerates the actual level of PSS by a big margin. Likewise, given the high elasticity of PSS with respect to changes in GDP[6], the increasing trend of real PSS should be attributed mostly to the

[5] The figure, calculated from Ministry of Economy and Production of Argentina data, represents the average for the 1991-2000 period.

[6] According to World Bank (2000:97), the elasticity coefficient for PSS for the 1980-97 period (1.3) was much higher than the coefficient for government expenditure (0.95).

expansion of the Argentine economy during this period, rather than the government's commitment to socioeconomic problems. In fact, the procyclical characteristic of PSS was confirmed during the crisis when at a time it was most needed PSS decreased from 22 percent of GDP in 2001 to 17.1 percent in 2002 (Table 7).

Table 7. Social Sector, Education and Health Spending of Argentine Government, 1991-2002

	1991	1993	1995	1997	1999	2000	2001	2002
Public Social Spending/GDP (%)	17.1	20.2	21.2	19.8	21.6	21.2	22.0	17.1
Education Expenditure/GDP (%)	3.6	4.1	4.3	4.3	4.9	5.0	5.2	4.3
Health Expenditure/GDP (%)	4.3	4.6	5.0	4.5	5.1	4.9	5.1	4.4

Source: Ministry of Economy and Production of Argentina website at http://www.mecon.gov.ar/peconomica/basehome/infoeco_ing.html

Both education and health spending as a percentage of GDP expanded throughout the course of Convertibility Plan (Table 7). Education spending/GDP ratio rose from 3.6 percent in 1991 to 5.2 percent in 2001. However, the situation worsened after the 2001 crisis; the ratio decreased to 4.3 percent in 2002. Considering the GDP itself has declined by 11 percent in 2002, educational expenditures plunged by 28 percent in absolute terms with obvious ramifications for the quality of education. Another factor of concern was that 72 percent of all households and 90 percent of poor households have reduced their spending on school materials after the crisis (World Bank, 2003: 20).

Public expenditure on health as a share of GDP increased during the 1990s, except for the 1996-1998 period, from 4.2 percent in 1990 to 5.1 percent in 2001, and then declined to 4.4 percent in the following year of crisis, representing a fall of 22 percent in real terms.

3.2. Social Assistance Programs

Argentina has been implementing social assistance programs targeted to poor families for over two decades. In 1998, there were 58 targeted programs in Argentina covering a wide range of areas including health, employment, training, education, shelter, clothing, and cash grants,[7]. Despite this thematic richness, the low level of funding combined with the politically manipulated, scattered and inefficient structure of programs prevented them from providing a reliable safety net for the poor. Table 8 shows that during the 1997-2001 period TSS contracted by a massive 13.2 percent in real terms. Seen in conjunction with the rise in the absolute number of people in extreme poverty, this has meant a fall in TSS per poor person by more than 50 percent after 1997 (Table 8).

Although TSS as a percentage of GDP rose after the 2001 crisis, its real level remained almost constant (Table 8). Since there was a sharp increase in the number of poor people during the crisis period, per poor person spending in the first year of the crisis declined further to one half of its level in 2001.

[7] See World Bank (2000: 152-162, Annex 1) for short contents of all of these 58 programs.

Table 8. Public Expenditure on Targeted Social Programs, Argentina, 1997-2002

	1997	1998	1999	2000	2001	2002
Targeted Social Spending/GDP (%)	1.6	1.6	1.4	1.5	1.5	2.4
Real Targeted Social Spending Index (1997=100)	100.0	100.5	89.3	92.3	86.8	87.0
Real Targeted Social Spending Per Poor Person (1997=100)	100.0	96.0	76.5	72.2	49.5	23.6

Source: SIEMPRO (2002: 20, Cuadro 3 and Cuadro 4).

Argentine government's main social policy program after the crisis was an expanded version of a previously implemented social workfare program named *TRABAJAR.* The new program, *Jefes y Jefas de Hogar,* provided employment opportunities for unskilled labor, the majority of whom being poor, through infrastructure projects with a wage rate lower than the ongoing market rate. Galasso and Ravallion (2003: 15) have estimated that the new program has reached two million people and caused the extreme poverty rate to decline by two percentage points.

The Argentine government seems to have given a faster social policy response than the Indonesian government had done to the 1997 crisis. Although the budget resources allocated fell short of coping with the gravity of the problem, a social assistance program was put into implementation in April 2002, only a few months after the eruption of crisis. However, the interim period was full of events that were reminiscent of the Indonesian case. There were widespread public protests, looting and street violence, contributing to political instability and the eventual resignation of the government. As in the case of Indonesian Social Safety Net program, the new government's main concern in introducing the social assistance program was to contain the social explosion and restore law and order.

The response of the IMF and the World Bank to the Argentinean crisis bore a close resemblance to that in Indonesia. The IMF did not seem to be interested in social policy matters with the social assistance program receiving IMF approval only after its announcement by the new government. Likewise, the World Bank supported the program with a $600 million loan, but only six months after the program was put in action.

4. Turkey : Social Policy as a Missing Component in Post-Crisis Programs

The Turkish economy has been characterized by boom and bust cycles, during which periods of rapid growth were followed by sharp contractions or economic crises. This pattern of growth did not change after 1980 when the transformation of the economy from an inward-looking and state-dominated one to an outward-oriented and market-based one began under the auspices of Bretton Woods Institutions. If anything, this pattern was reinforced by the move towards capital account liberalization as an integral part of this transformation in 1989 after which economic performance became increasingly dependent on the volatility of short-term international capital flows.

Against this background, Turkey experienced three major economic crises during the 1994-2002 period; first being in 1994, second in November 2000 and the third in February

2001. 2000 and 2001 crises are generally viewed together as the 2000-2001 crisis since they were separated only by a few months and were closely related with each other. These crises were initiated by sharp capital outflows from Turkey, causing the financial markets to collapse in a short period of time. The effects of the crises spread quickly from the financial sector, to real sectors such as manufacturing and then to socioeconomic indicators affecting the welfare of the entire population. Among the most common effects of these crises were a deep contraction of the economy, a sharp rise in inflation and unemployment and a fall in real wages. The crises were typically followed by the introduction of stabilization and structural adjustment programs under BWI supervision. Some of the typical measures taken as part of these programs such as suppression of real wages and reduction of public employment and spending in social sectors exacerbated the negative effects of the crises.

The main objective of this section is to analyze the socioeconomic effects of the 1994 and 2000-2001 crises in conjunction with the impact of the ensuing stabilization and structural adjustment programs, and the respective response of governments, BWI as well as the Turkish people to the crises.

4.1. Socioeconomic Effects of the 1994 and the 2000-2001 Crises

4.1.1. Labor Market

4.1.1.1. 1994 Crisis

Turkey's labor market could hardly be considered as a rigid one prior to the 1994 crisis (Şenses, 1996: 83). In 1993, the share of wage employment in total employment was slightly more than one-third, and the ones with access to a social security scheme accounted for a mere 42 percent of the total number of employed persons, representing formal employment. Yeldan (2001: 96) has estimated that even in the manufacturing sector, which generally contains the highest share of formal employment among all sectors, the share of formal employment in total employment was only 57 percent in 1993.

The impact of the 1994 crisis on the labor market was felt more on real wages than employment (Table 9). The stabilization program introduced in April 1994 shortly after the outbreak of the crisis also contributed to the sharp fall in real wages, partly through the introduction of a wage freeze in the public sector. Unemployment increased from 7.8 percent in 1993 to 8.2 percent in 1994 while underemployment rate rose from 6.9 percent to 8.2 percent. During the same period, manufacturing employment fell both in public and private enterprises, by 7.4 percent and 2.2 percent, respectively. Meanwhile, all real wage indicators fell by more than 20 percent, except public sector gross wage which declined by around five percent.

Although the economy was quick to recover with an eight-percent growth rate in 1995 real wages continued to fall with different intensities reflecting to some extent the effect of the stabilization program which, while losing some of its early momentum was still in force. Real civil servants' salaries and the minimum wage declined by around five percent, private sector gross wages fell by 14 percent, and public sector gross wages fell by 21 percent in 1995 (Table 9). On the other hand, as the economy entered a recovery phase, employment started to pick up and unemployment and underemployment went down to 6.9 percent and 6.7

percent respectively, in 1995. Employment in the private manufacturing sector which rose by more than 10 percent surpassed its pre-crisis level, while manufacturing employment in the public sector continued to fall[8].

Table 9. Labor Market Indicators, Turkey, 1993-1995

	1993	1994	1995
Unemployment Rate (%)	7.8	8.2	6.9
Underemployment Rate (%)	6.9	8.2	6.7
Manufacturing Employment Indices (1992=100)			
Of Private*	100.6	98.4	108.0
Of Public	93.8	86.9	74.9
Real Wage Rate Indices (1993=100)			
Minimum Wage	100.0	78.6	74.4
Private Gross Wage	100.0	79.9	68.4
Public Gross Wage	100.0	94.7	74.5
Civil Servants' Net Salary	100.0	78.0	74.3

*: For establishments with more than 9 workers

Sources: Unemployment and employment figures are compiled from the Household Labor Force Survey results and Manufacturing Industry Statistics of the State Institute of Statistics available at State Statistics Institute website (www.die.gov.tr). For real wage indices; IMF (1998: 148, Table 36).

Although the economy was quick to recover with an eight-percent growth rate in 1995 real wages continued to fall with different intensities reflecting to some extent the effect of the stabilization program which, while losing some of its early momentum was still in force. Real civil servants' salaries and the minimum wage declined by around five percent, private sector gross wages fell by 14 percent, and public sector gross wages fell by 21 percent in 1995 (Table 9). On the other hand, as the economy entered a recovery phase, employment started to pick up and unemployment and underemployment went down to 6.9 percent and 6.7 percent respectively, in 1995. Employment in the private manufacturing sector which rose by more than 10 percent surpassed its pre-crisis level, while manufacturing employment in the public sector continued to fall[9].

4.1.1.2. 2000-2001 Crisis

Turkey experienced a short-lived boom during the first ten months of 2000 under the exchange-rate-based stabilization program, which was launched on December 9, 1999. Although the November 2000 crisis brought the economic expansion to a halt for the rest of the year, average growth rates of real GNP and manufacturing output were over six percent for the year as a whole. This had a positive but limited impact on employment indicators. In the manufacturing industry, for example, while employment in the private sector declined by 1.4 percentage points, public sector employment continued its downward trend with a 5.4

[8] Neoliberal economic policies which required the state economic enterprises to be shut down, privatized or under-invested were largely responsible for this loss of employment in the public sector (Şenses, 1996: 85-86).

[9] Neoliberal economic policies which required the state economic enterprises to be shut down, privatized or under-invested were largely responsible for this loss of employment in the public sector (Şenses, 1996: 85-86).

percentage points fall in 2000. Unemployment for the country as a whole decreased to 6.9 percent in 2000 from 8.3 percent in the previous year and underemployment fell from 9.8 percent to 7.4 percent in the same period (Table 10).

Real wages presented a mixed picture in 2000. While the minimum wage and civil servant salaries decreased by 14 percent and 11 percent in real terms respectively, private sector wages increased by one percent and wages of public sector workers rose by seven percent (Table 10). Although the stabilization program aimed to restrain wages through a forward indexation mechanism, this could not be implemented in the public sector and in some of the private sector firms as agreements were mostly bound in the previous year (Uygur, 2001: 12).

Table 10. Labor Market Indicators, Turkey, 1999-2002

	1999	2000	2001	2002
Unemployment Rate (%)	8.3	6.9	9.1	11.5
Underemployment Rate (%)	9.8	7.4	6.5	6.1
Manufacturing Employment Indices (1992=100)				
Of Private*	91.7	90.3	82.5	84.4
Of Public	89.0	83.6	78.2	70.9
Real Wage Rate Indices (1993=100)				
Minimum Wage	123.9	105.8	91.1	98.4
Private Gross Wage	92.8	93.8	74.8	...
Public Gross Wage	105.0	112.3	99.3	90.2
Civil Servants' Net Wage	95.1	84.1	81.0	85.6

*: For establishments with more than 9 workers

Sources: Unemployment and employment figures are compiled from the Household Labor Force Survey results and Manufacturing Industry Statistics of the State Institute of Statistics available at the website of State Institute of Statistics (www.die.gov.tr). Real wage indices are from Undersecretariat of Treasury (2003: 34, Table 1.1B).

In February 2001, the country was hit by perhaps the most severe of its crises to which the Turkish government responded with a comprehensive structural adjustment and stabilization program (The Strengthened Program[10] of April-May 2001), signaling a deep recession. TSP aimed to reduce the public sector expenditures by cutting public employment and suppressing real wages. These measures, combined with the adverse effects of the crises themselves, produced negative results for the working population, as reflected in employment and wage indicators of 2001 (Table 10). Although the underemployment rate declined slightly, the overall unemployment rate reached 9.1 percent. Private and public manufacturing employment indices fell by 8.6 percent and 7.7 percent, respectively. On the wages front, private sector workers were the hardest hit, experiencing a real wage loss of around 20 percent in 2001. Minimum net wage and public sector wages have declined by 14 percent and 11 percent, respectively. The least affected section of the labor force was the civil servants,

[10] The program is known as 'Program for Moving to a Stronger Economy (PMSE)' in Turkey. We use the name 'The Strengthened Program', since TSP, which is structured in the May 2001 Letter of Intent, is in some respects different from the PMSE, which was announced in mid-April. There will be further information on this issue in the following sections.

who saw their real salaries decrease by less than four percent. Real wage losses of such proportions have meant that all wage categories were below their 1993 levels.

Interestingly, the recovery of 2002, with real GNP growth of 7.8 percent and manufacturing output growth of more than 10 percent, failed to prevent unemployment from rising further to 11.5 percent in 2002 (Table 10). Although there was a slight improvement in private manufacturing employment, public employment in this sector continued to decrease as the retrenchments in state enterprises were sustained as a part of the stabilization program[11]. Since 2002 was an election year, the government somewhat relaxed its tight incomes policy and increased civil servants' salaries and the minimum net wage by 5.7 percent and eight percent, respectively.

4.1.2. Income Distribution and Poverty

In the absence of periodic household income and consumption surveys to provide systematic data for examining in detail the trends in income distribution and poverty and the impact of crises on them we draw on the three surveys available for 1987, 1994 and 2002. Apart from the comparability of surveys, the fact that the effects of the crises cannot be isolated from those of other events that took place in the long intervals between the surveys poses formidable difficulties for our examination.

4.1.2.1. Income Distribution

Between 1989 and 1994, the government pursued an expansionary economic strategy, which was based on significant wage increases for labor, and high interest income gains, artificially low input prices and low taxes for the capitalist class. This strategy came to a halt with the financial crisis of early 1994. The expansionary strategy and the subsequent crisis resulted in a sharp deterioration in income distribution during the 1987-94 period.[12] While the share of the richest quintile rose by nearly ten percent, income shares of the first four quintiles declined. The Gini coefficient increased from 0.44 to 0.49 and the ratio of income share of the richest quintile to the poorest increased from 9.6 to 11.2 (Table 11).

The overall deterioration in income distribution stemmed from the urban areas. While the richest urban quintile increased its income share from 50.9 percent in 1987 to 57.2 percent in 1994, all other urban quintiles saw their shares falling. Consequently, the urban Gini rose sharply from 0.44 to 0.52 and Top 20/Bottom 20 ratio increased from 9.4 to 11.9. On the other hand, rural income distribution improved slightly between 1987 and 1994. Rural Gini fell from 0.42 in 1987 to 0.41 in 1994, and the Top 20/Bottom 20 ratio declined from 9.2 to 8.5. These improvements were due to the increasing shares of the poorest two quintiles in rural areas.

[11] As a result of continuous lay-offs and privatizations, the number of workers in the state-owned manufacturing enterprises in 2002 was less than half of that in 1992.

[12] Information is based on the total household nominal income data, as collected by the SIS Household Income and Consumption Expenditure Surveys (HICES) of 1987 and 1994.

Table 11. Income Distribution and Inequality Measures, Turkey, Urban and Rural, 1987, 1994 and 2002[13]

	Turkey			Urban			Rural		
Quintiles	1987	1994	2002	1987	1994	2002	1987	1994	2002
1st (Poorest)	5.2	4.9	5.3	5.4	4.8	5.5	5.2	5.6	5.2
2nd	9.6	8.6	9.8	9.3	8.2	9.7	10.0	10.1	10.3
3rd	14.1	12.6	14.0	13.6	11.9	13.9	15.0	14.8	14.7
4th	21.2	19.0	20.8	20.7	17.9	20.5	22.0	21.8	21.7
5th (Richest)	50.0	54.9	50.1	50.9	57.2	50.4	47.8	47.7	48.0
Gini Coefficient	0.44	0.49	0.44	0.44	0.52	0.44	0.42	0.41	0.42
Top20/Bottom20	9.6	11.2	9.5	9.4	11.9	9.2	9.2	8.5	9.2

Sources: SIS 1987 and 1994 Household Income and Consumption Expenditure Survey Results and 2002 Household Budget Survey Results, which are available at: http://www.die.gov.tr/TURKISH/SONIST/HHGELTUK/hhgeltuk.html, SPO (2001: 19, Tables 11,12) and Yükseler (2003: 3, Table 1).

The period between 1994 and 2002 was marked with economic instability. Volatile growth rates, high interest rates and chronic high-inflation, which the governments of the period continuously tried to bring down with unsuccessful stabilization programs, were the major characteristics of the economy during this period. The 2000-2001 crisis further exacerbated the situation; the economy contracted drastically in 2001 by nearly ten percent and inflation reached 68.5 percent.

Although the end year of the period under consideration, 2002, was one of recovery, one would expect the overall result of a period with such characteristics to be in the direction of higher inequality. However, the results of the 2002 Household Budget Survey (HBS), as presented in Table 11, are in open contradiction with these expectations. According to the HBS results, in 2002, overall income distribution was more equitable than in 1994. The Gini coefficient and the Top 20/Bottom 20 ratio declined to 0.44 and 9.5, respectively, from 0.49 and 11.2 in 1994. This improvement was due to the rising income shares of the first four quintiles in urban areas, as the richest quintile's share declined.

However, there are serious doubts over the validity of the argument that income inequality, particularly inequality in urban areas, was reduced between 1994 and 2002. The most important issue here pertains to the shrinkage of the share of financial asset income by 36 percent from 1994 to 2002, according to the results of 1994 HICES and 2002 HBS. (Yükseler, 2003: 9, Table 6). This result is not plausible as the main characteristics of financial markets have not changed. Public debt increased continuously, offering high real interest rates on public debt instruments. Furthermore, this period was characterized by a sharp increase in transaction volume of financial markets and the share of financial assets in GNP. Underreporting of financial income by the richest quintile may be a more plausible explanation for the anomalous results derived from the 2002 survey[14]. Yet another reason to

[13] In 2002, SIS reduced the size of the survey sample and made some changes in the survey, with the aim of converting the large scaled HICES to an annual income and consumption survey called Household Budget Survey (HBS). Hence, the results of these two surveys may not be directly comparable. See Yükseler (2003: 2) for a discussion of the differences between 1994 HICES and 2002 H BS.

[14] See Yükseler (2003) for a detailed discussion.

doubt these results comes from poverty indicators discussed in the following section, which show that poverty, particularly urban poverty, has risen sharply from 1994 to 2001. Had the incomes of the poorest segments of the population grown as the HBS results suggest, such an increase in poverty incidence could not have taken place[15].

4.1.2.2. Poverty

There are only a handful of studies on Turkish poverty[16]. Nearly all of these studies use HICES data, but different methodologies, and more importantly, none of them makes intertemporal comparisons *i.e.* between 1987 and 1994 or between 1994 and 2002, except Dağdemir (2002). For the post-2001 crisis period, the only study measuring the level of poverty is a World Bank report (World Bank, 2003a), which is based on Household Consumption and Income Survey (HCIS) conducted by the Bank itself. This study's methodology is the same as that of another report published by the Bank (World Bank, 2000a), making them comparable. Hence, the poverty analysis here is based on Dağdemir's study for the 1987-1994 period, and two World Bank reports for the 1994-2002 period[17].

Dağdemir (2002: 469) uses two poverty lines. The first one is based on the minimum calorie requirement of an individual, and called the minimum food cost (MFC). The second one adds some other necessary non-food expenditures to MFC, and reaches to basic needs cost (BNC), which is roughly 50 percent higher than MFC. His findings according to the MFC line suggest that there was a rise in urban poverty from 6.9 percent in 1987 to 8.7 percent in 1994 (Table 12). However, a fall in rural poverty from 21.2 percent to 20.2 percent has countervailed this rise, and the general poverty level of the country has remained constant at 11.5 percent from 1987 to 1994. According to the BNC line, both the urban and the rural poverty rates have increased from 14.3 percent to 20 percent and from 41.5 percent to 42.5 percent, respectively. These rises have generated an increase in the overall poverty incidence in Turkey, from 27 percent in 1987 to 29.5 in 1994. These results show that although poverty was mostly a rural phenomenon, urban poverty worsened significantly during the 1987-1994 period, most probably as a result of the 1994 financial crisis, which had a much bigger impact on urban sectors.

Table 12. Poverty in Turkey, Urban and Rural, 1987 and 1994 (percent)

	Turkey		Urban		Rural	
Poverty Line	1987	1994	1987	1994	1987	1994
Minimum Food Cost	11.5	11.5	6.9	8.7	21.2	20.2
Basic Needs Cost	27.0	29.5	14.3	20.0	41.5	42.5

Source: Dağdemir (2002: 472, Table 1).

[15] Another reason for doubting the survey results is the rise in luxury consumption expenditure that could be observed in daily life as reflected in mass media.

[16] See Erdoğan (2002) for brief summaries of all of the ten studies on Turkish poverty during 1990s.

[17] In April 2004, State Institute of Statistics published a poverty report based on the 2002 HBS available at http://www.die.gov.tr/TURKISH/SONIST/YOKSL/yoksul.htm. However, this report's findings are not comparable to the World Bank (2000a) report –or any other study currently available– because of methodological differences.

Both World Bank reports use four poverty lines: i) an internationally standard poverty line of "One-Dollar-A-Day" per capita; ii) a minimum food basket cost line; iii) a basic needs basket cost line; and iv) a relative poverty line set at one-half of national median income[18]. All poverty indicators worsened between 1994 and 2001 (Table 13) with the sole exception of extreme poverty based on the "One-Dollar-A-Day" line, falling from 2.5 percent in 1994 to 1.8 percent in 2001. As the World Bank (2003a: 11) itself has noted, however, with such small numbers the difference is within the standard error of the samples. The 1994-2001 period was also characterized by a sharp deterioration in urban poverty which nearly tripled from 6.2 percent in 1994 to 17.2 percent in 2001 (Table 13). This reflected the severe impact of the 2000-2001 financial crisis on the urban poor through highly restricted job opportunities and the upsurge in food prices by 80.2 percent that was bigger than the increase of 68.5 percent for the general price index (Şenses, 2003: 104-105). Similarly, there was a sharp rise in the economic vulnerability rate as measured by the basic needs cost line, increasing from 36.3 percent in 1994 to a massive 56.1 percent in 2001[19].

Table 13. Poverty in Turkey, 1994-2001 (percent)

	Turkey		Urban	
Poverty Line	1994	2001	1994	2001
$1/day per capita (at 1985 PPP prices)	2.5	1.8		
Local cost of minimum food basket	7.3	...	6.2	17.2
Local cost of basic needs basket	36.3	56.1		
One-half of national median income	15.7	21.5		

Sources: World Bank (2000a: 36, Table 1; 2003a: 11-23)

4.1.3 Social Spending-Education, Health and Social Assistance

In Turkey, public expenditure on social sectors[20] consists mainly of three categories: education, health, and social assistance[21].

4.1.3.1. 1994 Crisis

The 1994 crisis and the subsequent April 5 Stabilization Program resulted in reductions in all categories of social expenditure (Table 14). Between 1993 and 1996, public social spending as a proportion of GNP declined from 7.2 percent to five percent while its share in

[18] The World Bank reports provide only aggregate data, without the urban and rural distribution. The only exception to this is the urban food poverty rate given in the 2003 report which, however, fails to provide data on the overall food poverty rate.

[19] This shows the majority of the Turkish population was facing the risk of falling into poverty. This threat was much bigger in the Southeast region with a vulnerability rate of 93 percent (World Bank, 2003a: 23).

[20] Social assistance spending covers direct or in-kind transfers made to the poor and vulnerable segments of the population by the government. Social Assistance and Solidarity Fund (SASF), Social Services and Child Protection Agency, Old Age and Disability Assistance Scheme and the Green Card Scheme are the four major social assistance mechanisms/institutions covered here.

[21] Transfers to the social security institutions are here excluded from social spending as they emanate from the operational deficiencies of the social security institutions and are not the outcome of government's deliberate social policies.

total government expenditure fell from 29.8 percent to 19.1 percent.[22] Educational spending was the worst affected category, decreasing from 4.1 percent to 2.5 percent as a share of GNP and from 16.7 percent to 9.4 percent as a share of government expenditures during the same period. This, together with the decline in health and social assistance spending during the same period reflects as much the adverse effect of the crisis as the inaction of successive governments in the face of severe economic crisis.

Table 14. Education, Health and Social Assistance Expenditures of Turkish Government, 1993-1996

	1993	1994	1995	1996
Public Social Spending/GNP (%)	7.2	6.0	5.4	5.0
Public Social Spending/Government Expenditure (%)	29.8	25.9	24.6	19.1
Education Spending/GNP (%)	4.1	3.1	2.7	2.5
Education Spending/Government Expenditure (%)	16.7	13.5	12.3	9.4
Health Spending/GNP (%)	2.9	2.7	2.5	2.4
Health Spending/Government Expenditure (%)	12.0	11.5	11.3	8.9
Social Assistance Spending/GNP (%)	0.3	0.2	0.2	0.2
Social Assistance Spending/Government Expenditure (%)	1.1	0.9	1.0	0.8

Sources: State Planning Organization, Main Economic Indicators, 1950-2003, online edition, which is available at http://ekutup.dpt.gov.tr/ekonomi/gosterge/tr/1950-03/esg.htm; Ministry of Health (2003: 68); SHP (2002: 27, Table 14); World Bank (2000a: 60, Table 2); BYDK (2003: 14); http://www.emekli.gov.tr/ISTATISTIK/65yas.html; http://www.muhasebat.gov.tr/mbulten/T4-2-6.htm.

Table 15. Education, Health and Social Assistance Expenditures of Turkish Government, 1999-2002 (percent)

	1999	2000	2001	2002
Public Social Spending/GNP	8.1	7.8	7.8	8.1
Public Social Spending/Government Expenditure	22.5	20.9	16.9	19.0
Education Spending/GNP	4.2	3.8	4.0	4.1
Education Spending/Government Expenditure	11.8	10.0	8.6	9.5
Health Spending/GNP	3.3	3.5	3.2	3.5
Health Spending/Government Expenditure	9.1	9.3	6.9	8.1
Social Assistance Spending/GNP	0.6	0.6	0.6	0.6
Social Assistance Spending/Government Expenditure	1.5	1.5	1.4	1.4

Sources: Same as Table 14.

4.1.3.2. 2000-2001 Crisis

There was a fall in the share of public social spending in total government expenditure from 20.9 percent in 2000 to 16.0 percent in 2001. Although public social spending as a proportion of GNP in 2001 maintained its level in the previous year (Table 15), this actually represented a fall in absolute terms as GNP declined by 10 percent in that year. A similar

[22] The fact that there was a 23.5 percent fall in per capita social spending in 1994 alone indicates the severe impact o f the crisis.

pattern was observed in education spending. Education spending to GNP ratio had even a slight increase in 2001, but decreased in absolute terms and as a share of government expenditure. While health spending decreased in both measures, social assistance spending remained almost constant as a share of GNP and government expenditure. These highly aggregate figures reveal that social expenditures were somewhat better protected during the 2000-2001 crisis as compared with the 1994 crisis although social policy was not among the priorities of the government, as discussed in the next section.

4.2. Responses to the 1994 and 2000-2001 Crises

Despite the adverse socioeconomic effects of the 1994 and 2000-2001 crises, governments have, as many governments before them, failed to take any major social policy measures to deal with the situation. Instead, they were primarily concerned with macroeconomic stabilization, hoping that the economic recovery would trickle down to the socioeconomic indicators. This approach has not changed even in the setting of the 2000-2001 crisis during which the possibility of social explosion was openly discussed at the highest level of state authority.

In tackling the question why active social policies were not integrated into the post-crisis stabilization and structural adjustment programs, we now consider the post-crisis responses of the governments, civil society and the BWI to the crises.

4.2.1. 1994 Crisis

The April 5 stabilization program introduced shortly after the outbreak of the 1994 crisis did not include any measures to cushion the negative effects of the crisis. If anything, its fiscal austerity component, emphasizing wage suppression and cuts in public spending, may have exacerbated the initial impact of the crisis on the poor and the vulnerable groups. The government's decision to transfer 74 percent of the income of the Social Assistance and Solidarity Fund (SASF) to the general budget in 1994 (Şenses, 1999: 439, Tables 1-2) was also indicative of the government's insensitivity in this respect.

The attitude of BWI was characterized by a similar lack of concern and insensitivity. Although the IMF did not actively participate in the design of the April 5 program, it supported it with a stand-by credit. While the absence of any IMF documents on the program or its implementation precludes us from passing firm judgment, it is likely that the Fund approved the program without any reservations as social issues were not yet on the policy agenda of the IMF. The World Bank, on the other hand, was preoccupied with the privatization and social security reform components of the program through sectoral reform loans. The only World Bank document available on the 1994 crisis and the ensuing stabilization efforts does not contain any statement on their socioeconomic effects (World Bank, 1996). Instead, it commends the labor compensation and relocation plans of the government in the context of the privatization program as a tool for gaining political support for that program (World Bank, 1996: 48-49). World Bank's limited interest in socioeconomic issues seems to have been prompted primarily by the smooth functioning of the privatization program rather than protecting the low income groups.

The immediate reaction of civil society to the crisis was confined to the demonstrations of labor unions in 1994 (Şenses, 2003: 111). Despite the initial ineffectiveness of these demonstrations, public anger against the crisis and the stabilization program produced an important result: "a major dislocation in Turkish politics" in the December 1995 elections (Cizre-Sakallıoğlu and Yeldan, 2000: 501). According to the authors of the latter study, the winner of the 1995 elections, Welfare Party (WP) with an openly Islamist stance, owed its success to the reactive voting of the urban poor. In the absence of notable leftist alternatives, WP gained the support of the low-income sections of the population with its main slogan of 'Just Order' and a solid stance against the inequalities within the economic system. This enabled the WP to more than triple its votes from around six percent in the previous elections to 21 percent in the 1995 elections. However, the coalition government led by the WP did not change the course of economic policies in the direction of equality as the WP had promised. The only notable success of the WP in this regard was its resistance to its coalition partner's requests to use SASF's resources for other purposes[23].

4.2.2. 2000-2001 Crisis

When the country was hit by the first of the twin crises in November 2000, the government was already implementing an exchange rate based stabilization program with the full support of the IMF and the World Bank. The program did not include any measures on the social policy front. Neither did the revised version of the program, which was announced in December 2000, contain any statements about the possible negative socioeconomic effects of the November crisis let alone any measures to deal with them.

After the eruption of the February 2001 crisis, this revised program was also abandoned and a new stabilization program was prepared under the leadership of the new Minister of Economic Affairs, Kemal Derviş. The new program was announced internationally on May 3, 2001 through the Letter of Intent of the Turkish government to the IMF. The Letter of Intent contained the details of the economic policies to be implemented under the new program – The Strengthened Program (TSP), as it was called in the letter of intent. However, the social policy intentions of the government were mentioned in the last paragraph and were confined to only three sentences. Here the government stated its intentions to improve the social protection programs with World Bank assistance to reduce the negative impact of the crisis on the vulnerable segments of the population. Interestingly, this phrase was not included in the previous version of the program[24], which was announced to the Turkish public in mid-April as the Program for Moving to a Stronger Economy (PMSE). Instead, in that version reducing the public debt burden was declared as a tool for reducing income inequalities and poverty in the long-term. The difference between the two versions may be due to the discussions the government may have had with the World Bank in the interim period.

The intentions of the government seemed to be materializing when the World Bank approved a $500 million Social Risk Mitigation Project (SRMP) loan in August 2001. SRMP was aimed to improve the social safety net mechanisms both institutionally and financially in order to mitigate the negative effects of the crisis. The Bank agreed to make an immediate disbursement of $100 million to support the ongoing social assistance programs of the SASF on conditions that the government shows a satisfactory macroeconomic performance and

---

[23] At the same time, the WP was accused of using the resources of SASF for political purposes. See Şenses (1999: 445-446) for details.

[24] The version of TSP dated May 3 2001 is available at the IMF website: http://www.imf.org/external/np/loi/2001/tur/02/index.htm The first version, PMSE, is available at Central Bank's website: http://www.tcmb.gov.tr/yeni/duyuru/eko_program/program.pdf.

fulfils the initial conditions of the SRMP (World Bank, 2001a: 23). The rest of the loan was going to be used for the institutional development of the safety net mechanism and two new safety net programs: Conditional Cash Transfers and Local Initiatives.

Although the magnitude of the first part of the loan fell drastically short of providing a cure for the negative effects of the crisis[25], the second component of the SRMP had the potential of contributing to the development of the social assistance system. However, the available evidence[26] shows that the project could not be implemented as planned. An audit report on SASF has stated that the SRMP funding was not available to the SASF for 2001, and the amount of credit obtained from this source in 2002 was less than $3 million (Prime Ministry High Auditing Council–BYDK, 2003: II). Since the initial disbursement of $100 million was planned to be transferred directly to the SASF until the end of 2001, this means that the implementation of SRMP was delayed for a long period.

The report by the BYDK (Turkish acronym for Prime Ministry High Auditing Council) does not provide information about the reasons for the lack of funding, but it is most likely that the Turkish government failed to fulfill its initial commitments for the loan, leading to the suspension of the disbursement by the Bank. Considering that the first of the two conditions, macroeconomic performance, was found satisfactory for other loans of the World Bank (World Bank, 2003b: 2-3), the problem seems to be related to the fulfillment of the initial conditions of the SRMP associated with the SASF. Most important of these conditions was an increased funding for ongoing SASF operations by the government. On this issue, the BYDK (2003: II) has reported that 40 percent of the 2001 income of the SASF was diverted to the general budget of the government. This is a replica of government strategy followed after the 1994 crisis. Considering that the 2000-2001 crisis has created a much heavier impact on the poor, and that the program was designed by a team led by the ex-Vice President of the World Bank who was responsible for the Bank's Poverty Reduction and Economic Management Unit, the reallocation of poverty alleviation funds to other areas indicates that Turkish governments have maintained their insensitive attitude to social policy even when the poor households' need for assistance was bigger than ever.

A major point of criticism for the World Bank in this context stems from the motives of the SRMP. The Bank has openly declared that the social pressures emanating from the negative effects of the crisis would constitute a major risk for the economic reform program of the government, but strengthening the safety net through the Bank's SRMP would help the government to gain political support (World Bank, 2001a: 11). So, it seems that the name of the loan, Social Risk Mitigation, originates from the risks for the economic reform program caused by the society, rather than the risks for the society caused by the program.

IMF has preserved its silence on the social front also in the aftermath of the 2000-2001 crisis. IMF statements on the strengthened program and its implementation have seldom included references to socio-economic issues, and when they did, those sections of the statements would be quite short, generally reiterating World Bank's views[27].

---

25 In 2001, $100 million was approximately equal to 0.1 percent of GNP or a quarter of the total spending by the SASF in that year.

26 World Bank did not publish any reports on the implementation of the SRMP after the cited Project Appraisal Report of August 2001 until August 2004, even though there were at least three reviews of the project planned for the interim period. While this prevents a comparison of the BYDK (2003) data with the Bank's, it may at the same time point to implementation problems.

27 For example, when the journalists asked Michael Deppler, Director of the European I. Department of the IMF, about the possible political implications of a reduction of public employment due to its huge social costs, he

Public reaction to the 2000-2001 crisis was more intense than that of the 1994 crisis. The demonstrations were held in many provinces and some of them involved violence and damage to property (Şenses, 2003: 111). Interestingly, organized segments of the self-employed were leading these demonstrations, instead of trade unions, and one of the most affected groups, the poor, were not involved. Another interesting feature of the demonstrations was that protests were not directed only against the government, but also the IMF and the World Bank. In any case, the demonstrations faded away after the announcement of The Strengthened Program. But before they faded away, the possibility of social explosion was seriously discussed at different layers of the society[28]. Such a possibility may explain the initial rhetorically active position of the government for pursuing stronger social policies.

As in the case of the 1994 crisis, public reaction to the economic situation was sharply reflected in the following general elections, which took place in November 2002. None of the three parties constituting the coalition government that was in office during the crisis period could take enough votes to jump over the 10 percent threshold for entering the National Assembly. Moreover, only two parties, both of which unrepresented in the National Assembly during the crises, were granted this right. Justice and Development Party (JDP), which was one of the successors of the Welfare Party, won a clear majority of seats in parliament by collecting 34 percent of the votes, while the Republican People's Party (RPP) came in second with 19 percent. During the election campaign, JDP was distinctive with its focus on income inequality and poverty issues. This enabled it to collect the reactive votes of the poor and vulnerable segments of society, who bore the brunt of the crisis. As in the case of its ancestor, Welfare Party, the main factor behind JDP's success was the public reaction against the crisis and the stabilization programs. However, once in power, the JDP government seems to have lost its earlier fervor for poverty alleviation Şenses (2003a: 333).

5. Conclusion

Although the economic crises became common since the early 1990s, their socioeconomic effects have been largely neglected as a research subject. This neglect partially reflects the priorities of the hegemonic neoliberal approach in the economic field, which is promoted by Bretton Woods institutions. On the other hand, it can be partially attributed to the difficulties in the analytical assessment of the effects as they are not easily quantifiable, weak in terms of data and blended with the effects of other events. Due to these constraints, this study is confined to the socioeconomic indicators with sufficient data, such as those of labor market, social expenditures, poverty, and income distribution. Moreover, our

responded that there were certain aspects of the program for reducing and equally distributing its negative impact. This statement resembles the views of the Bank on the relation between the SRMP and the need for political support. Transcript of the press meeting is available at http://www.imf.org/external/np/tr/2002/tr020204.htm.

[28] At the National Security Committee meeting on 29 June 2001, for example, the military wing of the committee presented a report to the government members. It warned them about the negative effects of the economic program on the public, stating that "there may emerge a social explosion in the near future". The results of a public opinion survey, on the other hand, showed that 59.7 percent of the respondents believed that "there would be a social explosion in the coming days". See http://arsiv.hurriyetim.com.tr/hur/turk/01/06/30/turkiye/01tur.htm and http://www.radikal.com.tr/haber.php?haberno=16817&tarih=07/10/2001 respectively for these newspaper articles.

analysis covers the pre- and post-crisis economic programs, responses of the public, governments and the BWIs to the crises, since all of these have influenced the magnitude and the direction of socioeconomic effects.

Our assessments of the socioeconomic indicators of three countries that have been deeply affected by the crises show that the effects are devastating in general. However, our findings also indicate that there is a variety of experience among these countries with the magnitude and duration of the effects of crises varying across different sectors and income groups in individual countries. Some socioeconomic indicators have moved in different magnitudes and sometimes even in different directions. For example, Indonesian income distribution improved after the 1997 crisis. A comparison of Turkish labor market indicators between the 1994 and the 2000-2001 crises demonstrates that there can be diversity between different crisis episodes in the same country. While the 1994 crisis affected real wages mostly, both the real wages and the unemployment worsened after the 2000-2001 crisis. This variety of experiences indicates that one should avoid easy generalizations, and work through the individual country indicators –for each crisis episode– in detail. Likewise, one should take note of the different reactions of domestic governments, the general public and international organizations to crises in different countries.

Nevertheless, our results show that there are some common socioeconomic effects of crises as well. An increase in unemployment due to the plunge in labor demand, sharp falls in real wages and social expenditures, and worsening of poverty are the major common effects.

Post-crisis responses of governments, Bretton Wood Institutions and the public constitute a set of major determinants of socioeconomic effects. These responses also vary between different countries and between different crises. Sensitivity of governments to the issue depends on many factors. Relative importance of socioeconomic issues on the social agenda stands out as a major factor. For example in Indonesia, poverty alleviation and equitable growth were important issues for the society unlike in Argentina and Turkey, and the country recorded a significant success in those areas between 1967 and 1997. This should have been conducive to Indonesian government's positive attitude in the post-crisis period. On the other hand in Turkey, economic growth and informal solidarity networks within the society were traditionally assumed to be sufficient to alleviate the poverty, inducing a passive stance for the government in this respect.

It is observed that the BWIs are not very sensitive to the matter. Socioeconomic issues are known to be outside the interest areas of IMF historically. The Fund's increasing interest in poverty and inequality that has recently developed within the context of the so-called Post-Washington Consensus remained rhetorical and did not transform to effective action. Although the World Bank, which focuses more on social issues, seemed more sensitive to the negative socioeconomic effects of crises, the size of resources allocated by this institution for this purpose has been very small compared to the devastating impact of the crises. This problem has raised doubts over the sincerity of the Bank's behavior. It seems that the World Bank's interest in this area is for reducing the political frictions in the public against the neoliberal reforms rather than improving the living standards of the low-income population groups. On the other hand, insensitivity of BWIs to social issues is in part caused by the passive stance of governments. Indonesian experience has demonstrated that if the government of the crisis-hit country makes the socioeconomic effects a priority, the attitude of BWIs changes remarkably. It is in this context important that negotiations of domestic governments with these institutions should be more transparent. This would at least enable us to apportion the blame for inaction on the poverty front with a smaller margin of error.

Within this framework, public reaction to the economic crises and their socioeconomic effects is a major factor affecting the responses of the governments and the BWIs, hence the nature of economic policies implemented in the post-crisis period. The forceful reaction of the Indonesian people, which even resulted in a regime change, led to the government's sensitive approach to the social issues and the lessening of BWIs' reluctance to allow social safety net measures. The reaction chain of this process is illustrated in Figure 1. The significant decline in government's sensitivity as the reactions subsided over time indicates that it requires a constantly reactive public to build up a pro-poor political command. On the other hand, public reactions in Argentina and Turkey did not result in significant action by governments. Responses of the governments to those reactions came out to be ineffective in Argentine case and rather rhetorical in the Turkish case. In Turkey, which arguably has at least by developing country standards better democratic credentials the more substantial public reaction is expressed through the ballot box, with political parties with poor records on the socioeconomic front swiftly removed from power. This does not guarantee however that the new party that takes over will stick to its election promises once in power. It would however be simplistic to argue that it is only in closed political regimes that street protests constitute the main public reaction as mass demonstrations which can aptly be described as social explosion have taken place in both Indonesia and Argentina with different degrees of political openness. Hence, the initial pattern and the end result of public reactions are not the same everywhere.

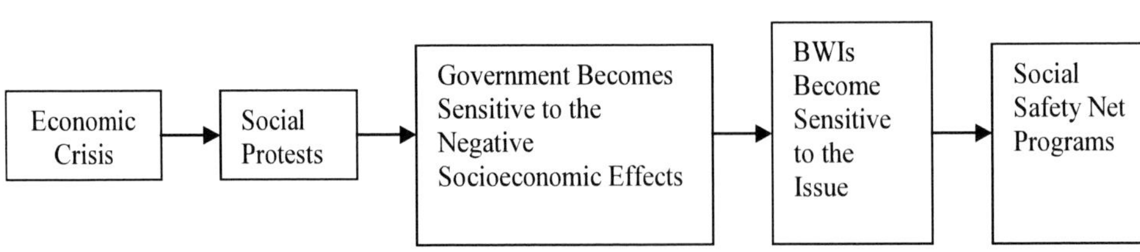

Figure 1. Reaction Chain – From Social Protests to Safety Net Programs.

The discussion so far should not in the least be interpreted to support the argument that economic growth and macroeconomic stability are not required for alleviating the adverse socioeconomic impact of crises. On the contrary, success in those spheres would obviously contribute to mitigating the adverse effects of the crisis on the low income groups, especially if the growth has pro-poor, equitable features. But it should also be recognized that success in these spheres is not sufficient and needs to be supported by active government policies on a broad front, aimed primarily at employment creation, protection of social expenditures that are of particular relevance for low income households and more generally at poverty alleviation. The Indonesian experience has demonstrated that an active social policy stance by the government can be very effective in coping with the adverse impact of the crisis. It has also shown that even within the straightjacket of IMF programs there is room for poverty alleviation as long as the political will is present. Without denying the significance of such relief effort by the government, one should also concede that this is the maximum that can be tolerated under the neoliberal framework which shies away from tackling the more fundamental ownership and distribution problems and thus fails dismally to remove large sections of the population from abject poverty.

Considering the scale of negative socioeconomic effects of economic crises which may extend well beyond the short term, international institutions and domestic governments should seek ways to avert crises, but also be ready for them. Since the crises often erupt rather unexpectedly and cause panic at both the national and the international levels, governments should get prepared in advance by drawing emergency plans. These plans would comprise arrangements ranging from building up an up-to-date socioeconomic database to the setting up of flexible safety net mechanisms that would expand during crises.

On a grander scale, preventing the negative effects of economic crises is identical with the objective of implementing equitable economic and social policies. This objective is, however, confronted by formidable obstacles headed by the skewed power relations in both the national and international spheres (Öniş and Şenses, 2005). In this regard, democratization of relations in both spheres is essential to prevent the negative effects of crises or more generally to reach a fair allocation of resources. At the national level, this task requires the poor to get organized politically as an effective pressure group and press for their rights. This calls for the need for a new type of democracy opening up the channels that have hitherto blocked such organization. At the international level, it requires the developing countries to have a strong voice in the global economic environment and change the decision making processes in Bretton Woods Institutions in a genuinely pro-poor direction[29].

REFERENCES

Altimir, O., L. Beccaria and M. G. Rozada (2002). "Income Distribution in Argentina, 1974-2000", *CEPAL Review*, Vol.78, December, pp. 53-82.

BYDK (T.C. Başbakanlık Yüksek Denetleme Kurulu) (2003). *Sosyal Yardımlaşma ve Dayanışmayı Teşvik Fonu 2002 Yılı Raporu*, Ankara: BYDK.

Cizre-Sakallıoğlu, Ü. and E. Yeldan (2000). "Politics, Society and Financial Liberalization: Turkey in the 1990s", *Development and Change,* Vol. 31, pp. 481-508.

Dağdemir, Ö. (2002). "Türkiye Ekonomisinde Yoksulluk Sorunu ve Yoksulluğun Analizi: 1987-1994", in C. C. Aktan (ed.), *Yoksullukla Mücadele Stratejileri,* Ankara: Hak-İş.

Dhanani S. and I. Islam (2000). "Poverty, Inequality and Social Protection: Lessons from the Indonesian Crisis", *UNDP/United Nations Support Facility for Indonesia Recovery (UNSFIR) Working Paper 00/01*, Jakarta: UNDP.

Dinerstein, A. C. (2001). "Roadblocks in Argentina" *Capital and Class*, No.74, pp. 1-7.

Erdoğan, G. (2002). "Türkiye'de ve Dünyada Yoksulluk Ölçümleri Üzerine Değerlendirmeler", in C. C. Aktan (ed.), *Yoksullukla Mücadele Stratejileri,* Ankara: Hak-İş.

Frankenberg, E., K. Beegle, D. Thomas and Suriastini, W. (1999). *Health, Education and the Economic Crisis in Indonesia*, RAND Working Paper, Santa Monica, USA: RAND Cooperation.

[29] See IMF (2004) for the disproportionate weight of industrialized countries in the decision making processes of the IMF and the World Bank.

Foster, J., J. Greerand and E. Thorbecke (1984). "A Class of Decomposable Poverty Measures", *Econometrica*, Vol. 52, pp. 796-766.

Galasso, E. and M. Ravallion (2003). *Social Protection in a Crisis: Argentina's Plan Jefes y Jefas,* Working Paper No.11/03, Washington DC: World Bank.

Hill, H. (2000). *The Indonesian Economy*, 2nd ed. Cambridge: Cambridge University Press.

IMF (1998). *Turkey: Recent Economic Developments and Selected Issues,* Staff Country Report, No. 98/104, Washington, D.C.: IMF.

IMF (2002). *Indonesia: Selected Issues*, IMF Country Report No. 02/154, Washington, D.C.: IMF.

IMF (2004). "Do developing countries have a say at the IMF?", *IMF Survey*, Vol. 33, No. 3, February 16, pp. 33-37.

Koyuncu, M. and F. Şenses (2004), " Kısa Dönem Krizlerin Sosyoekonomik Etkileri: Türkiye, Endonezya ve Arjantin Deneyimleri, *Çalışma ve Toplum*, No 3, pp. 11-52.

Lanjouw, P., M. Pradhan, Saadah F. Sayed H. and R. Sparrow (2001), *Poverty Education, and Health in Indonesia*, World Bank Policy Research Working Paper 2739, Washington, D. C.: World Bank.

Manning, C. (2000). "Labour Market Adjustment to Indonesia's Economic Crisis: Context, Trends and Implications", *Bulletin of Indonesian Economic Studies*, Vol. 36, No. 1, pp. 105-136.

Mussa, M. (2002). *Argentina and the Fund: From Triumph to Tragedy*, Washington, DC: Institute for International Economics.

Öniş, Z. and F. Şenses (2005). "Rethinking the Emerging Post-Washington Consensus-A Critical Appraisal", *Development and Change,* Vol. 36, No. 2, pp. 263-290.

Pastor, M. and Wise, C. (1999). "Stabilization and its Discontents: Argentina's Economic Restructuring in the 1990s", *World Development*, Vol. 27, No.3, pp. 477-503.

Pritchett, L., S. Sumartoand and A. Suryahadi (2002). "Targeted Programs in an Economic Crisis: Empirical Findings from the Experience of Indonesia", *Social Monitoring and Early Response Unit (SMERU) Working Paper*, Jakarta: SMERU.

SIEMPRO (2002). *Estructura y Evolución del Gasto Social Focalizado: 1997-2002*, Informe de Gasto Social No. 4, Consjo Nacional de Coordinación de Póliticas Sociales, Presidincia de la Nación, Argentina.

Sosyal Demokrat Halk Partisi (SHP) (2002). *Yoksulluğu Yenmek için Acil Plan*, Ankara: SHP.

SPO (State Planning Organization) (2001). *Sekizinci Kalkınma Planı, Gelir Dağılımının İyileştirilmesi ve Yoksullukla Mücadele Özel İhtisas Komisyonu Raporu*, Ankara: SPO.

Sumarto, S., A. Suryahadi and W. Widyanti (2002). "Design and Implementation of Indonesian Social Safety Net Programs", *The Developing Economies*, Vol. XL-1, pp. 3-31.

Şenses, F. (2003). "Economic Crises as an Instigator of Distributional Conflict: The Turkish Case in 2000-2001", *Turkish Studies*, (4) No. 2, p. 92-119 and *The Turkish Economy in Crisis*, Z. Öniş and B. Rubin(ed.), Frank Cass, London, 2003, p. 92-119.

Şenses, F. (2003a). "Yoksullukla Mücadelenin Neresindeyiz?: Gözlemler ve Öneriler", A. H. Köse, F. Şenses, and E. Yeldan (ed.), *İktisat Üzerine Yazılar I–Küresel Düzen: Birikim, Develet ve Sınıflar,* İstanbul: İletişim Yayınları.

Şenses, F. (1996). "Structural Adjustment Policies and Employment in Turkey", *New Perspectives on Turkey,* Vol. 15, pp. 65-93.

Şenses, F. (1999). "Yoksullukla Mücadele ve Sosyal Yardımlaşma ve Dayanışmayı Teşvik Fonu", *METU Studies in Development,* Vol. 26, No. 3-4, pp. 427-451.

Tabor, S. R. and M. H. Sawit (2001). "Social Protection Via Rice: The OPK Rice Subsidy Program in Indonesia", *The Developing Economies,* Vol. XXXIX-3, pp. 267-294.

Tjiptoherijanto, P. and S. S. Remi (2001). "Poverty and Inequality in Indonesia: Trends and Programs", Paper presented at International Conference on the Chinese Economy, Beijing.

Turkish Ministry of Health (2003). *Health Statistics 2002*, Ankara: Ministry of Health.

Turkish Undersecretariat of Treasury (2003). *Treasury Statistics, 1980-2002*, Ankara: UT.

Uygur, E. (2001). "Krizden Krize Türkiye: 2000 Kasım ve 2001 Şubat Krizleri", *Türkiye Ekonomi Kurumu Tartışma Metni, 2001/1*, Ankara: TEK.

Yeldan, E. (2001). *Küreselleşme Sürecinde Türkiye Ekonomisi: Bölüşüm, Birikim, Büyüme*, İstanbul: İletişim Yayınları.

Yükseler, Z. (2003). "2002 Hanehalkı Bütçe Anketi: Gelir Dağılımı ve Tüketim Harcamalarına İlişkin Sonuçların Değerlendirilmesi", *Türkiye Ekonomi Kurumu Tartışma Metni, 2003/6*, Ankara: TEK.

World Bank (1996). *Turkey: Challenges for Adjustment*, Report No. 15076-TU, Washington D.C.: World Bank.

World Bank, (1999). *Report and Recommendations of the President of the International Bank for Reconstruction and Development to the Executive Directors on a Proposed Social Safety Net Adjustment Loan in the Amount of US$ 600 Million to the Republic of Indonesia*, Report No. P7307-IND, Washington, D.C.: World Bank.

World Bank (2000). *Poor People in a Rich Country: A Poverty Report for Argentina,* Washington D.C.: World Bank.

World Bank (2000a). *Turkey: Economic Reforms, Living Standards and Social Welfare Study*, Report No. 20029-TU, Washington, D.C.: World Bank.

World Bank (2001a). *Project Appraisal Document on a Proposed Hybrid Investment/Adjustment Loan in the Amount of US$500 Million to the Republic of Turkey for a Social Risk Mitigation Project/Loan,* Report No. 22510-TU, Washington, D.C.: World Bank.

World Bank (2003). *Argentina – Crisis and Poverty 2003*, Poverty Assessment Report, Report No. 26127-AR, Washington D.C.: World Bank.

World Bank (2003a). *Turkey: Poverty and Coping After Crises*, Report No. 24185-TR, Washington, D.C.: World Bank.

World Bank (2003b). *Turkey Country Economic Memorandum Towards Macroeconomic Stability and Sustained Growth*, Volume II: Main Report, Washington D.C. : World Bank.

In: Argentina: Economic, Political and Social Issues
Editor: Jeanne B. Haverland
ISBN 978-1-60456-469-3

Chapter 4

LIFELONG LEARNING AND CITIZENSHIP EDUCATION IN ARGENTINA: A CHALLENGE TAKEN UP BY NON-GOVERNMENTAL ORGANISATIONS (NGOS)

Josefina Ostuni

INTRODUCTION

This chapter has been planned and structured on the basis of common ideas present in definitions of lifelong learning. In it, the main aspects and characteristics of Argentina's situation will be exemplified. The context will be the hardships that the democratic process has gone through - and is still going through - in the search for its consolidation. Such a context will help to understand the social movements called upon to contribute to a more participative democracy. Non-governmental organisations have perceived education as the driving force that will contribute to solving the existing deficiencies.

The educational system, in its formal and non-formal modalities, and with its particular contents, plays an influential role so that lifelong learning may become gradually consolidated and may be regarded by the citizens as a satisfier fulfilling various needs.

The main topics upon which this chapter will pivot are: the background to Argentina's situation; Argentina's educational system; education as satisfier; the role of NGO's: a case study; and leisure time and lifelong learning.

Brief Overview of Argentina's Situation

In order to analyse the social learning within which non-formal education is included, it is convenient to to make a short reference to the historical, political, social and economic context underlying the growth of several organisations that share a common denominator: the concern for the education of the citizens aimed at enabling them to face a reality which is not always favourable to them.

Argentina, as with most of the Latin American countries, has unfortunately lacked continuing democratic practices. The long authoritarian periods of its history have had an effect upon the slow re-conditioning of citizens' actions.

The history of Argentina's reality shows traumatic situations at times and more hopeful ones at other times. Bringing to memory the most recent episodes, it is possible to set up certain significant thresholds. The period between 1976 and 1983 was marked by a succession of authoritarian regimes during which all constitutional guarantees and rights were suspended. The return to democratic practices in 1983, and the subsequent respect for civil rights, meant for Argentina's citizens the beginning of an era perceived with great optimism. The efforts aimed at consolidating the liberties of citizens and democratic rule were not enough to get the proper balance between the political, economic and social areas. Besides, the long years of lack of democratic practices gave rise to an immature society in addition to the subsistence of certain structural vices that were not consistent with the democratic mode. However, such a highly esteemed wealth as liberty and participation of citizens could not be overlooked.

In 1992, the country's critical economic situation led to the decision to adopt the neo-liberal model or system, without introducing it in a suitable way so as to avoid the maladjustments which unfortunately occurred. Even when at the beginning there was a period of apparently favourable reaction on the part of the economic components, the social problems were multiplied and became more and more complex every time. The impact of globalisation on the local elements created de-stabilizing effects.

Throughout this period, democratic and representative rule seemed to be responding to the expectations of Argentinians; nevertheless, the citizens were only being considered at pre-election times. The dominance of an elite democracy was the expression of a distorted system which could not go without notice by the citizens. This situation is described by Peruzzotti (2002: 91) in a very graphic statement:

> Argentine society and politics are in a fluid state where new and old identities and practices chaotically live alongside one another.

Therefore, an economy restricted more and more to reduced groups was the cause of a wide sector of society becoming increasingly marginal, thus producing the feeling of dissatisfaction which gave rise to a complex predicament that could not be easily solved. Thus arose movements of citizens of all kinds, in order to find a way to air their demands and to cry for an answer in view of their unfulfilled needs.

The strong impact of this political, economic and social context upon the educational system turned it into a box of resonance in which successes and deficiencies could be detected. Such was the understanding of the numerous organisations created to act in support of democratic stability. Education was taken to be one of the synergic satisfiers *par excellence*, and was consequently granted a privileged standing by all such organisations.

Argentina's Educational System

Starting in the 1970s, UNESCO put special emphasis on the concept of 'lifelong learning', which has been considered a key concept in the 21st. century. The extensive studies published in different papers (e.g. Williams and Gerber, 2002, and Cantell and Rikkinen,

2003) about this concept allow us to pinpoint the criteria that define the conceptual nucleus. From those criteria, there have been attempts to circumscribe such features as: lifelong duration, learning how to learn, individual stimulus and strengthening to act with self confidence, creativity and enjoyment in different circumstances, roles and environments. Also, importance is given to the inclusion of the social dimension within learning, learning in society, respect for diversity, all of which contributes to lay down the foundations for peace.

These theoretical guidelines will help to analyse what is happening in Argentina in the field of education. No doubt the educational process must be approached holistically without neglecting any of its several phases, both in formal and in non-formal education.

The educational reform undertaken by Argentina in 1993 by means of the so-called Federal Law of Education sets the organisation and the unity of the National System of Education. In it, it is proposed the formation of free citizens, critical participants, creators and transformers of society, ...defenders of the democratic institutions and the environment. Besides, it is stated that the system must be flexible, articulated, fair, open, prospective, and oriented to satisfy national needs and regional diversity.

Argentina's educational system has formally incorporated the principles of lifelong education as understood in the underlying tenets of the educational reform. However, in practice there is no materialisation of the proposals. The system provides for various instances: elementary education, education for youth and adults, and social learning (Llosa, 1996: 70).

Elementary education is essentially formal, and in it the conceptual, aptitudinal and attitudinal contents are taught, which will provide the basis for future actions. Even though the different curricular subjects are to develop teaching strategies in order to reach the goals of the Law, special reference is made in particular to one of them, because it is most closely related to the concern for the civic formation of the citizens. It is *Ethics and Civic Formation*, included within the area of the social sciences as stated in the official document. This subject tries to 'recover practices given at school but which had not been duly legitimated in prior curricular designs'. The purpose is to shape citizens on the basis of democracy and pluralistic life.

The Federal Law of Education in its Article 15 states the following objective: 'To favour the individual, social and personal growth aimed at responsible actions, with a compromise towards society, and a consciousness of the duties and rights, and respectful of others.' This goal is taken into consideration in the contents of the subject *Ethics and Civic Formation*, as stated in its objectives:

- Attend to the growth of the human beings in order to make conscious use of their freedom oriented with a social sense.
- To form responsible citizens, engaged in the search for the common well being.
- Promote the development of a democratic lifestyle based on participation and dialogue, with the aim to reach at shared decisions within the framework of the universal values laid out by Human Rights.

The difference between this proposal and the seemingly similar one contained in previous curricula is the following: whereas the latter simply intended to make known the constitutional norms, the sense given to *Ethics and Civics Formation* in the new educational scheme, instead, tries to make students analyse critically such norms within a socio-historical context in which they are inserted. In addition, the need to shape free citizens, able to intervene and make decisions, is fully stressed.

The *education for youth and adults* is taken care of both by formal and non-formal education. It is necessary to clarify that in Argentina education for adults - formerly given slight attention only for short periods of time - was aimed at those over 15 years old who, for social and economic reasons, were excluded from the regular educational process. In other words, it was oriented essentially to provide literacy. From the standpoint of the specialists (Sirvent, 1996: 67), this role in formal education has become weakened by the educational reform.

It has been often remarked that the economic factor is the main cause for the crisis affecting formal education, even though such a concept would imply a very simple approach to the situation. The problem is much more serious, with a series of factors interacting over a lengthy process, and which at present are evidenced as having a strong influence. All in all, it must be acknowledged that the contributions of formal education are important even though they are not enough.

The *social learning*, the other instance approached by the educational system in Argentina, should not be taken separately from the rest of the system which it accompanies, and must be articulated with the others in order to be efficient.

Citizens have become aware of the numerous problems of the country's reality. Through projects of non-formal education, citizens' groups provide labour training, professional updating, political and social awareness, in addition to tending to the growing sector of the population which, freed of their normal duties due to their age, find it difficult to reposition themselves in their new status.

Education as a Satisfier: The Role of NGOs

The political, economic and social picture of the country, as the origin of the crisis, has created inside the people a wider and wider range of dissatisfactions. In Max Neef's approach (1987: 40-51), which considers needs satisfaction not with a linear but with systemic criterion, education is placed as a synergic satisfier, that is, it favours the satisfaction of other needs. Education aimed basically at satisfying the axiological need for understanding also contributes to cover other needs: protection, participation, creativity, identity, freedom. These are axiological needs to which another synergic satisfier also responds: democracy. Both of these satisfiers also coincide in the way they are fulfilled in interacting fields: formal in the case of education and participative in the case of democracy.

These have been the fundamentals of the non-governmental organisations that came to life and placed their confidence in education with the hope that it would be the essential instrument to give birth to that egalitarian country proclaimed by the constitutional norms.

These institutions are receptors of one of the ideals of the makers of the country's organisation who relied on education as the powerful engine for progress. The nation's Constitution states such an ideal when it decrees education to be a right of all citizens and to be the path that leads to the achievement of economic, social and political changes for the country that was dreamed about.

Peruzzotti (2000: 88-89) very well describes the features of such organisations:

> These associations emphasize a reflexive politics of identity that has as its main objective the democratization of social practices and of identities. They define themselves as associations of 'citizens' whose goal is to create a spirit of civility among the population. A major goal of their activities is to modify entrenched authoritarian patterns as well as privatist tendencies to move in the direction of a culture of active citizenship that could strengthen the democratic institutions. Their notion of participation is removed from any mobilizational or movementist undertones, emphasizing instead autonomous organisation and reflexive and pluralistic forms of action.

These concerns were not limited only to Argentina. Many Latin American countries also understood that the consolidation of their democracies demanded unified action. The new democracies were confronted with many difficulties, ethnic and racial conflicts, irresponsibility, delinquency and apathy, all of which led the different countries - despite their different realities - to adopt the compromise to defend the democratic foundations, and to strengthen them beyond their frontiers in a common effort favoured by the new technologies in communication.

Their concern took the form of a meeting called '*Pan American Civitas. Education for Democracy*'[1], which was held in Buenos Aires in 1996. It was attended by representatives of twenty North and South American countries, and its goal was to set up a network of experts, from both governmental and non-governmental organisations, in order to strengthen the democratic values, civic participation and free-market economy throughout the Americas. It is important to point out that among its organisers was Conciencia, an institution whose activities will be described below.

NGOs undertake a valuable action in the form of non-formal education in defence of democratic principles and their application. Many of them have put into motion strenuous actions that have deserved the recognition of the people. Reference will now be made to some of them.

Conciencia[2] was founded in 1982, when the return to democracy was coming into being. At the beginning it was formed by women citizens, but men were later incorporated. It is a non-governmental organisation without financial or political aspirations. It is simply a civic movement that decided to educate and to mobilise citizens for better and efficient participation. In addition, it is determined to defend republican life and to live in democracy 'as an effort of dialogue, responsibility and freedom.'

It acts in the city of Buenos Aires and in 14 of the provinces. Besides, it has promoted the creation of similar organisations in several Latin American countries and keeps close bonds with other entities inside and outside the country. *Conciencia* aims at reaching different social sectors, such as trade unions, entrepreneurial organisations, governmental and educational institutions, etc. through different mechanisms.

Its educational programs are varied. Some of them are aimed at participants in formal education, such as the 'U.N. Model', 'I have P.O.W.E.R.', 'Citizens' Responsibility', etc., all of which are aimed at training younger people in participation and decision-making. Other

---

1 Information obtained from: http:/www/civnet.org/civitas/panam/baout.htm (accessed February 2003).

2 I thank the Head of the Mendoza branch of Conciencia who supplied all the information and the material about this organization.

programs, for citizens in general, are made up of courses and seminars, debates and lectures, forums, etc.

The 'Forum of Citizens' Interest' (FIC) is worth mentioning. It allows participants to deal with issues at great depth and to adopt a well-founded option. To achieve this aim, documents are provided on a topic to be studied and different alternatives for analysis are presented. From them, participants may adopt a decision. The forum is a space for moderated and orderly debate that provides the ground for respect by disagreement. Furthermore, it helps citizens to know which public policies should be adopted, based upon deliberation which, not being coincidental, evaluates those alternatives that better lead to the best decision for the well-being of the community. One such 'Forum of Interest' was held in Buenos Aires in 1999 on the topic 'Argentine Women and Their Challenges in Present-Day Society: Traditional Roles or Public Leadership?' In 1996, in Buenos Aires, another Forum of great significance was titled 'Education at the Crossroads: Which Way to Educational Excellence?' This forum was conducted in the 1990 decade as a reaction to the results of successive questionnaires that recurrently referred to education as one of the most severe problems in Argentina. In one of those documents (Mooney, 1996: 14), the fundamental philosophy for Conciencia's actions may be found:

> the exercise of our citizenship is not done on Election Day, even though this is an important event that contributes to the strength of our democracy and to the continuity of the State of Rights. But that is not enough. The word *politics* not only refers to governmental action but also encompasses all *our common effort* aimed at solving our *common issues.*

Special mention must be made of the document furnished by Conciencia together with the Konrad Adenauer Foundation on 'Civil Society Facing Political Reform for the Argentina of the XXIst Century'. Such a proposal was elaborated by consensus from various contributions and was presented to the authorities to help deal with the serious crisis the country was going through at the end of 2001.

The importance of the environment and the people's role in such a field was interpreted and developed in a far-reaching plan of action by FARN[3] (*Foundation for the Environment and Natural Resources*). It was founded in 1985 and encourages the different sectors to assume their responsibilities in environmental protection. Citizens' participation is one of the main topics of *FARN* 's work, since it is the citizens who must comply with and enforce the laws, agree upon policies and assign resources to prevent environmental problems. Its objective is to provide training on legal and institutional aspects of sustainable development. It also promotes the dialogue between various social actors in the search for the suitable decisions for both public and private organisations.

Another organisation is *Poder Ciudadano*[4] (Citizen's Power), whose central idea is that 'in order to have better leaders there must exist better citizens'. It undertakes vast action in defence of citizen's rights, and it develops wide educational activity through courses and through the media, with the purpose of defending the rights of people when they are subdued by some governmental measure.

Its principle is to train citizens so that they become involved in public affairs and in the control of justice. As the organisation itself declares, 'it turns schools into generators of

---

3 Information obtained from: http:/www. Farn.org.ar (accessed February 2003).

4 Information obtained from: http:/www. Poderciudadano.org.ar (accessed February 2003).

knowledge, into promoters of constructive leadership, into generators of young people who will be acting as agents of social changes and as the foundations of a culture of pacific conflict resolution. It also turns society into an ideal space for the build up of citizenship.' That is, *Poder Ciudadano* is an organisation carrying out its activities in several areas related to government so that greater transparency in the exercise of power is achieved.

As can be seen, these and other existing institutions, which by the constraints of this chapter cannot be fully analysed, share common functions among which can be mentioned: the exercise of participation; education and training; search for areas of exchange; defense of democratic principles; distinctive search for a better quality of life; - all of which are best achieved through lifelong learning.

Alongside this type of organisation, suitably projected and planned, there are those popular organised movements - neighbourhood or living quarter associations - which spontaneously come about due to the urge to satisfy needs of subsistence, food, housing, and labour. The Government, under the pressure of the external debt, seems incapable of satisfying these needs.

The need of subsistence is reinforced by that of belonging, since the feeling of 'the place of residence' gives coherence to such popular movements. These local groups, faced with the homogenising forces of globalisation, lack the means, and the continuity, to act efficiently. It has been asserted (Ostuni, 2000: 68-69) that the local actors require an attitude of participation and co-operation that is only achieved through education. The exercise of lifelong education oriented towards the training of the citizens within a framework of their problematic reality reinforces the cultural values and consolidates the sense of identity, both of which are necessary to put a barrier to the threatening force of globalisation. These groups, which are urged by their vital problems, struggle to obtain specific satisfiers which may cover their immediate needs. In most of such groups, education is in a deficit; they need support to understand that education is the driving force in order to achieve longer-lasting and more efficient goals.

Studies carried out in the province of Mendoza (Molina de Buono, 1996: 259-281) have recorded the existence of more than 800 *neighbourhood groups* which became more numerous since the return of democracy. Most of them grew out of the demand for housing or services, although many died out when such demands were satisfied or when leadership clashes came about. Other groups, more committed to the development of the neighbourhood, live on by performing other social functions. It is interesting to point out that such groups, operating in an urban environment, are less tied to their area than those acting in rural contexts. The latter, though smaller in number of participants, show greater perception of the sense of identity with their land.

Max Neef (1986: 17), highlighting the role of these social actors in the participation in the government of their land, has remarked:

> Our emphasis on 'social democracy' or rather on 'democracy of everyday life' does not arise from a neglect of 'political democracy' but from the conviction that only by rescuing the 'molecular' dimension of what is social (micro-organisations, local spaces, relations on a Human Scale) does it make sense to think about the possible ways for the existence of a political order sustained upon a democratic *culture*

The neighbourhood groups mentioned above, which sometimes take the form of shanty-town groups, constitute a space for social learning which has not been developed to its true potential. It is an area upon which the educational system shall have to work more intensively.

Leisure Time and Lifelong Learning

One of the aspects related to lifelong learning is that of leisure time. For several decades the issue of *leisure time and space* has been approached by sociologists, planners, etc. and as a result a bulky bibliography exists. The meaning of *leisure time* as defined in a dictionary is that of 'free time, period of rest within everyday activity'. Max Neef (1986: 42, 47) considers leisure time as a need of axiological order, which may be directly or indirectly satisfied by synergic satisfiers such as 'democratic community organisations', 'didactic games', 'cultural television', etc. It is a private space, or one of encounter, where the human being tries to relax or have fun. Such time may be devoted to education, to community life, to listening to music, to watching TV, to reading, to shows, to sports, to walks. It is a time devoted to the spiritual, to creativity, to the development of everyone's potentials. In short, it is a time devoted to the individual's self-realisation.

For Dumazedier (Llosa, 1996: 71) free time is associated with three functions: a) rest as repair of fatigue from some compulsory activity; b) entertainment through recreational activities in order to overcome boredom; and c) social and personal growth and development. It is this last one function which refers to participation in social or group activities for permanent formation; also, it includes the transformation of individuals and of their social environment. Education for leisure time corresponds with the social learning that makes up an educational system.

Longer life expectations and retirement from work at an age when people still dispose of great vitality both pose the problem of time availability without knowing how to channel it. It has been said that 'Yesterday they had no leisure time; now that they have it, they do not know what to do with it' (Chadlender, 1973: 118). This predicament has mobilised many retired citizens on their own initiative to create groups or centres within which activities are planned for their members to take part in. But the solution to the dilemma of what to do during one's leisure time has often come from educational institutions that have understood the need to fill such empty space of life by means of well-planned didactic proposals.

One such program with such an objective is that of 'Classrooms for Leisure Time'. Even though it is organised by universities, which guarantees their quality, they constitute one kind of non-formal education. The purpose is to fill up leisure time with pleasure-giving activities as well as to incorporate new or renewed learning. They include both humanistic and practical subjects. Several Argentine universities have implemented this type of program and engage themselves in permanent contact through periodical meetings in which they exchange and share experiences, and thus they are able to follow-up the learning process, for instance, by setting up workshops. Attendees to such courses, quite numerous indeed, include mainly middle- and upper-middle-class groups, since a fee has to be paid. This is the reason why not-so-well-off participants are unintentionally excluded.

At this point, reference must be made again to the economic and social situation. The extremely serious crisis in Argentina, which produced the extinction of the labour source, has brought about a high rate of unemployment. It is at this point that Sauvy's (Chadlender, 1973: 174) remark can be applied: 'Forced leisure time is as unpleasant as forced labour'. Those sectors of population with leisure time that is neither voluntary nor dutifully acquired are pushed to search for temporary work that may provide them with their basic subsistence. Since such sectors are left more and more excluded from the educational system, from training programs and from updating schemes, and consequently they suffer from negative feedback, their possibilities to be inserted into the demands of new labour markets are equally diminished.

On the other hand, the free time of mature-aged citizens retired from work is not always synonymous with leisure time. The meager salaries of retired citizens prevent them from using that time to engage in activities or attend courses that may enable them to pursue learning in a pleasant way. Despite this discouraging picture, there are Retired Citizens' associations that try to compensate for this negative situation. In them, cultural and tourist travel programs are organised which contribute to improve the senior citizens' quality of life.

Conclusion

Lifelong learning in Argentina constitutes an objective - sometimes not explicitly manifested - that is developed through the articulation of the different stages of the educational system, both in its formal and non-formal modalities. The political, economic and social context in which the country has lived – and still lives – gave rise to the growth of a variety of non-governmental organisations that in general rely on education as the best means to contribute to the consolidation of democracy to overcome the mistakes of the past and the present. Citizens' inertia and immaturity caused by long periods of democratic crisis demanded intensive action to remove that passivity. During two decades of democratic stability, an evaluation of Argentina's citizens' behaviour shows achievements and deficiencies upon which hard work has to be exercised so that lifelong learning may become an achievement of society at large.

The protagonism of local actors, in their struggle for identity and existence, gives ground to think of them as the leaders of local power. Despite this, the global flux acting upon the local areas are a de-stabilising force for their struggle. The overflows - sometimes chaotic ones - of local citizens in their pursuit of participation in defence of their interests are showing their vulnerability. Only education can give them the capacity to participate efficiently.

The process of lifelong learning in Argentina is evolving especially along its social dimension through the citizens' tenacious decision to participate, to intervene in order to modify the deficiencies of the social, political and economic context in which they are inserted.

References

Cantell, H. and Rikkinen, H. (2003) Lifelong geographical education, In R. Gerber, (ed.) (2003) *International Handbook on Geographical Education*, Dordrecht: Kluwer Academic Publishers.

Chalendar, J. (1973) *La planificación del tiempo* [Time planning], Madrid: IEAL.

Dirección General de Escuelas – Gobierno de Mendoza (1999) *Renovación Curricular en la Provincia de Mendoza-Propuesta Curricular de Ciencias Sociales para el tercer ciclo de la EGB* [Curricular changes in Mendoza Province. Curricular Proposal for Social Sciences for 3rd level of BGE], Mendoza: Dirección General de Escuelas.

Gerber, R. and Williams, M. (2002) Geographical education and the challenge of lifelong learning. In R. Gerber and M. Williams (eds.) (2002) *Geography, Culture and Education,* Dordrecht: Kluwer Academic Publisher.

Llosa, S. (1996) Educación de adultos y tiempo libre [Adults' education and free time], *Revista del Instituto de Investigaciones y Ciencias de la Educación*, Buenos Aires: Facultad de Filosofía y Letras, v, 8, 69-79.

Max-Neef, M. *et al.* (1986) *Desarrollo a escala humana, una opción para el futuro* [Development on the human scale. An option for the future], Uppsala: Centro de Alternativas de Desarrollo (CEPAUR), Fundación Dag. Hammarskjold.

Ministerio de Educación (2000) *Programa Nacional de Innovaciones Educativas. Propuestas para el aula. Material para docentes. Formación ética y ciudadana.* [National Programme of Educational Innovations Proposals for the classroom. Teachers' resources. Ethics and civic formation], Buenos Aires: Ministerio de Educación de la Nación.

Molina de Buono, G. (1996) Las uniones vecinales en San Martín, Junín y Rivadavia. Aportes para evaluar su participación en el desarrollo local. [Neighbourhood groups in San Martín, Junín y Rivadavia. Contributions to the evaluation of their action in the local development]. In M. Furlani de Civit, y M. Gutiérrez de Manchón (eds.) (1996) *Mendoza: una Geografía en transformación,* Mendoza: ExLibris.

Mooney, L. (1996) *Conciencia. Educación en la encrucijada* [Education at the Crossroads], Buenos Aires: Ediciones Santillana.

Ostuni, J. (2002) La significatividad del lugar desde la enseñanza de la Geografía [Local meaning from Geography teaching] *Anales de GAEA Sociedad Argentina de Estudios Geográficos. Homenaje al Dr. Raúl Rey Balmaceda*, Buenos Aires, GAEA Sociedad Argentina de Estudios Geográficos, 21-22, ii, 63-75.

Peruzzotti, E. (2002) Towards a New Politics: citizenship and rights in contemporary Argentina, *Citizenship Studies*, 6, 1, 77-93.

Sirvent, M. (1996) Educación de jóvenes y adultos en un contexto de ajuste [Youth and adult education in an adjustment context], *Revista del Instituto de Investigaciones y Ciencias de la Educación*, Buenos Aires: Facultad de Filosofía y Letras, v, 9, 65-72.

In: Argentina: Economic, Political and Social Issues
Editor: Jeanne B. Haverland
ISBN 978-1-60456-469-3

Chapter 5

RURAL DEVELOPMENT PROGRAMS IN ARGENTINA AND ITS INSTITUTIONS (IN THE CONTEXT OF NEOLIBERAL ACROECONOMIC ADJUSTMENT)*

Mabel Manzanal*
CONICET, Facultad de Filosofía y Letras, UBA, Argentina

ABSTRACT

Rural development begins in Argentina together with the restoration of democracy in the 1980s, but the first actions only started to be developed in the 1990s. Since then, different programs have followed and overlapped. These programs are precisely the purpose of our study.

This paper discusses the resultant rural strategies of the main rural development programs of Argentina in the context of the neoliberal macroeconomic adjustment. It identifies its institutions and analyses whether the actions that are being carried out are suitable or not, and if the assistance to help the rural poor (promoted by international financing organisms) is feasible in face of the negative impact of the neoliberal policy over the small and medium farmers. Besides, this paper looks into and develops questions about the suitability of local and provincial institutional structures for satisfying the institutional demands of rural development programs.

Our starting point is the macroeconomic transformation of the 1990s, which affected the agricultural activity and brought about permanent processes of re-structuring and de-structuring of the public and private institutions linked with rural development management.

* This paper is part of an ongoing research, under the direction of the author, related to Rural Development Programs in Argentina. The research is funded by the Consejo Nacional de Investigaciones Científicas y Tecnológicas –CONICET- and the Universidad de Buenos Aires –UBA-, Argentina.
* Researcher from CONICET, Facultad de Filosofía y Letras, UBA (Address: Rojas 575, 1405 Buenos Aires, Tel/Fax 54 11 4431-1257, e-mail: postmaster@manzan.ba.ar).

Introduction

In Argentina, during the mid-1970s, precisely in 1976, with the overthrow of the constitutional government of Isabel Perón, and the take-over of the military dictatorship, with Martínez de Hoz as Minister of Economy, a new economic model began to develop. This new model coincided with the onset of a neoliberal policy that would progressively replace the Keynesian model and the policy of the Welfare State that had been applied during the three previous decades. The advent of neoliberalism would bring about a policy of structural adjustment which, with differences, would go further than the succeeding governments that followed since that time, and would imply an increase in the socioeconomic and social inequities.

It was since the debt crisis of the early 1980s that this policy could achieve total legitimacy at national and international levels. However, it was since Carlos Menem´s first presidency -and more precisely, with Minister Domingo Cavallo's Convertibility Plan of 1991- that a model with social and economic viability emerged based on the objectives of the Washington Consensus, and designed to meet the commitments of the external debt. During the previous period, even when the adjustment was already running, it could neither be fully performed nor applied in the orthodox terms of the Mememist period either. Internal and external factors prevented it from being established during the military dictatorship as well as during the democratic government of Raúl Alfonsín. The causes were the lack of social consensus and the instability of the economic and social situation that did not offer enough guarantees to the external investor. On the other hand, this was both cause and consequence of the successive economic crises, of the hyperinflationary periods and of the unsuccessful negotiations with the International Monetary Fund (IMF) and even with local businessmen.

The convertibility plan included the privatizations and de-regulations that led to the dismantling of public bodies of institutional and political control. In this context, the population with the lowest incomes suffered severe impacts in their socioeconomic situation. Even vast sectors of the middle classes added up to the masses of those excluded from the productive system.

The unemployment rate in May 1989 (when Menem became President) was 8,1 % and in October 1999, when he finished his two governmental periods, it increased to 13,1% (with an underemployment rate of 14,3%). The highest unemployment rate of this governmental period was in May 1995 (18,4%). Then, it decreased, with some ups and downs, although it always kept above the two digits, reaching 21,5% in May 2002.

The notorious increase in unemployment and the violent transformation of a wide social sector into exceeding population opened the door to a succession of poverty, hunger, insecurity and social riots that dominated the scene in the mid-1990s. In some provinces, the unemployment rates were close to, or even higher than 20% -Jujuy, Tucumán, Bahía Blanca, Mar del Plata, Salta, Concordia, Gran La Plata, Gran Santa Fe, Río Cuarto, Gran Rosario, Gran Catamarca-. It was a process of national de-structuring expressed in impoverished provinces with high debts.

Besides, the adjustment and restructuring was escorted by institutions adequate to its own interests. The viability of the model was possible because it acted through degraded institutions; through which Argentina would have no chance to develop its economy or to insert itself in the competitive global context.

This leads us to ask ourselves about the feasibility, in the mid-term, of the self-sustainability of the potential improvements in the income and/or in the occupation of the families of poor farmers that are promoted by different Programs of Rural Development existing in Argentina since the 1980s. Which is the scope and the feasibility of the strategies of rural development in Argentina in the context of the neoliberal socioeconomic adjustment? Do proposals centered in the expansion of production and agricultural productivity of poor families achieve their productive inclusion or do these families remain in their situation of poverty and exclusion? Is it only an economic problem or is it also affected by the present institutional weakness in Argentina?

Neoliberalism, Institutions and Development Policies

The neoliberal period led to a gradual process by which the State abandoned its traditional roles of promoting development and guaranteeing equality of opportunities in education, health and housing.

Widespread privatizations and de-regulations were the main instrument of this policy to ensure a differential profitability and, consequently, intensify the concentration of capital. Concessions, powers and advantages in prices and conditions were granted to private investors, frequently in strategic areas such as natural resources, transport, energy and communications.

At the same time, the National State restricted itself in its competence as a market regulation entity, for example, by disarticulating the regulatory institutions for food and raw materials (grains, meat, cotton, *yerba mate*, tobacco). The State also gave in specific functions of the Central Bank, as happened with the convertibility plan by Minister Cavallo. From then on, the dollar became the actual exchange standard.

Likewise, the participation of international organizations was encouraged for the funding of specific projects and programs. This involvement reached even the design and implementation of such projects. This contributed to the increase of the external debt because *funding came through international loans*. Jointly, the government fostered the implementation of social policies by NGOs (non-governmental organizations) under the argumentation that this would imply operational benefits due to their lower operating costs and NGOs would contribute to increase the participation of civil society in public issues.[1]

The programs aimed at the rural poor were inserted in the context described above, with a growing social polarization and with a State that disregarded and/or lacked instruments for the implementation of a national development policy. Some of them (as the PNEA -Program for Small Producers of the Argentine Northwest-, PRODERNEA -Program of Rural Development of the Argentine Northeast-, PSA -Agricultural Social Program-, PROINDER -Program of Rural Development Initiatives-) were intended to implement and reach an integral proposal of productive transformation and improve the income or standard of living of the rural poor. These strategies are contradictory at a national scale since they are part of

[1] In the rural environment there are few NGOs specialized in rural development with many years of expertise. The NGOs dealing with family farmers tend to have a lower scope regarding the number of beneficiaries and the kind, diversity and extent of the services they offer; occasionally they can exceed 2.000 beneficiaries by NGO. Those with most experience are: INCUPO –Institute of Popular Culture -, INDES -Institute of Social Development and Human Promotion -, FUNDAPAZ –Foundation for the Development of Justice and Peace.

macroeconomic processes characterized by the systematic discrimination and exclusion of the small agricultural producing sector.

These processes were not restricted to Argentina; they appeared in the whole of Latin America with local, national and regional specificities. Latin America was the first goal of the Washington Consensus, of the macroeconomic adjustment. Chiriboga (1997: 14-17) in a specific analysis of the subject says: "...the fiscal austerity that characterized the reforms in the Region has implied an important decline in the supply of public services, such as roads, communications infrastructure, electrification, irrigation, education and rural training... *With only a few exceptions, what characterizes the Region as result of the economic reforms, is the weakening, and even the vanishing, of sector-aimed policies and of organizations in charge of supporting the agricultural producers...* The implemented reforms have not been able to promote an alternative institutional system in support of small agricultural producers either. In fact, the main effect was a big reduction in loans programs, technical assistance or commercialization among this kind of producers" (translation and italics are ours).

RURAL DEVELOPMENT IN ARGENTINA

The State concern for implementing programs to improve the situation of the families of the poor agricultural producers had it first attempt in the democratic period that began in 1973 with a Program of Re-conversion of Small Holding Areas, which, unfortunately, had a short duration due to the sudden political changes typical of that period. The rural development issue would re-appear ten years later, with the following democratic period (by the end of 1983).

Previous programs –from the 1960s and early 1970s- had different characteristics. The concern about poverty was minor, having as a priority the insertion and sectorial, agro-industrial, mercantile and capitalist development of family producers with a certain degree of capitalization. They were plans of colonization of integral rural development, such as that of the Río Dulce in Santiago del Estero or that of the Institute for Development of the Lower Valley of the Río Negro -IDEVI-.

Lombardo and Tort (1998: 6) mention the Agricultural National Program -PRONAGRO- designed by the National Secretary of Agriculture, Livestock and Food -SAGPyA- in 1984, as the first case in the period of democratic restoration under the radical administration of Raúl Alfonsín. However, they say it could not be fulfilled because of the opposition of the middle and large farmers of the Pampas and also for the economic plan known as Austral.

The first actions in rural development of this period could be performed only at the beginning of the 1990s; we are referring to the PNEA, although its design began in the mid-1980s, with the return of democracy.

In 1987, the Coordination Unit for Research Projects and Plans for Small Holding Producers was established within the National Institute for Agricultural Research -INTA- dependent on SAGPyA. This unit was aimed at generating and validating agricultural and forestry technology for these producers. This was a totally new experience for the INTA since, until then it had only assisted medium and large producers.

In all aspects: institutional, professional, programmatic and political, rural development is a recent experience (just a bit longer than a decade). Actually, it was only towards the 1980s that Argentina began to be considered a country with rural poverty.

The reason for this fact may be traced in the historic development of the country that had shown, until then, an economic dynamics very different from the rest of Latin America. Its extraordinary and varied agricultural production and its scarce population marked the initial difference. Since the end of the XIX century and well into the XX, the gross domestic product and the foreign currency came from exports of grains and meat, and these products (in the hands of medium and large farmers) had a differential profitability in the world due to the natural high productivity of the Pampas. The economic dynamism resulting from the period of the substitution of imports is also very important to build the image of a rich country: the development policies and the Welfare State of the 1950s to 1970s allowed for the insertion of many small rural producers in the dominant economic model, either producing food for the growing domestic market or migrating and finding jobs in the new national industry. This caused an early urbanization centered in the main Pampean provinces: Buenos Aires, Santa Fé and Córdoba. It was a period of massive migrations from the country to the city responding to the intense employment demand from the industries located in the most urbanized areas (Manzanal 1993: 28-34).

In the mid-1970s, a process of structural transformation started together with the beginning of the neoliberal model. Since then, a set of measures, historically demanded by the most concentrated exporting sector, began to be systematically implemented: the dissolution of the Grain and Meat Board, the elimination custom duties to exports, the establishing of a unique exchange rate and the reduction of the custom duties to imports. The impacts of these measures varied according to the productive insertion type (agro-exporting or domestic). Those producers related to the domestic market had to face the recessive effects of the crisis on this market.

Therefore, the exporting agriculture began to grow rapidly. The fishing activity had also a very important dynamics in relative terms. Oilseeds and cereals showed the biggest productive increases while the traditional products (meat and regional crops) lagged behind.

At the same time, the socioeconomic situation of the small producers worsened due to the decrease in the process of their products as a result of the adjustment, the de-regulation and the privatizations. The small producers were affected by: a) the elimination of quotas for sowing, harvesting, manufacturing, and marketing of traditional production. b) The suppression of the grant they received through the Commerce Employees' Family Grants Office -CASFEC- as in the case of the cotton producers. c) The decrease in the resources distributed as overprice for tobacco producers. d) The absence of subsidized loans as a result of the privatization of the provincial banks. e) The implementation of a regressive tax system, which implied a heavier load for the small producers (the biggest revenue comes from taxes on consumption such as the Value Added Tax -VAT). f) The trend to the elimination of informal economy, in which the small producers were operating at that time.

The Beneficiaries of Rural Development Programs

One of the characteristics, or requirements, of the programs to alleviate rural poverty promoted by the international funding organizations is the focus on the potential beneficiaries. Soverna and Craviotti (1998: 18) affirm that in the projects of rural development, "focalizing" is a requirement to guarantee that the benefits of a project be directed to those that meet the poverty criteria defined for each case.

To focus on the programs' beneficiary groups it is necessary to define, beforehand, the potential population universe, its relative importance and its location. Then, the Programs set up their respective eligibility criteria. However, this task has turned out to be very complex for different reasons, ranging from the theoretic-methodological difficulties emerging from the different conceptualizations and interpretations of the beneficiary subject to the inadequate data base available.

There is a great diversity of situations that compose the universe of agricultural family production, as well as an overlap of different interpretations that try to identify and make the concepts of peasantry, small agricultural holding and rural poverty, operational.

Neiman (1997:1 a 4) when he refers to "rural poverty" says that: "it does not refer exclusively to geographical contexts of relative isolation, to institutional deficiencies and/or to social subjects typical of the country, but it refers to a more complex notion given by the present re-structuring of the activity" (translation is our). He emphasizes that the trends towards globalization and re-conversion imply: (i) an expansion of the non-agricultural rural activities; (ii) modifications in the relation capital-labor that accelerate the decrease in the welfare of the rural population and make the labor markets more flexible; and (iii) an increase in the regional differences due to the fragmented and unequal character of the current development.

Carballo (1996:57) states that the agricultural family production is: "a heterogeneous universe that includes families producing for their own consumption as well as units with important levels of capitalization totally connected with markets" (translation is our).

Based on data from the Population Census of 1991, the SAGPyA (1997[a]:4) estimated that in that moment there were 128.000 poor agricultural rural families (that is to say with Unsatisfied Basic Needs -UBN-).[2] This figure refers to family heads in rural zones and includes small producers as well as temporary workers.[3]

In spite of the complexity of the respective informative and methodological context, we know through different indicators (information surveyed locally in different provinces) that the poor farms have decreased considerably lately. This is a consequence of the neoliberal policy that made many small producers leave their farms and led to the bankruptcy of their economic activities. These holdings are located basically in the northern and northeastern provinces.

Finally, ¿what do Argentine small family farmers cultivate? They do not produce the basic food included in the household expenses. Cereals, meat, and oilseeds are grown by the capitalist agricultural sector. The small family producers of the non-pampean economies

---

[2] This national estimation was made within the SAGPyA to calculate the target population for the PROINDER program.

[3] However, to identify and quantify the peasant families, or small holdings or small family producers, it is better to use data from Agricultural Census that include specific data from families working in an agricultural holding (unfortunately, the Agricultural Census was carried out 14 years ago, in 1988).

produce basically traditional agro-industrial crops. According to Carballo (1991: 157) at the end of the 1980s they produced: 10% of sugar cane production, 15% of grapes for wine, 25% - 30% of cotton, and 10% of tobacco. They also raised *yerba mate*, tea, vegetables, sheep and goat stocks.

This production must have decreased considerably in the last decade because of the degradation of the small holding sector and the increase in the participation of the large agricultural holdings in the total volume of these products.[4] Since the liberalization and deregulation of the market, the productive boom of cotton, sugar cane, tobacco and *yerba mate* is well known. This expansion was shown in the notable productivity increases led by big agricultural companies, many of them new in the sector.

THE SPECIFICITIES OF THE RURAL DEVELOPMENT PROGRAMS

The different rural development programs described in this paper can be situated in the general context described above. These programs do not constitute a State policy given that there is no legal and institutional framework that gives consistency to the development model, designs the strategy, coordinates the particular actions of each program and rules its institutional, administrative and territorial organization as well as its respective benefits.

The current rural development programs whose target population are the small poor agricultural producers and which have an "integral" strategy for the transformation and the productive insertion of the sector and whose loans and subsidies have a central role, are: the PRODERNEA (prolongation of the PNEA, ended in 1997), the PSA and the PROINDER (enlargement of the PSA). Additionally, we can mention the PRODERNOA (Program for Rural Development of the Argentine Northwest) with similar characteristics to the PRODERNEA but centered in three provinces of the Northwest (Jujuy, Salta and Catamarca) and that has not started yet (although the loan contract was signed in the year 2000).

We must mention that within the SAGPyA there are other programs such as Peasant Woman from the Argentine Northwest, Rural Change, Small Holding Unit, Pro-Huerta, Project for the Restructuring of Tobacco Areas (PRAT), Forestry Project of Development (CAPPCA), and Regime for the Promotion of Forest Plantations (RPPF). But, generally, these programs are not basically aimed at small producers, or they lack an integral strategy for their transformation, or their main component is the technical assistance instead of loans and subsidies.[5] Anyway, they should be taken into account in other analyses related to the small holdings population because some of them support or complement their own actions with the ones of the programs analyzed in this paper. For example, in certain activities or locations the PSA, the PNEA, the Small Holding Unit, the Pro-Huerta and the Peasant Woman have shared the implementation of their projects.

In other areas of the national and provincial public sector, there are also programs that benefit small producers. This is the case of the Secretary of Social Development of the Presidency, with the Participative Fund of Social Investment -FOPAR- and the Participative Fund of Capitalization -FONCAP-; and the Ministry of Labor with the Youngsters' Project

[4] The lack of a new Agricultural Census prevents us from giving accurate information on this issue.

and the Work Plan. They matter precisely because, together, they contribute to the different services and actions directed to the small agricultural producers. However, these benefits cannot be adequately profited from due to the absence of a policy and a coordinated strategy.

We will now introduce some characteristics of the main current programs which are the subject of this paper. The following data were obtained from SAPyA (1996: 69 - 82):

1. Prodernea

This Program is an extension of the PNEA and, therefore, has many things in common with it. The PNEA was one of the first experiences in rural development and although its design began in 1984, it was implemented only at the beginning of 1991 and it concluded in 1997.

The institutional organization of both programs was based on a National Coordination Unit, with headquarters in the SAGPyA, and the implementation bodies were the Agriculture Ministries of Chaco, Corrientes, Formosa and Misiones (in the PNEA Chaco was not included). Both were funded through a loan from FIDA – BID (International Fund for Agricultural Development –Inter-American Development Bank) subscribed by the Nation and transferred to the provincial governments by the SAGPyA. The provinces were responsible by law of the external debt, guaranteed by the Federal Co-participation, and they implemented the Project through their agriculture Ministries and contributed with counterpart resources (SAGPyA; 1999).

The PRODERNEA (and the PRODERNOA as well) are aimed at a group of small agricultural producers whose economic level is higher than that of the beneficiaries of the PNEA. Its objective is to increase the family income and the self-management capabilities of small producers and indian population of the region. This goal is achieved through the diversification and re-conversion of the production, an improvement in the access to the markets, the establishment of a special fund for small producers and the empowerment of small producers' organizations.

The provincial governments are responsible for its implementation; having started by the end of 1998 and lasting for 5 years (Pfr. SAGPyA; 1997: 62 and ss). In fact, in January 1999 it began in Misiones only. Apparently it should be deferred beyond the year 2003 due to the delays in its implementation. The provinces joined gradually, one per year (in May 2002 Corrientes had not started the Program yet and Formosa had not disbursed the money). Only Chaco and Misiones were able to start with the Program.

In this project, the national Director was replaced twice (February 2000 and April 2001) according to the political modifications at the national level (and therefore in the SAGPyA). This has implied a delay in the implementation.

The disbursements for Misiones amounted to u$s 650.000 until November 2001 (from a loan of u$s 16 million). Chaco went through political problems and difficulties in the technical implementation. As this province was not included in the previous stage of the

[5] Besides, they usually have a wider definition of target population (Rural Change, Pro-Huerta, PRAT) or have only one specific component for small producers (CAPPCA, RPPF) within other broader actions (Pfr. SAGPyA, 2000).

PNEA, it had less availability of people with expertise specific in strategies and actions for small producers.

The program demanded a strong effort from technicians with producers, because it was based on a loan that required repayment. And this meant a lot of technical support and training from the National Unit which was somewhat dismembered because of the political changes derived from the removal of most of the technicians that had worked in the PNEA for many years. Similarly, in some of the participating provinces, there may have been interference from the provincial government with the decisions related to the projects.

During 1999, another project -the PRODERNOA- was designed. It was approved by FIDA in September 1999, with similar characteristics to the PNEA and the PRODERNEA but intended for 3 provinces of the Northwest: Jujuy, Salta and Catamarca. The loan contract was signed in November 2000 but the project has not started its activities yet. Salta, Jujuy and Catamarca have not approved the law allowing them to receive the loan, and therefore the respective contract with the SAGPyA was not signed either (this loan has no commitment commission). The debt is of about u$s 5 million for Jujuy (being its counterpart 2 million), u$s 4,5 million for Catamarca (u$s 1,5 million counterpart) and u$s 8 million for Salta (u$s 3 million counterpart)

One important difference between the PRODERNEA and the PNEA is that the former is aimed at producers with entrepreneurial skills, that is to say, producers with a higher economic profile.

2. PSA

By the end of the 1990s another line of action was born within the SAGPyA for the rural poor: the PSA, which started in April 1993 without due date and with national scope. The whole country is included with the exception of Santa Cruz and Tierra del Fuego.

When the PSA started working, the PNEA was already running in the northeastern provinces with similar strategies and target population. During the first half of the 1990s, the PSA and the PNEA were the most important programs focused on the poor small agricultural producers, and so it was necessary for both programs to agree on coordinated guidelines to avoid overlapping and friction among provinces. Key informants state that these guidelines could not always be fulfilled. This demonstrates the need to develop a unique policy for the target group with a central coordination.

The main support for the PSA comes from funds from the national budget. In the beginning $10 million were assigned for the launching of the sub-programs. Later it received annual funds of about $ 4 and $9,5 million, depending on the year. The amount transferred to the beneficiaries (accumulated up to the end of 2001) was approximately $28 million (SAGPyA, 2000: 40).[6]

Its goals are: (i) contribute together with the small agricultural producers to the search of alternatives to face the economic crisis; and (ii) increase the income of small agricultural producers and promote its organized participation in political decisions about programs and projects.

[6] Due to the convertibility plan, between 1991 and the end of 2001 all figures in pesos are equivalent to US dollars.

The PSA works through a decentralized structure composed by a National Technical Coordination Unit -UTCN-, the National Coordination Committee and the Advisory Council on the national level; and a Provincial Technical Coordination Unit -UTCP- for each of the 21 participating provinces. In each UTCP there are representatives from the provincial governments, the INTA, the NGOs and the producers. The provincial coordinator of each UTCP depends on the UTCN.

In the National Coordination Committee there are representatives from other programs of the SAGPyA, the INTA, the Inter-American Institute for Agricultural Cooperation -IICA-, the Inter-Cooperative Agricultural Confederation Ltd -CONINAGRO-, and the main NGOs related to rural development.

3. Proinder, Project of Rural Initiatives

In the mid-1990s a new stage started which focused on groups of extreme poverty through donations or subsidies. The most representative example is the PROINDER, with headquarters within the SAGPyA but funded by the World Bank -WB-. This program is an extension of the PSA. Its principal component, a granted fund, depends on the PSA.

In early December 1998 the PROINDER was formally launched, being its total funding budget u$s 100 million, being 70 % provided by the WB and the rest by the Nation. Its ending is expected by the year 2003.

This program was being designed for many years, as happened with the PNEA. In 1994 the diagnostic stage started (Soverna and Craviotti, 1998:3). In the preliminary versions of this program the "improvement of income" was not included among its objectives. However, in the last revision, it appeared as a goal but without any quantification. Its explicit objective is: "to improve the standard of living of the rural poor population in a framework in which such population may participate in an organized way in the decision-making which affects them and in conditions of sustainability of natural resources and the environment". Some of its intermediate objectives are: increase quantity and/or quality of the production, inclusion of new productive activities, improvement of the production for self-consumption, better positioning in the market, better equipments.

Its main component is a fund (FAIR–Fund of Support to Rural Initiatives) that subsidizes investments of beneficiaries. This is its main difference with the PSA that gives loans that require repayment. This Fund has an application methodology similar to the one applied in the PSA: the beneficiaries, gathered in groups, participate in the diagnosis, design, implementation, follow-up and evaluation of sub-projects or initiatives (Pfr. Soverna and Craviotti, 1998: 2).

As the main component of this program is based on subsidies for rural workers and vulnerable population (Indians, women and young people) it may be considered as a new trend in the design of rural development programs. The emphasis is on rural poverty in general, and not on agricultural producers only, and the actions are oriented towards assistance rather than towards self-sustainability. The heterogeneousness and seriousness of poverty in rural environments reduce the concern about production and agricultural holdings as an exclusive issue. Therefore, we can conclude that the concern is focused on "assisting and alleviating the situation of extreme poverty" of the poor living in rural environments (working in the agricultural sector or not) rather than on making structural transformations.

This approach is also evident in the transfer of PROINDER funds to the Program for the Recovery of the Productive Capacity of the Small Producers affected by floods (PROEMER) during 1999, although its aim was to alleviate the social emergency situation brought about by the natural disaster related to El Niño phenomenon. The PROEMER, which started functioning as a PROINDER component since August 1998, received U$S 31 million that were distributed as individual subsidies to 39.000 producers in emergency situation in the following provinces: Corrientes, Santa Fe, Misiones and Santiago del Estero.

The lack or scarcity of additional national resources to face this social problem led to the use of PROINDER funds, which were originally intended for other objectives. This transfer of funds had direct effects in the delay in the implementation of the original components of the PROINDER until the end of 1999. Additionally, this fact is somewhat connected with the low priority assigned to this project by some groups related to the political power.

The following tables show a summary of some variables that characterize the three current programs (the PNEA, ended in 1977, is not included).

Table 1. National Programs of Rural Development in Argentina, Institutions in charge and Target Population

Acronym	Institution in Charge// Executing Institution	Target Population
PSA	SAGPyA//SAGPyA	159.712 small producers
PROINDER	SAGPyA//SGPyA	127.565 families with UBN related to agricultural production.
PRODERNEA	SAGPyA// SAGPyA y Provincial Agricultural Ministries	41.700 families with agricultural holdings of less than 25 hectares[7] has in the provinces of Misiones, Formosa, Corrientes and Chaco and 10.550 indian families from Misiones, Chaco and Formosa.

Source: SAGPyA (2000: 37) "Los programas nacionales de desarrollo rural ejecutados en el ámbito de la SAGPyA", *Serie Estudios e Investigaciones 1*, PROINDER, Buenos Aires.

Table 2. National Programs of Rural Development in Argentina, Target population, Eligibility criteria, geographic location and assistance types

ACRONYM	TARGET	ELEGIBILITY CRITERIA	LOCATION	SERVICES OR ASSISTANCE TYPE
PSA	none	Groups of at least 4 families in Patagonia, 6 in the rest of the country, the producer works in the agricultural holding, permanent household in the holding, lack of permanent salary job and contract of transitory labor only in moments of high demand, extra-holding income coming from transitory labor or handcraft not surpassing the salary of rural worker, income level coming from holding not higher than two monthly rural worker salaries, and capital level not higher than $20.000, excluding family household and land.	National scope, except Santa Cruz and Tierra del Fuego.	Technical assistance. Training. Marketing Support. Assistance with solidary payback of $200 per family, $2.000 per self-consumption projects group. Loan up to $1.200 per family, $50.000 per group in associative productive initiatives.

[7] 1 hectare ("ha") is equivalent to 2.5 acres

Table 2. (Continued)

ACRONYM	TARGET	ELEGIBILITY CRITERIA	LOCATION	SERVICES OR ASSISTANCE TYPE
PROINDER	40.000 small producers and transitory poor workers.	Rural household, the producer works in the agricultural holding, not hiring more than 60 annual wages, family work outside the holding, not higher than 270 annual wages, fixed capital not higher than $15.000, livestock existences not higher than 500 sheep or goat heads or 50 cattle heads, not having a shed of brick or metal sheets of more than 50 m2, have any of the needs listed in the UBN indicator.	National, except Santa Cruz and Tierra del Fuego. Focus per department	Funding not reimbursable for investment initiatives. Limits of $200 per family and $4.000 per group for self-consumption projects; $1.500 per family and $22.500 per group for projects of community use and/or holding infrastructure, and $1.500 per family and $50.000 per group for projects of community use infrastructure. Technical assistance. Training. Marketing support. Institutional empowerment.
PRODERNEA	10.570 small producers' families and 3.450 indian families.	Small producers with some productive resources and entrepreneurial management skills but who face multiple limitations. Requirements: living in the rural area corresponding to the Project and working in their own holding with predominant use of family labor, working in an agricultural holding of up to 25 ha or bigger but with only 25 ha of apt land; not to be in debt with the PNEA or other credit programs; most of the family income should come from the agricultural holding, with possible outside income complement from a family member; keeping a productive structure with a clearly commercial orientation, that can exist together with self-consumption production (the latter represents a minor part in the family income). Indian communities are also eligible, whether they practise agriculture, handcraft, fishing, hunting or recollection.	Chaco, Corrientes, Formosa and Misiones. Focus per department except in Chaco.	Credit up to $5.000 per producer and $50.000 per group; lower limits in innovative activities or rural non-agricultural. Promotion of organization and technical assistance. Training and communication. Commercial and agro-industrial development. Support Fund to indian communities. Gender consideration and activities with rural youngsters.

Source: SAGPyA (2000: 38-9) "Los programas nacionales de desarrollo rural ejecutados en el ámbito de la SAGPyA", *Serie Estudios e Investigaciones 1*, PROINDER, Buenos Aires.

Table 3. National Programs of Rural Development in Argentina, operating period, total amount and funding agencies

N°	Acronym	Starting Date	Ending Date	Total Ammount	Funding Agency and % Of Funding
1	PSA	April 1993	Still operating	Subject to budget items. $ 9 million per year (average).	National Government (SAGPyA)
2	PROINDER	May 1998	May 2003	$100 million	75% BIRF 25% National Government
3	PRODERNEA	January 1999	January 2004	$36 million	45.7% FIDA 52.6% Provinces 1.6% SAGPyA

Source: SAGPyA (2000: 41) "Los programas nacionales de desarrollo rural ejecutados en el ámbito de la SAGPyA", *Serie Estudios e Investigaciones 1*, PROINDER, Buenos Aires

Some Limitations of the Rural Development Programs

When analyzing the operation of all these programs, it is clear that there is overlapping of objectives, territory coverage, subjects and actions and, therefore, we can conclude that the coordination and complementation among them has not been enough so far. Without any doubt, there is no institutionalized rural development policy, producing as a result a sum of different programs and actions rather than a coordinated strategy aimed at common objectives.

If we compare the strategy of rural development programs with the social and regional impacts of adjustment policies in Argentina, some contradictory aspects arise. For example:

1) There is no national, regional or local instrumentation to face the restrictions posed by a recessive, concentrated and highly competitive market, especially for small family producers, who have no control over it.
2) There is a lack of regional diagnosis indicating the specific and essential actions to be developed in each zone to be promoted, as well as the particular projects of rural development for target groups. The programs work without any coordination with regional or provincial development policies that could act as framework and boost it. At the provincial level, we notice a lack of connection between public organizations and institutions in charge of rural development and small producers' organizations and support NGOs.
3) The information about small producers at national and provincial levels is not updated; this brings about ignorance about the productive and socioeconomic characteristics of small producers and agricultural transitory workers. This is consistent with the lack of a national strategy of rural development defined in a coordinated and centralized fashion and, at the same time, of provincial strategies.
4) The loan or subsidy amounts given to the beneficiary families do not match up with the necessary resources to start with the modifications the sector needs to overcame its situation of poverty and structural deficiency. The two most important national programs have distributed $1.200 (the PSA) and $1.700 (the PNEA[8]), in average per family. These amounts can be very important for each family. Due to the low annual income of most of these small producer families, these subsidies may represent more than 30 % of their total annual income, plus the additional value that it is cash. Nonetheless, they do not mean or allow structural changes in the productive development of small producers.
5) The total amount destined for loans and subsidies is small if compared with the funds assigned to training for organization, for the productive, technical, administrative and financial activity in the agricultural holding, and for the development of self-consumption orchards –Rural Change, Small Holding Unit, Pro-Huerta, Peasant Woman (some of them may have been lacking funds for a long time and particularly at present -2002). Although the poor agricultural producer families have received some assistance, this does not mean that they have been able to find "solutions" or autonomy to become independent because each small producer needs *loans, specific technical assistance and multiple*

[8] These figures were equivalent to US dollars until the devaluation of January 2002.

actions performed in a coordinated fashion. Furthermore, there are about 100.000 poor agricultural producer families that require an improvement in their productive conditions and standard of living to achieve a self-sustainable insertion in the market and not just a simple relief. During the year 2001 the PSA distributed $917.927 in direct financial assistance (loan or subsidy), the PROINDER $2.823.273, and the PRODERNEA $807.937.[9]

6) They reach a limited number of beneficiaries. The available data regarding the number of beneficiaries of the running programs is imprecise and overstated: between 1991 and 1997 the beneficiaries from the PNEA were 8.000 and those from the PSA were 39.000 families between 1993 and the end of 1998. However, we cannot assure that this information is accurate or free from overlaps because beneficiaries are not identified year by year. They usually sum up the beneficiaries of the whole period under analysis, or all the "operations" (loans, technical assistance, and training) and consider this as the "total amount of assisted families". This procedure gives as a result a total amount quite higher than that resulting from individual follow-up, name by name, independently from the benefits each person/family has received. According to data from the year 2001, there were 11.046 beneficiaries in the PSA, 11.721 in the PROINDER and 1.447 in the PRODERNEA (figures with similar problems, including loans, technical assistance, training, adaptive experimentation)[10].
7) There is an overlapping and multiplication of actions that do not compose a consistent policy. As we have already mentioned, there is a sum of different programs which only in particular cases reach some coordination. As a consequence, the beneficiaries find it difficult to understand the different operating modes of each program.
8) Most programs are funded through an increase in the external debt. The social and economic consequences implied by this fact demand that these programs be directed to a real productive transformation of the poor small producer sector. That is to say, debt would only be acceptable when changed for growth and a better participation of the small producers in the gross national product; because debt means an economic embargo on the development of the country and endangers the potential of future generations. This is not to question the generation of the debt itself. On the contrary, we accept it replaces the lack of resources in the national budget for social policies. Additionally, the responsibility of these programs in the debt increase is actually lower due to their tiny amounts. It is clear that the groups of higher economic power are the true beneficiaries from the increase in the external debt.
9) If rural projects do not lead to structural transformations and remain as relief programs, they can turn into facilitators of political patronage. The "relief" to extreme poverty situations favors the discretionary acting of local administrations. The patronage spoils the projects really intended for reinforcing values and labor culture in the country. One example is what is going on in some

[9] Source: PROINDER, SAGPyA Institutional Strengthening Area, data base. It should be taken into account that during 2001 the budget for all programs was low due in part to the restrictions in the availability of resources imposed by the national government.

[10] Source: PROINDER, Fortalecimiento Institucional, SAGPyA, Base de datos.

> areas with the "Work Program" of the National Ministry of Labor which gives transitory subsidies to the unemployed. It is common that poor agricultural producers participate in these programs given that, due to the seasonal characteristic of their jobs they appear as "unemployed" in different moments of the year (although, in fact, they are not unemployed). When these producers get used to obtaining a fixed monthly subsidy, they refuse to do their normal activities because of the effort and uncertainty they represent. This situation is very common in provinces with a high component of public jobs. We have seen this in La Rioja, Catamarca and Formosa, where the rural population that used to work in the country and now receives a public salary or an unemployment subsidy, is moving away from the possibility of re-inserting themselves as producers because they are getting accustomed to another kind of life and job dynamics having the security of getting a salary every month without the sacrifice and uncertainty associated with agricultural work.

Most of the restrictions mentioned above are the result of and can be explained within the framework of the present neoliberal policy. Thus, dividing little money among many people and reaching more beneficiaries has to do with the political interests of governments, their lack of resources due to the adjustment and their lack of interest in the problem of poverty. For governments, reaching more people is a goal that favors political consensus. Additionally, the increase in the number of beneficiaries could also benefit the officials from international funding agencies as an indicator of their efficiency and professional productivity.

Furthermore, the rural development programs are not the only ones that reach the beneficiary population, because it is trapped in a productive and economic framework where most impacts are negative and come from the macroeconomic adjustment. Frequently, the beneficiary population feels that the adjustment-associated loss in acquired and universal rights (in subsidies to their products, in health care, in education services and welfare system) surpasses the benefits they receive through focused social programs. This situation worsens when the benefits only apply to some sectors, to those that fit with the "eligibility criteria" for being the poorest.

The adjustment and the de-regulation had other consequences for small producers: many of the social benefits they received for free during the Welfare State, have at present to be bought from the private sector. That is why families claim for the lost social benefits, such as the social security that cotton, tobacco and *yerba* producers obtained from their regulating institutions. They also feel unsafe and chased by the State because they are neither registered under any Welfare System nor pay taxes, when, in fact their condition of economic marginality means they do not have the capability to make regular monthly payments because their income is seasonal and rarely higher than $ 6.000 or $ 7.000 per year[11]. We knew that the General Tax Office has pressed the producers with rural inspections when they deliver their products to the stockpilers.

[11] Amounts equivalent to US dollars until January 2002. From then on, incomes kept their values in pesos but remained highly devaluated compared to the dollar (to July 2002 the relation peso-dollar was $3,6/ dollar)

FINAL REMARKS: THE POSSIBLE DIRECTION OF FUTURE ACTIONS

The characterization made above suggests that it is not very probable that the mentioned rural development actions turn into self-sustainable benefits for the poor agricultural sector. As they are designed so far, it is not very likely that these actions enable poor families to:

(a) Improve their income in the mid-term in a self-sustainable way.
(b) Achieve their "actual" productive integration.
(c) Overcome their historical instability, precariousness and flexibility as regards labor.
(d) Have their social security guaranteed.

The rural development strategy described in this paper is not designed to be imposed on or overcome the obstacles and conditions of the macroeconomic context, which systematically tend to the exclusion, marginality and invalidation of the agricultural small producer sector.

Of course, there are mechanisms to face these processes: institutions, groups and NGOs that are trying to do it, but in order to succeed they have to fight an "unfair battle" with sectors of higher economic and political power with other objectives.

It is also true that the beneficiaries themselves, through their stronger participation in the decision in different programs, are a very important factor in order to achieve these transformations. Furthermore, if we consider that most programs have components to promote the organization, training and participation of beneficiaries with the aim of de-structuring the historic limitations they have been facing. The way to achieve this goal is by giving them skills, power and knowledge so that they can assume responsibilities, make decisions, have authority and, in the long run, build processes of change.

All this is feasible only if beneficiaries can organize themselves and make demands free from the assistance of their respective programs. This entails a participative capability totally different from the one they presently have. They have to overcome many restrictions (economic, social, political, ideological, educative and participative) imposed by the current economic development model, which is exactly the opposite of the empowerment and consolidation of the small producer sectors.

In other words, it seems that the rural development strategy and the economic policy are contradictory and they do not go after complementary objectives. Therefore, the explicit objectives of the rural development strategy are only apparent or their actual aim is to complement the adjustment with "relief".

This contradiction is more evident if we take into account that the present context is characterized by a weakening of social popular movements, a new organization or "social stabilization" where the "social change" issue is not relevant.

Then, the viability of a change in favor of the excluded -or precariously included,- majorities is higher if it emerges from the political action of these majorities rather than from their economic action. That is why their organizational empowerment against the negative consequences of the model (such as reduction in income, unemployment, insecurity, the deterioration of education, health and environment) is so important. In order to re-insert the groups "invalidated" by the present situation in the social game (Pfr.Castel; 1997: 23), they also have to play a relevant role through their opposition to the model that excludes them and stops them from being part of society as a whole. It is only through this action that the State will be able to play a suitable role.

Consequently, we should ask ourselves if there is another way of action in the present restriction context. We think there is.

First, if we consider that the production is *really* important for the training and labor re-insertion of these families but resources are scarce: Why not focus only on projects which actually promote integral cooperative or group work in the use of land, raw materials, and labor, in the agroindustrial transformation and in marketing? That is to say, carry out an exhaustive survey of the projects to be approved in order to choose the best.

This might imply accepting a lower number of beneficiaries and focusing only on those with potential to generate a real socio-productive transformation, knowing they can turn into a multiplying model for future projects and beneficiaries; exactly the opposite of the disappointment resulting from a succession of unfulfilled goals. Precisely, in a previous paper (Manzanal; 1998:73) we concluded regarding a frustrated experience of joint marketing of vegetables among peasants from Cachi, Salta: "The frustrated experiences add restrictions to the already existing ones."

Furthermore, the opposition between universal and focused policies has no support. On the contrary, they could complement each other, as Rubén de Dios (1998:130) affirms. Focusing *should mean solutions, actual transformations,* if not; the focused programs act as a double exclusion instrument. On the one hand, because of the magnitude of the potential beneficiaries they leave out, as this author says. On the other hand, because they do not provide any solution for the target population, producing a drawback in trust, in organizations, and in the will of participation.

Within the same line of action, programs should promote participation and commitment from the beneficiaries. This can only be achieved by applying "transparent" methods in all decisions and actions. For example, the generation of debt associated with programs and projects -which although minor is not innocuous- should be known about by the beneficiary population. Precisely, because these programs foster their participation and they should participate with full knowledge of the present and future possibilities and limitations. From our contacts with producer families we found out that most of them had no idea of the origin of the funds they were receiving. We think that if they learnt about it, their attitudes and demands regarding objectives and results would surely change and, probably, the need to promote actions tending to modify their marginal, socioeconomic and productive insertion would be more relevant.

The suggested way of acting requires a social agreement that guarantees a high degree of consensus, awareness and commitment from the involved population about the priorities and distribution of resources for social purposes. This leads, again, to the need of coordination and complementation among State programs. It is a priority that should not be ignored in order to favor short-term group and personal interests or in order to show differential results by government areas. Even when there have been many compilations about programs with external funding depending on different State Secretaries, there have been no results regarding complementation and coordination among them. We believe this is so because high governmental areas put specific and personal interests before the interests of society as a whole.

Therefore, it is urgent to train and inform about issues such as types and origin of funding, type of fostered activities and coordination and complementation among programs.

In short, make the beneficiary population participate through ways of democratic representation.

It is from this knowledge that the beneficiaries can participate in the decision-making, which leads to transparent procedures and the decline of patronage and of individual or corporative advantages. In addition, the awareness of the beneficiaries about the processes they are involved in, is the first step in the understanding of their socioeconomic framework and, therefore, in the search for alternatives and solutions to their own problems.

Obviously, the feasibility of these training processes requires a long maturing time, which we think should be measured in decades rather than in five-year-periods, as it is the case with the programs analyzed in this paper (generally 4 to 5 years terms).

Besides, these programs work under strict schedules that are compatible neither with participation and training processes nor with the intrinsic characteristics of the target population. In particular, in Manzanal (ibid: 74) we affirmed that these families need a continued assistance instead of training from teams that may change or disappear within a short term: "The processes aimed at training, awareness, participation and organization of the sectors require time; a slow, consistent, sustained and long practice... a decade in the history of marginality suffered by these families and in their family life cycle is a very short time. However, it is too long in terms of the actual projects currently being performed".

So that rural development actions may build effective and sustainable improvements in the standard of living of the rural poor, it is necessary for these actions to have connection and coordination with one another.

This means that we need *a rural development "policy" that is part of a local and regional development strategy and fosters the commitment and the effective participation of beneficiaries in its different stages.*

Organizing and implementing several public programs from a central strategy would avoid many problems related to the scarcity of funds and, basically, it would reach beneficiaries with proposals *according to* their capacity to assimilate different projects; *integral*, due to the coordination among different areas; *sustainable* in the long term because of the addition of resources; and *decisive* in order to achieve the initial objectives. This would also avoid the excess of bureaucracy.

No doubt this is a difficult task because it implies an effort at organizing technical and human resources available individually and unequally in each State area and/or in each program.

However, the most important fact is that we need will and decision from high political levels. This implies not only the intention of "coordination", but, basically, *determination* to face the socioeconomic transformation of the rural poor as one of the priorities in the State policy.

The advance towards the opposite interests, typical of every process of change, demands: (i) *a deep knowledge about the specific problem*, (ii) *to allow the participation* of the different involved sectors (producers, officials, technicians), (iii) to have the *capability to manage* conflicts of interests, and (iv) *to show determination and strength* to initiate a real transformation to improve the previous situation.

REFERENCES

Aspiazu, Daniel (1994) "La industria argentina ante la privatización, la desregulación y la apertura asimétrica de la economía", en D. Aspiazu y H. Nochteff, *El desarrollo ausente*, Tesis, Buenos Aires, 1994.

Basco, Mercedes (1997) *Modalidades de asistencia técnica a los productores agropecuarios en la Argentina*, IICA, Buenos Aires.

Carballo, Carlos (1991) "Los pequeños productores y el desarrollo rural en la Argentina", en *Realidad Económica 110*, IADE, Buenos Aires.

-------------------------(1995) "Programa Social Agropecuario y Cambio Rural. Dos intentos para atenuar la crisis entre los agricultores familiares", en *Realidad Económica 136*, IADE, Buenos Aires.

Castel, Robert (1997) *La metamorfosis de la cuestión social. Una crónica del salariado*, Paidós, Buenos Aires.

Chiriboga, Manuel (1997) "Desafíos de la pequeña agricultura familiar frente a la globalización", *Perspectivas Rurales 1*, Univerisidad Nacional, Heredia, Costa Rica.

Chudnovsky Daniel, López, Andrés y Porta, Fernando (1995) "Más allá del flujo de caja. El boom de la inversión extranjera directa en la Argentina", en *Desarrollo Económico Revista de Ciencias Sociales*, N° 137, abril-junio, IDES, Buenos Aires.

De Dios, Rubén (1998) "Políticas para la pequeña producción agropecuaria o el derecho a permanecer", *Realidad Económica 158,* IADE, Buenos Aires.

Forni, Floreal y Neiman, Guillermo (1994) "La pobreza rural en la Argentina", Documento de trabajo N° 5, mimeo inédito, CEPA (Comité Ejecutivo para el Estudio de la Pobreza en la Argentina), Ministerio de Economía y Obras y Servicios Públicos, Secretaría de Programación Económica, Buenos Aires.

González, María, Pagliettini, Liliana et al (1996) *Habitat rural y pequeña producción en la Argentina. Situaciones de pobreza rural y pequeña producción agraria,* Subscretaría de Vivienda, Secretaría de Desarrollo Social, Buenos Aires.

Kosacoff, Bernardo (1995) "La industria argentina, un proceso de reestructuración desarticulada", en Pablo Bustos (comp.), *Más allá de la estabilidad,* Fundación Friedrich Ebert, Buenos Aires.

Lombardo, Patricia y Tort, María Isabel (1998) "Estrategias de intervención para pequeños y medianos prodcutores agropecuarios en la década del ´90", mimeo *Jornadas Extraordinarias de Estudios Agrarios 'Horacio Giberti',* Facultad de Filosofía y Letras, Universidad de Buenos Aires.

Manzanal, Mabel (1993) *Estrategias de sobrevivencia de los pobres rurales*, Biblioteca Política Argentina, Centro Editor de América Latina, Buenos Aires.

------------------------ (1995) "Desarrollo y condiciones de vida en asentamientos campesinos. El caso de Cachi en los valles calchaquíes salteños", Buenos Aires: Tesis de Doctorado, Facultad de Filosofía y Letras, Universidad de Buenos Aires.

-------------------------(1998) "Vicisitudes de la comercialización de hortalizas entre los pequeños productores agropecuarios. El caso de la producción de tomate fresco en Cachi, Salta", *Realidad Económica 153,* enero/febrero, Buenos Aires.

Murmis, Miguel (1995) "Pobreza rural: datos recientes y diversidad de situaciones ocupacionales", mimeo PROINDER, Dirección de Planeamiento y Desarrollo Agropecuario, SAGyP, Buenos Aires.

Neiman, Guillermo (1997) "Empobrecimiento y exclusión. Nuevas y viejas formas de pobreza rural en la Argentina", mimeo, I Congreso Internacional de Pobres y Pobreza en la Sociedad Argentina, CEIL - UNQ, 4 al 7 de noviembre.

Petras, James y Vieux, Steve (1995) *¡Hagan juego!,* Icaria - Más Madera, Barcelona.

Redar Argentina (1993) "Boletín Redar Argentina, Red de Agroindustria Rural", Año 2, N° 3, INTA, Buenos Aires.

----------------------- (1994) "Boletín Redar Argentina, Red de Agroindustria Rural", Año 3, N° 5, INTA, Buenos Aires.

------------------------(1994a) "Boletín Redar Argentina, Red de Agroindustria Rural", Año 3, N° 6, INTA, Buenos Aires.

SAPyA (1992) "El minifundio en la Argentina", Dirección de Planificación y Desarrollo Agropecuario (inédito), Buenos Aires.

------------(1996) "Programas y proyectos agropecuarios y pesqueros", Dirección de Planeamiento y Desarrollo Agropecuario, Buenos Aires.

SAGPyA (1997) "Programa de Crédito y Apoyo Técnico para Pequeños Productores Agropecuarios de Noreste Argentino, Informe Final", Unidad Nacional de Coordinación PNEA, Buenos Aires.

------------- (1997a) "Proyecto de Iniciativas Rurales, PROINDER, Resumen del proyecto", Dirección de Desarrollo Agropecuario, Buenos Aires.

....................(1999) "Políticas para pequeños productores con potencial empresarial en el norte argentino", Gobiernos Provinciales, FIDA, SAGPyA, mimeo, setiembre 1999, Buenos Aires.

.....................(2000) "Los programas nacionales de desarrollo rural ejecutados en el ámbito de la SAGPyA", *Serie Estudios e Investigaciones 1*, PROINDER, Buenos Aires.

Soverna, Susana y Craviotti, Clara (1998) "Los estudios de caso: su utilidad para el análisis sociológico y la formulación de programas de desarrollo rural", mimeo *Jornadas Extraordinarias de Estudios Agrarios 'Horacio Giberti',* Facultad de Filosofía y Letras, Universidad de Buenos Aires, agosto de 1998.

In: Argentina: Economic, Political and Social Issues
Editor: Jeanne B. Haverland
ISBN 978-1-60456-469-3

Chapter 6

HUMAN RIGHTS AND PSYCHOLOGY ETHICS CODES IN ARGENTINA

Andrea Ferrero
National University of San Luis, Argentina

ABSTRACT

This work considers the importance of ethics in the practice of psychology. Within this general framework, this paper takes into account the central role that human rights take in the main professional ethic codes of psychology in Argentina, like in many other ethic codes from other countries. The particular inclusion of these topics in Argentinean ethic codes of psychology is analyzed in this case not only as the inclusion of general ethical principles that guarantee personal and community welfare. It is specially considered that the permanent direct or indirect reference to human rights in those Codes is related to the '70 dictatorial government that, as in many other Latin-American countries, established a terror system, in which personal and social rights were seriously damaged, causing a deep wound in society.

Key words: psychology - ethic codes - human rights - Argentina

Psychologist's scientific and professional community agree in the importance of ethics in the professional psychologist's training. It has also been stated that an ethical practice of psychology, as any other profession, must consider some general principles as *Beneficence* and *Nonmaleficence*, *Autonomy* and *Justice* (Childress, 1998). Upon these basic principles most ethics codes in psychology includes Fidelity and Social Responsibility, Integrity, and Respect for People's Rights and Dignity (Leach & Harbin, 1997; Lindsay, 1996; Loewy, 2003, Pettifor, 2004, Waring, Bore & Munro, 2003). All these professional commitments are referred to the expectations of an ethical practice of psychology (Graham, 2001; Lindsay, 1996; Pettifor & Horne, 2001, Ferrero, 2003).

In some Latin-American countries these principles take a particular relevance. As it is known, between 1970 and 1985, military forces overthrew democratic governments and established dictatorial governments in many Latin-American countries, characterized by the illegal capture, torture, and forced disappearance of thousands of people. In Argentina there was a *coup* on March 24th, 1976, that ended in October 1983, when democratic elections were held. There were about 30.000 missing people, mostly students, teachers, workers, members of any political party, and even priests and housewives. From all professional fields, psychologists had the higher number of missing colleagues (Comisión Nacional sobre la Desaparición de Personas [National Commission for Missing People], 1984).

Some of those missing people recovered their freedom and state their testimonies about the inhuman life conditions in clandestine detention centers, the frequent torture sessions -in many occasions supervised by medical doctors-, and the all kind of abuses they had to suffer. There also were over 300 babies born in those centers, whose mothers were killed after the birth and the babies were adopted, specially by families related to the military staff. Up to day 77 of those babies, young men and women, have recovered their real identity and met their biological families due to the praiseworthy work done by the *Abuelas de Plaza de Mayo*, which central goal is to recover their grandchildren, those who they could not knew because their pregnant daughters or daughters in law were kidnapped by military forces. As the *Madres de Plaza de Mayo*, the grandmothers lost their sons or daughters, but they still hope to recover their grandchildren (Comisión Nacional sobre la Desaparición de Personas [National Commission for Missing People], 1984). All this facts left a deep wound not only in those who have been directly involved themselves or their relatives, but in the whole society as well.

There is no doubt that respecting human rights is everybody's duty, as it is stated in the main Right's Declarations, beginning with the *Universal Declaration Of Human Rights* (United Nations, 1948). Since that moment, many new right's declarations, conforming the so called "generations", arose with the intention to protect any kind of individual and community's right. It is necessary to remark that rights also means duties, as everybody's rights imply some one's else duties (Tugendhat, 1997).

So everyone, both as person and part of a community, is obliged to respect these declarations, but in case of a professional relation, these duties take become even more relevant because of the asymmetrical relation between the parts, and that is why there are many right's declarations which function is to preserve people's rights, also within mental health field (United Nations, 1990; 1991; 1997). Due to this principles, any professional practice -including psychology in any field of application-, must consider the relation between rights and duties, relation that is expressed by professional ethics codes (Dobson & Breault, 1998; Ferrero, 2005; Knapp & VandeCreek, 2003; Leach & Harbin, 1997; Lindsay, 1996). Within these specific professional principles there are also ethical regulations specially referred to research with human beings, which main interest is to protect the autonomy and the welfare of the persons involved in medical treatment and research, as the *Helsinki Declaration* (World Medical Association, 1975/2000), the *Belmont Report* (National Commission for the Protection of Human Subjects of Biomedical and Behavioral Research, 1979), the *International Ethical Guidelines for Biomedical Research Involving Human Subjects* (Council for International Organizations of Medical Sciences (CIOMS), 2002), and the *International Code of Medical Ethics* (World Medical Association, 1949/ 1983)

In Argentina the practice of psychology is regulated by provincial federal laws all over the country. Each province has got its own Board of Psychologists leading to licensure and has developed local Ethics Codes with very few differences between them (Klappenbach,

2004). In this country there are two Psychology Ethics Codes with national application. One of them, is the National Ethics Code, stated in 1999 by the *Psychologists' Federation of the Argentine Republic* [Federación de Psicólogos de la República Argentina] (Federación de Psicólogos de la República Argentina [Psychologists' Federation of the Argentine Republic], 1999), and the other is a regional one called *Ethical Principles Framework for professional practice of psychology in the Mercosur and Associated Countries* [*Protocolo de Acuerdo Marco de Principios Éticos para Psicólogos del Mercosur y Países Asociados*] and involves not only Argentina but other countries of the *Mercosur* (Comité Coordinador de Psicólogos del Mercosur y Países Asociados [Psychologists' Committee of Mercosur and Associated Countries], 1997). The *Mercosur* is a socio-economic and cultural Union of the southeast countries of South America: Argentina, Brazil, Paraguay and Uruguay as full members, and Chile and Bolivia as associated countries.

Even though the *Psychologists' Committee of Mercosur and Associated Countries* has not reached the goals showed by the *European Federation of Psychologists' Associations*, whose Metha Code of ethics "provides a model of common principles or values" (Pettifor, 2004, p. 267), such Committee has also began the hard task of providing a framework for common training and practice standards in psychology, and also a common psychology Ethics Code for the countries of the Mercosur (Hermosilla, 2000).

The Ethics Code of the *Psychologists' Federation of the Argentine Republic* is considered the most important reference for psychologist's professional conduct in Argentina, and includes a Preamble, five Ethical General Principles and many Ethical Standards referred to deontological duties: informed consent, confidentiality, record keeping, education and training, research, publication, advertising and human relations with colleagues and clients (Federación de Psicólogos de la República Argentina [Psychologists' Federation of the Argentine Republic], 1999). The *Ethical Principles Framework for professional practice of psychology in the Mercosur and Associated Countries* is also a valuable reference, and its main interests are five Ethical General Principles, which are exactly the same of the mentioned National Code *Mercosur* (Comité Coordinador de Psicólogos del Mercosur y Países Asociados [Psychologists' Committee of Mercosur and Associated Countries], 1997).

The importance of human rights in psychology's Argentinean ethics codes can be firstly appreciate in the *Preambule* of the National Code, where this matter takes a relevant place:

> "(Psychologists)... promotes for both the person and the society the absolute validity of Human Rights, the defense of the democratic govern system, and the permanent looking for freedom, social justice and dignity, that will produce an active, critic and solidarity person and society"... "(Psychologists)... do not permit, nor even take part willingly of any kind of discriminatory action" (Federación de Psicólogos de la República Argentina [Psychologists' Federation of the Argentine Republic], 1999) (Translation is ours).

Both ideas of this *Preambule* of the National Ethics Code of Psychology are clear enough from the very beginning about the importance of human rights in this Code.

As we have already mentioned, both Ethics Codes, the psychologists' *Mercosur's Code* and the Argentinean one, include the same five General Principles: *Respect for People's Rights and Dignity*, *Professional Competence*, *Professional and Scientific Commitment*, *Integrity*, *and Social Responsibility* (Comité Coordinador de Psicólogos del Mercosur y Países Asociados [Psychologists' Committee of Mercosur and Associated Countries], 1997;

Federación de Psicólogos de la República Argentina [Psychologists' Federation of the Argentine Republic], 1999).

These principles do not differ much from the General Principles of the *Ethics Codes* of the American Psychological Association and the European Federation of Psychologist's Associations. In fact, the general principles of the American Psychological Association Ethics Code are: *Beneficence and Nonmaleficence, Fidelity and Responsability, Integrity, Justice, and Respect for People's Rights and Dignity*. And the general principles of the EPFA Metha Code are: *Respect for a Person's Rights and Dignity*, *Competence*, *Responsibility* and *Integrity* (APA, 2002; EFPA, 1995; Knapp & VandeCreek, 2003; Pettifor, 2004).

Human rights is a central topic in the North-American end European psychology ethics codes, and South-American countries are not an exception as all of them includes their commitment to this matter. Of course that all above-mentioned general principles share, directly or not, a relation with human rights, as they protect general people's welfare related to any psychological practice (Ferrero, 2002).

But in countries like Argentina, where human rights have been seriously defiled, this professional commitment acquires a very particular meaning. From this perspective the inclusion of human rights in psychological ethics codes in Argentina has a particular value, as it makes reference to a very painful past and promotes a reflection in a professional community that is part of a society that has been seriously injured.

That is why in this occasion we consider the relation between the same five General Principles of the Argentinean ethical codes and human rights, with the intention of analyzing the underlying links, some kind of silent and omnipresent role of human rights in all of these principles (Federación de Psicólogos de la República Argentina [Psychologists' Federation of the Argentine Republic], 1999; Comité Coordinador de Psicólogos del Mercosur y Países Asociados [Psychologists' Committee of Mercosur and Associated Countries], 1997).

The first mentioned General Principle of both Codes is specifically referred to human rights. It is called Respect for people's rights and dignity, and states:

> "Psychologists has a commitment with the principles stated by the Universal Declaration of Human Rights. They will respect fundamental rights, dignity and worth of all people, and will not take part in discriminatory actions. They will respect people's right to privacy, confidentiality, self-determination, and autonomy" (Federación de Psicólogos de la República Argentina [Psychologists' Federation of the Argentine Republic], 1999; Comité Coordinador de Psicólogos del Mercosur y Países Asociados [Psychologists' Committee of Mercosur and Associated Countries], 1997) (Translation is ours).

As we have already mentioned, the need to give priority to human rights in Argentinean psychology ethics codes can be appreciated in the other four General Principles, which are mainly focused to different aspects of an ethical practice of psychology. So the second point referred to *Competence*, remarks the importance of professional competence itself and states:

> "(Psychologists)... "Must consider that the competence required in the treatment, teaching or researching of communities, may vary according to the diversity of those communities" (Federación de Psicólogos de la República Argentina [Psychologists' Federation of the Argentine Republic], 1999; Comité Coordinador de Psicólogos del Mercosur y Países Asociados [Psychologists' Committee of Mercosur and Associated Countries], 1997) (Translation is ours).

This shows that psychologists must not only have to develop a high qualified intervention, but that this one must seriously consider the respect for the own characteristics of the community in which it is held, act that involves the respect of any kind of individual or cultural differences.

The next General Principle is referred to *Integrity*, and states:

> "Psychologists will be aware from using notions that might conclude in denigrating or discriminatory cualifications" and "In their scientific and professional role they will make clear the role of any of the parts involved and will act according to that" (Federación de Psicólogos de la República Argentina [Psychologists' Federation of the Argentine Republic], 1999; Comité Coordinador de Psicólogos del Mercosur y Países Asociados [Psychologists' Committee of Mercosur and Associated Countries], 1997) (Translation is ours).

Both ideas are referred to the fact that professional and scientific *Integrity* must take into account the respect for the person involved in the practice and the need of honesty to make a clear set up of that practice.

Finally, the General Principle referred to *Social Responsibility*, establishes:

> "Psychologists exert their social commitment through the study of reality and promote and/or help with the development of laws and social policies that, from their professional specificity, might contribute to the welfare and development of the person and the community" (Federación de Psicólogos de la República Argentina [Psychologists' Federation of the Argentine Republic], 1999; Comité Coordinador de Psicólogos del Mercosur y Países Asociados [Psychologists' Committee of Mercosur and Associated Countries], 1997) (Translation is ours).

This last General Principle points out that the practice of psychology is related to the possibility of being part of policies that could formally guarantee people's welfare, and personal and community development.

The analysis of the main psychology ethics codes in Argentina shows the importance that human rights had at the moment in which they have been stated. This fact has consequences regarding the local practice of psychology as it is regulated by these Codes, and points out that an ethical practice of psychology must always take into account not only ethical procedures themselves, but also their origins. The central role of human rights in Argentinean psychology Ethics Codes reveals part of the history of this country.

References

American Psychological Association (2002). Ethical Principles of Psychologists and Code of Conduct. *American Psychologist*, 57 (12), 1060–1073.

Childress, J. F. (1998). El lugar de la autonomía en la bioética. [The place of Authonomy in Bioethics]. In F. Luna & A. Salles (Eds.), *Bioética. Investigación, muerte, procreación y otros temas de ética aplicada.* [Bioethic. Research, death, procreation and other matters of applied ethics] (pp. 133-144). Buenos Aires: Sudamericana. (Original work published in 1990).

Comisión Nacional sobre la Desaparición de Personas (1984). *Nunca más. Informe de la Comisión Nacional sobre la desaparición de personas.* [Never again. Report of the National Commission for Missing People]. Buenos Aires: Eudeba.

Comité Coordinador de Psicólogos del Mercosur y Países Asociados [Psychologists Committee of Mercosur and Associated Countries] (1997). *Protocolo de acuerdo marco de principios éticos para el ejercicio profesional de los psicólogos en el Mercosur y Países Asociados.* [*Ethical Principles Framework for professional practice of psychology in the Mercosur and Associated Countries*]. In Conselho Federal de Psicologia [Federal Board of Psychology], *A psicologia no Mercosul* [*Psychology in the Mercosur*] (pp. 11-14). Brasilia, Brasil: Author.

Council for International Organizations of Medical Sciences (CIOMS) (2002). *International Ethical Guidelines for Biomedical Research Involving Human Subjects.* Author.

Dobson, K. S. & Breault, L. (1998). The Canadian Code of Ethics and the Regulation of Psychology. *Canadian Psychology, 39* (3), 212-218.

European Federation of Professional Psychologists Associations (1995). *Metha-Code of Ethics*. Brusels: Author.

Federación de Psicólogos de la República Argentina [Psychologists' Federation of the Argentine Republic] (1999). *Código de Etica. (Ethics Code).* Buenos Aires: Autor.

Ferrero, A. (2002). Importancia de los derechos humanos en los códigos deontológicos de psicología en la Argentina [The importance of human rights in psychology ethics codes]. *Revista Argentina de Psicología, 45*, 33-41.

Ferrero, A. (2003). Consecuencias sociales y psicológicas de la globalización en Argentina. Una mirada desde la ética profesional [Social and psychological globalization's effects. An ethical point of view]. *Revista Iberoamericana de Educación, Salud y Trabajo, 4*, 253-264.

Ferrero, A. (2005). El surgimiento de la deontología profesional en el campo de la psicología [The beginnings of professional deontology in psychology]. *Fundamentos en Humanidades, 6,* (10/11), 169-177.

Graham, J. (2001). Caring from Afar: Expanding our Concept of Care in the Professions. *Professional Ethics: a multidisciplinary Journal, 9* (1), 31-60.

Hermosilla, A. M. (2000). Psicología y Mercosur: la dimensión ética de la integración y antecedentes del debate en Argentina [Psychology and Mercosur: ethical perspective of integration and framework for the debate in Argentina]. *Fundamentos en Humanidades, 1*, 2, 63-76.

Klappenbach, H. (2004). Psychology in Argentina. In M. J. Strevens & D. Wedding (Eds.), *Handbook of International Psychology* (pp. 129-168). New York: Brunner-Routledge.

Knapp, S. & VandeCreek, L. (2003). An Overview of the Major Changes in the 2002 APA Ethics Code. *Professional Psychology: Research and Practice, 34* (3), 301-308.

Leach, M. M. & Harbin, J. J. (1997). Psychological Ethics Codes: a comparison of twenty-four countries. *International Journal of Psychology, 32* (3), 181-192.

Lindsay, G. (1996). Psychology as an Ethical Discipline and Profession. *European Psychologist, 1* (2), 79-88.

Loewy, E. (2003). Education, practice and bioethics: Growing barriers to ethical practice. *Health Care Analysis, (2),* 11, 171-179.

National Commission for the Protection of Human Subjects of Biomedical and Behavioral Research (1979) The Belmont Report Office of the Secretary. Ethical Principles and guidelines for the Protection of Human Subjects of Research. Author.

Pettifor, J. L. (2004). Proffesional Ethics accross National Boundaries. *European Psychologist, 9* (4), 264-272.

Pettifor, J. L. & Horne, K. (2001). Professional ethics: Social responsibility or the status quo? In R. Roth & S. Neill (Eds.), *A matter for life: Psychological theory, research and practice* (pp. 449–46). Berlin: Pabst.

Tugendhat, E. (1997) *Lecciones de ética*. Barcelona: Gedisa.

United Nations General Assembly (1948). *Universal Declaration Of Human Rights*. Author.

United Nations (1990). *Tallinn Guidelines For Action On Human Resources Development In The Field Of Disability*. Author.

United Nations (1991). Principles for the Protection of Persons with Mental Illnesses and the Improvement of Mental Health Care. Author

United Nations (1997). *Standard Rules on the Equalization of Opportunities for Persons with Disabilities*. Author.

Waring, T., Bore, M. & Munro, D. (2003). Ethics and the practice of psychology. Regulating, educating and selecting the ethical practitioner. *Australian Journal of Psychology, Supplement 2003,* 463-475.

World Medical Association (1975/2000). *Declaration of Helsinki: Ethical Principles for Medical Research Involving Human Subjects*. Author.

World Medical Association (1949/1983) *International Code of Medical Ethics*. Author.

In: Argentina: Economic, Political and Social Issues
Editor: Jeanne B. Haverland
ISBN 978-1-60456-469-3

Chapter 7

SMALL AND LOCAL INITIATIVES IN SOUTHERN PATAGONIA: BEGINNINGS, CRISIS AND PERSPECTIVES

María Eugenia Cepparo de Grosso*
Facultad de Filosofía y Letras, Universidad Nacional de Cuyo
Consejo Nacional de Investigaciones Científicas y Técnicas
Ciudad Universitaria, Parque Gral. San Martín, Mendoza, Argentina

ABSTRACT

In the fragile environment of Southern Patagonian with limited opportunities for economic diversification, the predominant socioeconomic activities have focused on stock breeding in rural areas, and public services in urban ones. This particular investigation seeks to study specific actions, which relate to the agricultural conditions of the province of Santa Cruz.

Some of the processes that can contribute to this province's economic growth are: the public organizations and intervening communities' actions, and the producers' capability for innovation, decision-making and regulation. Thus, this investigation seeks to reflect on the positive and negative aspects that influenced both public and private organizations' activity, level of commitment and identity. It focuses on the organizations orientated to promoting local development and considerations of an environmental and cultural nature.

Keywords: Southern Patagonia, marginality, local development, innovative projects, economic diversification.

---

* E-mail: mcepparo@logos.uncu.edu.ar

Introduction

The province of Santa Cruz is characterized by a fragile natural and socioeconomic environment. The society in this province is traditionally orientated towards single-product farming in rural areas and public services in the urban centers. This report examines a small innovative project, developed by a group of social actors eager to generate activities adapted to prevailing agricultural limitations, in this southern province.

Producers' competence for idea formulation and transformation, together with the decision-making capacity and skills of public institutions and cooperatives, form part of the factors which have either stimulated or inhibited agricultural activity, in Santa Cruz. The objective of this report is to reflect upon the motives that justify the study of small communities in remote areas. It also looks at actions and the levels of commitment of public and private agents who are orientated towards an alternative form of local scale development, in the Gobernador Gregores district.

1. Reasons Justifying the Study of Declining Agrarian Projects in Marginal Territories

I think that it is necessary to answer a series of personal questions which have linked me, for several years, in my research into marginal territories in Southern Patagonia.

1. Why study such small agricultural projects, in a scarcely populated area with enormous limitations which does not have a crop growing tradition?
2. Why study a peripherally located space which is considered marginal from various points of view?

It is interesting to answer the first question from thematic, theoretical and methodological angles. This subject has never been dealt with in Santa Cruz. Thematically, the problem of reducing fruit and horticultural cultivated areas has only been looked at from an agronomical perspective. Theoretically, research related to this province's agriculture has never been considered a problem under the concept of marginalization. Methodologically, by way of direct contact between economic agents and social actors, and understanding their achievements and failures through fieldwork, surveys, interviews and personal life stories, we can obtain valuable information. This report also allows insight into current activities as they are evolving, at the same time as new farms are being created and pioneering efforts advance. It is also an enriching contribution to microscale geography where bottom-up and internal movement is giving rise to new activities, which are based on local resources and community interest.

With respect to the second question, its response enables us to compare studies dealing with marginality carried out in developed countries and the problems that affect developing and underdeveloped countries.

On the one hand, one can demonstrate that there is a general tendency by research organizations, interdisciplinary groups and especially geographers, towards studying areas with a high urban and industrial concentration, with intensive agricultural activity or with long agricultural traditions. Complex productive structures, substantial capital and technological investment and attractive job opportunities, among other factors, have influenced the tendency towards studying these phenomena and spaces. On the other hand, there is little research related to low density populations in rural areas that are working with new crops, and even more so if they are located in regions such as those included in this research.

In an international framework, after reading the papers published in the books by the IGU Commission on Dynamics of Marginal and Critical Regions, a growing interest by geographers in studying this region can be seen. Walter Leimgruber shows that continuing demands exerted on the land and its resources, the tendency towards international economic deterioration and the increase in centralized authority has intensified the appearance of marginal regions in developed and developing countries (Leimgruber, 1994, p. 1).

As pointed out by other members of the Group, integration between theory and practice is needed, and the transfer of knowledge from countries and institutions with more information regarding this subject, is necessary in order to get closer to resolving these problems (Furlani, 1996, p. XVII).

However the concept of marginality, diverse and complex in nature because of its multiple relationships, is the reason why this transfer of knowledge is both difficult and insufficiently carried out. The predominant subject matter in research by investigators in this Commission, especially those from developed countries, is also reflects a spatial imbalance. According to the papers published in the books by this IGU Commission, only 25% of the papers presented refer to problems related to marginality in underdeveloped or Third World Countries[1].

There is another group of researchers from various countries, including Switzerland, Sweden, Turkey, Finland and the United States, who are concerned about sustainability and the future of small communities within the context of present dynamic economics. Their work includes the relationship between space and society within a reduced, insecure or fragile natural environment.

Reference to this Commission or Research Group, shows that marginality also exists in developed countries, where it encompasses a variety of issues. This highlights the need to study these issues in question in affected spaces in developing and underdeveloped countries such as Argentina.

[1] In Latin America there are planning organisms which take care of the problems characterizing critical and marginal regions. Researchers such as Patricia Wilson of SIAP (Sociedad Interamericana de Planificación); F. Alburquerque Llorens of ILPES (Instituto Latinoamericano y del Caribe de Planificación Económica y Social), J. Rocatagliata, H. Bozzano and J. Coraggio from Argentina, Sergio Boisier y C. de Mattos from Chile; and Friedmann from the United States, amongst others, have various publications, mainly in the SIAP (Sociedad Interamericana de Planificación). Although they are not specialists in marginality, it is necessary to draw attention to the work being done by concerned specialists working on conceptual, methodological and technical changes in order to face and resolve different situations which affect sparsely populated or marginal countries in Latin America.

2. The Role of Social Agents in Marginal Spaces in Argentina

The macro-economic changes that have been taking place in Argentina since 1990, have deeply affected all the social players involved in productive processes. In the agricultural sector, adjustments to new economic measures have caused intense production and organizational changes. These adaptive strategies, not new to the Pampas' agricultural development, initiated new activities and led to a changing economic, social and political situations in the country (Nogar, 1998, p. 473). Regional economies, where there are varied and fragile environments with little diversification, outside the Pampas region, could not confront this demanding model with the same speed. Local impact in these regions also varied with regards to the commercialization of regional agricultural production and the flexibility towards change according to market demands.

Generally studies related to the influence of globalization on Argentina refer to either medium and large regions, or urban, industrial and intense rural activities. Little attention has been given to the consequences of globalization on the system's weaker units, that is: small settlements, peripheral and marginal areas or spaces where traditional cultural models have a strong influence over personal and community decision making. These places are those that run the risk of being underestimated by public and private policy makers. However, the influence of these powerful agents, the search for new and integrated markets, and the rapid advances in communication technology, have gradually allowed the incorporation of previously remote places into the world economic system. Despite these changes and the evidence of their benefits the following has happened: local communities could remain unchanged or they may immediately accept proposed guidelines which generally arrive from the outside, created by people who are often ignorant to local and regional potential and limitations.

Small societies cannot make use of many of the advances or of the decisions they are faced with. This is even more so in societies that are associated with agriculture in developing countries, such as Argentina, where there are a domination of imbalanced regional economies. Here, the conditions are either precarious or too weak to be competitive. In the most affected areas one finds:

a) areas cultivated by small producers without capital,
b) spaces which cannot progress agriculturally, often due to environmental factors, or
c) places with a historical evolution characterized by an irregular sequence of political and economic processes.

These processes are marked by interruptions, advances and withdrawals of interest and decisions. These characteristics are overlying and repeated, particularly in Southern Patagonia where communities are making an effort to adapt their "productive structures" to suit the economy's overall requirements.

In theory, in order to create an atmosphere suitable for change, one should look for strategic consensus between public and private agents, in the territory concerned. Alburquerque Llorens believes that the relationship between different agents with unequal negotiation power and capacity depends on the possibility to obtain organizational and technological innovations, and to accomplish the economic projection of their production (Alburquerque Llorens, 1995, p. 20). This association may be the key to developing new economic perspectives, or to reactivate those which have lagged behind.

It is evident that a large part of the responsibility of access to relationships, services and more advanced technology falls on the region's public officials. Applying this situation to Argentina, Rofman considers that the absence of this connection has been important in the level of economic, social and political delay, which affects many of the country's regions (Rofman, 1999, p. 11).

Due to the decrease in state intervention in Argentina, social actors have had to activate their own local initiatives. In some cases, state representatives have played the role of being their own agents in regional socio-economic development. They have integrated with producers, prompting and guiding attempts to re-evaluate their natural resources and social and cultural traits. In other cases a lack of presence and unfulfilled promises is prevalent. In both situations, local actors have been faced with the lack of experience and the weight of responsibility of carrying out and acting on the strategies and the initiatives of local development.

Local development needs both strong social and cultural ties in order to:

- satisfy needs through growth and equality,
- achieve community participation in decision-making and innovations,
- encourage municipal participation especially in medium and smaller towns or in rural service centres; and
- preserve community identity and its commitment to the place and its resources (Furlani & Manchón, 1996, p. 214).

3. An Example of a Local initiative with an Agrarian Base in Southern Patagonia[2]

3.1. The Role of Agriculture in Santa Cruz

This study follows the line of work which I began working on several years ago. It refers to projects that have been developed in Southern Patagonia, where the action of local actors has involved the development of intensive cultivation, and a method of integration between public and private agents.

Santa Cruz is the southern-most territory of continental Argentina. It is the second largest province in land area and one of the least populated in the Republic. It has a cold and arid climate, it is extensive at 240.000 km^2, and has extreme environmental features, making it a place which is difficult to populate and exploit economically.

Little transformation has taken place over the sparsely occupied Santa Cruz province. Sheep farming, which has been practiced by the population for a little more than a century, still dominates rural spaces. The first wave of inhabitants accepted the environment's limitations in order to economically exploit extensive sheep farming.

From the first half of the 20th century onwards, hydrocarbons and coal were exploited, but this did not generate any industrial activities. Later on, fishing created a few ports. While these developments were taking place the territory was "organized", from an urban point of view, in a network of peripheral towns connected by an elementary infrastructure (Cepparo, 1992, p. 77). There is a prevalence of pastoral activities in rural areas and tertiary activities in the towns, which are predominated by public administration.

The most noteworthy territorial impacts have been produced by sheep farming. There have been a long series of circumstantial and structural factors generated by successive economic crises. Also, poor grazing habits have intensified the propensity towards desertification.

This situation has motivated farmers and some government bodies to make decisions and to initiate measures in order to promote and strengthen other activities and production areas in recent years. Activities related to intense agriculture, tourism, mining and fishing are among the possibilities available to generate production diversification.

Agriculture here has always been inadequately represented. It is also limited to certain locations. Despite the accentuated arid conditions, there are places which are privileged by higher precipitation, abundant water in the rivers, special microclimates and the effort made by some producers. The appearance of dry-land farming or irrigated crops has given rise to small areas dedicated to intensive agricultural production and this has broken the monotony of rural activities. Berries and in particular cherries, which has a fledgling export market, are being cultivated in Los Antiguos. Varieties of green vegetables, with fast market placement in the local market are being grown at present in Rio Gallegos. Alfalfa and garlic crops as well as forestation activities have appeared in Gobernador Gregores.

These opportunities may give rise to new economic structures, which are potentially different from the traditionally exclusively ovine pastoral model (Figure 1).

3.2. The Gobernador Gregores District and its Agricultural Project

3.2.1. Beginnings of the Initiative

The area cultivated in Gobernador Gregores, which lies in the centre of Santa Cruz's plateaus, is advantaged by the abundance of water from of the Santa Cruz River and its confluence in the Chico River (Figure 2). The scale of its present usage is rather insignificant with respect to its potential. From the beginning, agricultural exploitation has always tended towards alfalfa and some horticulture. This has been in order to satisfy the needs of local inhabitants and livestock producers on neighboring "estancias".

[2] This project is the product of personal field study for the rural areas in the province of Santa Cruz with the use of surveys taken with producers and public officials during 2000, 2002 and 2004.

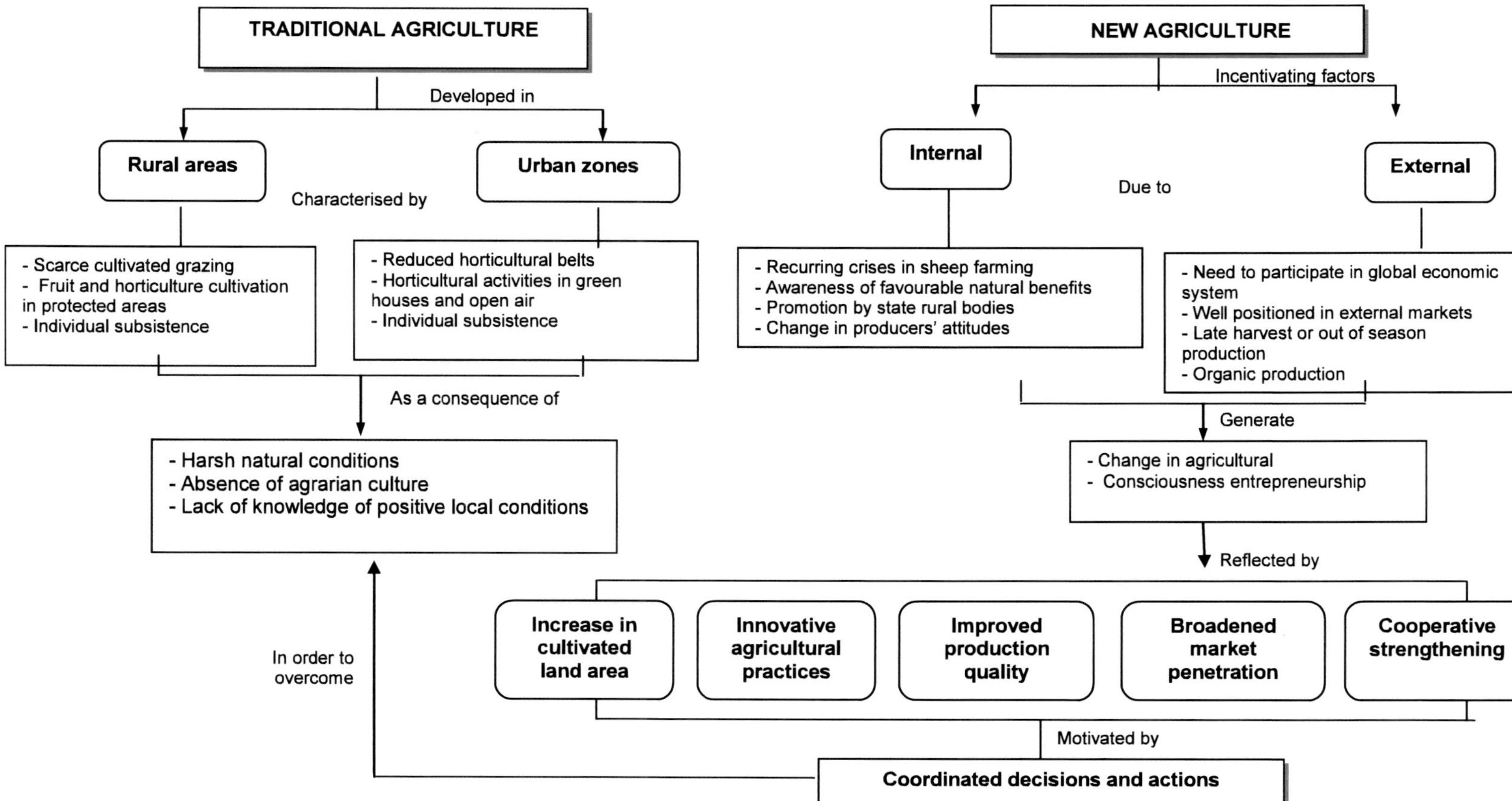

Source: Compiled by María Eugenia Cepparo.

Figure 1. Two agriculture models in the province of Santa Cruz.

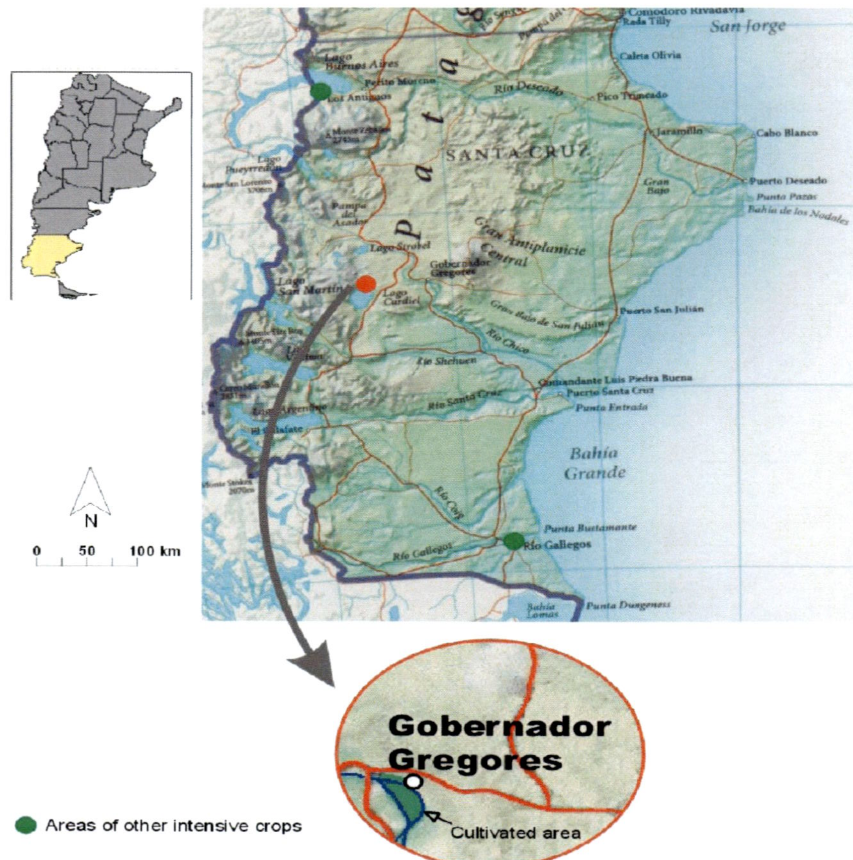

Source: Compiled by Maria Eugenia Cepparo based on Instituto Geográfico Militar 2001. Atlas Geográfico de la República Argentina, Buenos Aires, IGM. p. 99.

Figure 2. Gobernador Gregores and its area of intensive cultivation. Santa Cruz. Panagonia Argentina.

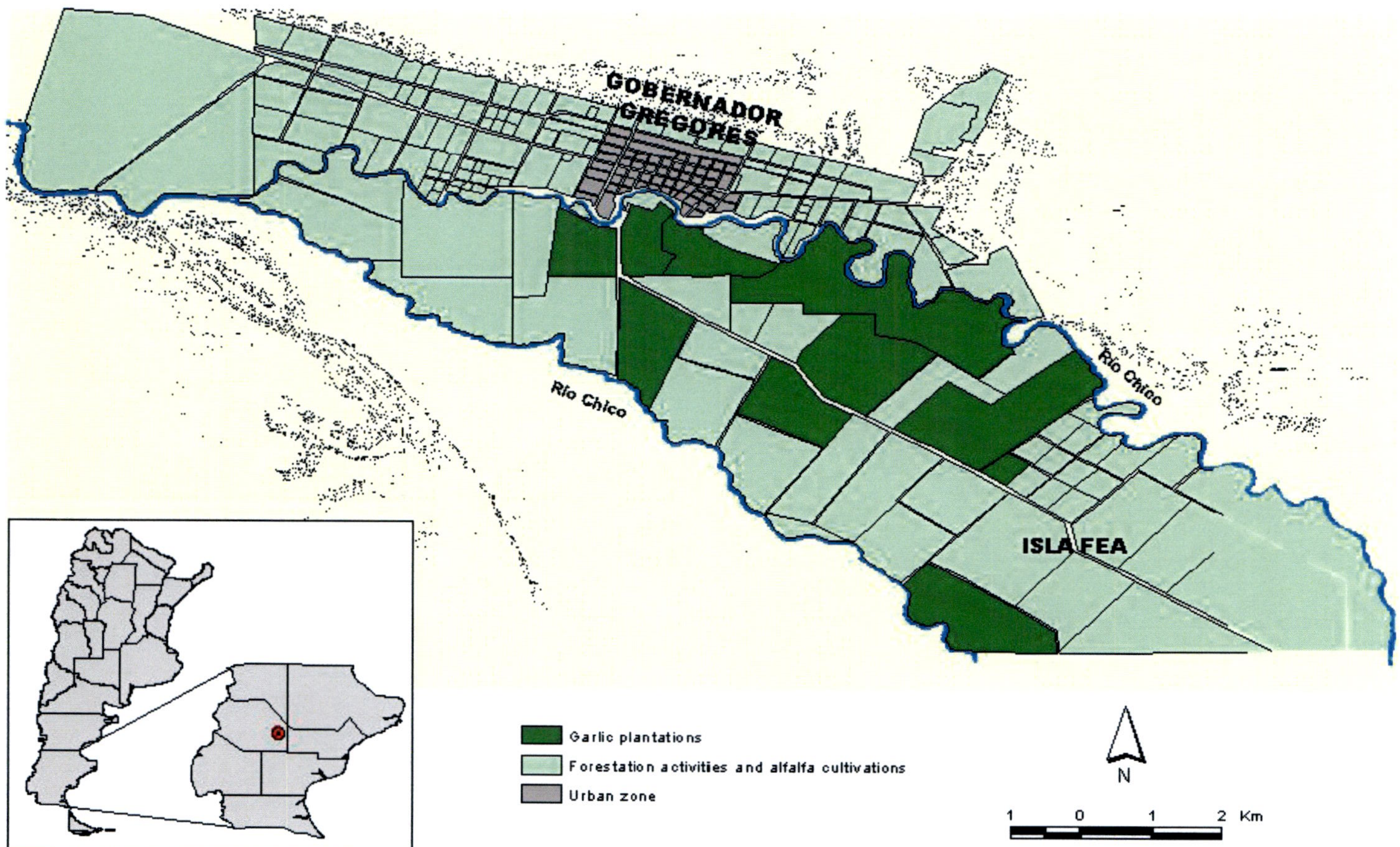

Source: Compiled by Mańa Cepparo based on Town Council Plans. Municipality of Gobernador Gregores, 2000.

Figure 3. Gobernador Gregores and its cultivated areas. Province of Santa Cruz. Patagonia Argentina. 2002.

The town's 2500 inhabitants are presently suffering from the consequences of overgrazing. More than 40% of the sheep farms, in the central and northern parts of the province, have been abandoned. The process of desertification on the Patagonian plateaus has caused this phenomenon, and rural workers have migrated. The traditional "chacras" (smallholding) production in Gobernador Gregores has been deeply affected by this process, because their main crop, alfalfa, has lost its markets. The rural exodus from the pastoral and agricultural sectors has also increased the number of employees in government organizations. More than 75% of the active labour force works in public administration, fundamentally in municipal and provincial sectors.

Some producers embarked on new ventures as a result of this crisis. Many began to cultivate a garlic variety which was not native to the region. The seeds, brought from Punta Arenas in southern Chile, were cultivated by a group of Croatian immigrants. The garlic bulbs are medium to large in size, have a violet and white colour and a pleasant smooth aroma. They are called "ajo violeta santacruceño" (Violet Santa Cruz Garlic). At first, the crops developed favourably. They did not show any symptoms of disease, tolerated frost well and had a similar performance to the main garlic production areas in the provinces of San Juan and Mendoza. There were also other factors which were beneficial to its cultivation: suitable soils, an agricultural tradition and abundant cost-free irrigation. The production from here was also available in the marketplace in the months when there was no supply from other production areas. At this point prices were higher and thus profitable.

The main cultivation incentive was the "Santa Cruz Garlic Programme", which was a result of Provincial Law N° 876, on 8 July 1994. Its contents included: the prohibition of the entry of seeds from outside the province, state loans, permanent technical assistance from the National Agricultural Technology Institute (INTA), and seed quality control.

Credit assistance was fixed between $8.000 and $20.000 (Argentine Pesos) per hectare. This covered the cost of the seeds and a large part of sowing expenses. The loan had a diminishing value, as the State was meant to be a promoter and not a crutch in this system. During the first four years -1995 to 1999- these amounts were maintained, and then were diminished to $2.000/ha, and only would be available only up until the time these crops could be consolidated. From 1999 a loan of $3.000/ha was provided. This was intended to aid harvest and post-harvest costs, which included selection and packing.

Two hectares of garlic were planted before the start of the Programme. This increased to 38 hectares in the 1996/97 season, following the loans, which totaled $230.600. In 1997, 100.000 kg of garlic was produced, with an average production of 6.000-7.000 kg /ha. In the 1997/98 season, 105 hectares were produced, using a total credit of $600.000. Approximately 100 labourers worked in the most productive seasons. Many of these workers are migrant labourers from other places, e.g. Bolivia. The plantations extended to Isla Fea and the banks of the Chico River in the General Gregores area (Figure 3). Alfalfa and oats had previously been cultivated on most of the plots here - the rest of the plots had previously been planted with carrot and potato crops. The Programme's success seemed to be guaranteed, even though its overseers were very cautious.

The "Santa Cruz Garlic Programme" facilitated the discovery of the comparative advantages of the province's climate for certain crops. Long cold winters, winds which constantly blow across virgin land, unpolluted water and the almost non-existence of diseases common to other places, made the use of pesticides unnecessary. These features have made this region into an ecological paradise without any additional production costs. Garlic seeds, flower bulbs, e.g. tulips, and other horticultural products such as potatoes are healthy and free from (chemical or other) contamination. These productions may be a future employment opportunity in the region. Also, these products could be sold to other areas in the country and the rest of the world, with quality and origin control certification, as is demanded by international markets.

The "Santa Cruz Garlic Programme" was the most important state project which promoted production expansion. It provided loans at low interest rates to those who were already cultivating garlic-seed or wanted to do so. These loans were offered by the government via the Agricultural Council and the Santa Cruz Provincial Bank. The loans were to be returned after each harvest. This plan was intended to last for 4 to 5 years.

At first, the seeds were overvalued – they were sold at between $4.50 and $5.00 per kilo. The reason for this was due to the enthusiasm created by the State loans and a supply of seeds, larger than the demand, was created.

The attractive initial price and high quality product, encouraged planting and technical aid provided by the State. Gobernador Gregores, with only 100 hectares of garlic farms, became one of the most important and highest quality garlic-seed producers in Argentina for a few years.

The majority of the producers used their profits for upgrading and improvements. These gains were used for the purchase and maintenance of machinery, irrigation-system improvement and the construction of sheds used for selection and packaging during the post-harvest stage. The profits were also used to extend the amount of cultivate land.

3.2.2. The Beginning of Problems

The problems began when the increased production saturated the local market. Assistance from INTA's agronomical engineers, brought in from other regions, helped resolve problems which in turn helped achieve higher productivity. Producers initiated different strategies in order to lower costs and compete in the domestic market. The average cultivated area was increased in order to achieve larger yields and superior crops. Soon afterwards the Chamber of Garlic Producers was founded, followed by the "Cañadón León" Cooperative. These institutions created and nurtured cooperative awareness and defended the sector's interests.

This Cooperative, comprising mainly farmers, was encouraged the community and created real employment sources. A small warehouse, provided by the government, was used. The infrastructure was basic and it had machinery for tilling, sowing and harvesting, as well machines for cleaning the garlic. Classification was done by simple equipment, and 10 kg boxes were packed by hand. The cooperative was responsible for making contacts within the national marketplace in order to commercialize the entire production. They also planned to make garlic paste[1].

When the loans ended, the project began to encounter serious problems. The farmers themselves had to go out into the national market. Here they encountered large volumes of garlic, from the traditional production areas in the country, which offered their goods at much lower prices. The timing of the search for foreign markets coincided with the Brazilian over-supply crisis where the product's value, of $0.80/kg, was very low. Competing with this price meant that production costs could not be covered. These events impeded further crop

---

[1] Opinions by Agronomical Engineer Oscar Maranzana, Subsecretary to the Production Division, Ministry of Economy, Santa Cruz Provincial Government, December 2000 and March 2002.

expansion and gave priority to garlic-seed production. Data from 2002 shows that prices fluctuated between $1.20 and $1.50/kg, and that the garlic was sold in Bahía Blanca, Cordoba and in the central market in Buenos Aires.

After the loans had been terminated, the benefits were carried over for one or two more years. Official credit institutions' debts were never paid back by the farmers. Of the 30 producers who were members of the cooperative in 1996, five cultivated garlic in 2000 and only two in 2002.

"Santa Cruz Garlic Programme" was only beneficial in the production stage. The provincial government was not aware of the other stages which involved industrialization, and marketing. Also, the cooperative's warehouse did not have the necessary size for storage, nor the infrastructure necessary for keeping the garlic fresh, until the products were sold during each season.

The Gobernador Gregores's case is a clear example of a small community with high expectations associated with an intense agricultural project. The system functioned while the programme operated. However, when loans were suspended, the initial boom died down and so did the interaction between public and private agents. Data from the 2002/03 harvest shows a notable decrease in the total area cultivated, where only 14 hectares of garlic were farmed.

Producers are currently waiting for new loans and subsidies in order to reinitiate their activities. The Cooperative does not have any leadership at present, and has not repaid their debts to the public institutions.

3.2.3. The Crisis Explained

The crises experienced outside the Pampas' economies are even more acute inside Southern Patagonia. In Gobernador Gregores the harvest volume was low in comparison to other production areas. The town is isolated from markets, there is a lack of basic infrastructure and tarred roads, and frequently, communications are interrupted due to weather conditions. These are factors which increase transportation costs[2]. The disadvantages of location, the high cost of materials and the domination of producers from other sectors, were the main problems encountered by the "Santa Cruz Garlic Programme".

There was a general understanding and coordination between public bodies and farmers as well as economic and technical state backing. However, they didn't achieve their goals; only a fictitious and temporary production was generated.

The producers enjoyed the success of this venture for only a few years. According to opinions from interviews, some of the economic and characteristic climatic problems in the region forced producers to return to fodder production. Only one producer, who has the largest amount of capital, has continued this endeavour. He has managed to establish international contacts and has begun commercialization with packaging as well as product diversification. The remaining farmers in the area have returned to producing alfalfa and oats and have doubts whether they will go back to garlic cultivation.

This situation has given rise to a series of questions regarding the causes of the project's weaknesses and interruptions.

- Was this project adequately promoted by government agents?

[2] Opinions by Gobernador Gregores Mayor, Agronomical Engineer Hector Spina, December 2000 and March 2002.

- Was the correct crop promoted?
- Was there a lack of unification by public policies and private agents?

Santa Cruz's community has always been strongly influenced by government bodies in their attitudes and initiatives. In the case of Gobernador Gregores, it was hoped to minimize the influence of these bodies minimized. However, the inhabitants asked for even more help and more time to return loans when they encountered their first problems. This confirms, firstly, that the community is used to depending on either public employment and/or livestock farming subsidies, and secondly, the population's weakness of identity in valuing their own resources, and their weakness in promoting their own local development. The provincial government only focused on short term planning and not on medium to long term strategies. Despite the fact that state bodies believed that the producers should be responsible for themselves, there was a lack of official guide-lines which should have included all the necessary steps. This was detrimental to product conservation and the production chain. Short term policies, and the lack of planning in the commercialization of the garlic, affected the continuity of this activity.

With respect to the crops, experiences and knowledge show that these crops reached expectations. They also have favorable comparative advantages; the plants are healthy and can be easily placed in the domestic market.

It is evident that in micro territories, such as Gobernador Gregores, it is necessary for local actors and public agents to agree on goals and to coordinate their planning. These initiatives should be based on the reality of environmental conditions, on the existing infrastructure, and market mechanisms. In these marginal spaces, the State should support potential economic sectors in order to prevent their weakening or disappearance.

CONCLUSION

My research in Patagonia has allowed me to confirm three points of view.

Firstly, I can illustrate the complexity and scope of marginality theory. It has allowed me to illustrate that there is no perfect union between reality and theories derived from developed countries.

Secondly, I can also show that there are certain signs of marginality, which exert more pressure, and thus are more influential than the impact of the global system. These signs are:

- Inconclusive community interest and incomplete participation in the state organizations' attitude.
- Local and regional environmental limitations. This factor impedes inhabitant and product circulation. This in turn hinders the advance of the productive boundary.
- Rural and small town exodus. These populations lack basic services and employment opportunities. They do not have authentic production alternatives.
- Abandonment or lack of interest by state agencies. This feature minimizes the importance of the amalgamation of policies. These factors retard local initiatives.
- The perception of abandonment. Communities have resigned themselves to this sensation, and tend to isolate themselves.

- -Isolation. This factor cannot always be measured as an absolute distance from regional centers. Distances may also be relative with regards to the proximity to basic services. Following my interviews with the region's inhabitants, I discovered that this provokes poor access or deprivation to technological innovations, and puts the preservation and continuity of local development projects at risk.

Thirdly, this study of the dynamics of an agrarian project in Southern Patagonia, allows me to put forward new reflections which may enrich the intrinsic relationships related to the concept of marginality. In marginal regions, I think that analyses should start with cultural characteristics. These include social attitudes and behaviour when confronting changes, risks and their alternative solutions provided by local and national agents. Often these solutions are neither integrated, harmonious nor coherent due to socio-economic and political conflicts and instability. These factors have proved to have more weight than environmental limitations.

I believe that there is no accurate definition of the marginality model. The questions formulated at the beginning of this paper have not been fully answered due to the confusing and complex reality and characteristics of Southern Patagonia. Finally I ask myself whether these regions have possibilities in the future. This is a difficult question to answer. Probably possible changes depend on the transformation in state organizations' attitude and continual community interest and participation. If this proposal becomes a reality, these regions could become a source of potential in the future.

REFERENCES

Alburquerque Llorens, F. (1995). *Espacio, territorio y desarrollo económico local.* Santiago de Chile: ILPES, Dirección de Políticas y Proyectos Sociales.

Andersson, L., Blon, T. (Ed.), (1998). *Sustainability and development. On the future of small society in dynamic economy.* Sweden: Motala Grafiska AB.

Arocena, J. (1995). *El desarrollo local, un desafío contemporáneo.* Caracas: Centro Latinoamericano de Economía Humana.

Cepparo de Grosso, M.E. (1992). "Hacia la búsqueda de relaciones más complejas entre las redes y los asentamientos de dos espacios australes fronterizos". In: *Anales del Instituto de la Patagonia*, v.22. (77-90). Punta Arenas, Chile: Universidad de Magallanes.

Cepparo de Grosso, M.E. (2000). "Desequilibrios y expectativas. Convivencia de dos procesos productivos de base agraria en la provincia de Santa Cruz". In: CD Rom *II Encuentro Internacional Humboldt,* Periferias, Regiones y Países, Mar del Plata.

Cepparo de Grosso, M.E. (2000). "El paisaje agropecuario de Santa Cruz. Una estructura territorial homogénea". In: *El Gran Libro de Santa Cruz.* (904-914). Madrid: Ed. Milenio.

Cepparo de Grosso, M.E. (2001). "Southern Patagonia facing globalization". In: *Globalization and marginality in geographical space.* (53-60). Aldershot: Ashgate.

Chang-Yi David Chang. Editor. (1994). *Marginality and development issues in marginal regions.* Taipei: National Taiwan University.

Claval, P. (1987). *Geografía humana y económica contemporánea.* Madrid: Akal.

Furlani de Civit, M.E., et al. (1991). "Las comunicaciones en las provincias de la frontera oeste argentina". In: *Boletín de Estudios Geográficos*, Vol. XXIV, n.87, *167-201*, Mendoza, U.N. de Cuyo.

Furlani de Civit, M.E. (1996). "Sinopsis". In: Furlani de Civit, M.E., Pedone, C. & Soria, N. (Eds.). *Development issues in marginal regions II: policies and strategies.* (XVII-XXVI). Mendoza: U.N. de Cuyo.

Furlani de Civit, M.E. & Gutiérrez de Manchón, M.J. (1996). "Posibilidades de desarrollo endógeno en centros menores de la provincia de Mendoza". In: *Mendoza una geografía en transformación.* (209-232). Mendoza: U.N. de Cuyo.

Furlani de Civit, M.E., Pedone, C. & Soria, N. (Eds.). (1996). *Development issues in marginal regions II: policies and strategies.* Mendoza: U.N. de Cuyo.

Furlani de Civit, M.E. & Gabay, E. (2003). El desarrollo local ¿utopía o realidad?. In: *CD Rom II Seminario Internacional "La Interdisciplina en el Ordenamiento Territorial.* Mendoza: CIFOT.

Jussila, H., Leimgruber, W. & Majoral, R. (Eds.). (1998). *Perceptions of marginality.* Aldershot: Ashgate.

Jussila, H. & Majoral, R. (Eds.). (2001). *Globalization and marginality in geographical space*, Aldershot: Ashgate.

Leimgruber, W. (1994). "Marginality and marginal regions: problems and definition". In: Chang-Yi David Chang. (Ed.).. *Marginality and development issues in marginal regions.* (1-15). Taipei: National Taiwan University.

Nogar, G. (1998). "Las estrategias adaptativas de los productores agropecuarios argentinos: el caso de la agroindustrialización de base rural". In: *Boletín de Estudios Geográficos.* Anejo del N° 93, T.II, *473-482*, Mendoza, U.N. de Cuyo.

Ostuni, J. (2002). "La significatividad del lugar desde la enseñanza de la Geografía". *Anales de la Sociedad Argentina de Estudios Geográficos.* (63-75). Buenos Aires, GAEA, v.21-22, T.II.

Revista Ventana Abierta, Río Gallegos, Año VII, n.60, *9-13*.

Rodríguez Gutiérrez, F. (1996). "El desarrollo local, una aplicación geográfica. Exploración teórica e indagación sobre su práctica". In: *Revista Eria.* Rev. Cuatrimestral de Geografía, Depto. de Geografía, U. de Oviedo, *57-73*.

Rofman, A. (1999). *Las economías regionales a fines del siglo XX.* Buenos Aires: Ariel.

Singh, R.B. & Majoral, R. Editor. (1995). *Processes, technological developments and societal reorganizations.* New Delhi: Oxford & IBH Publishing Co.

Vázquez Barquero, A. (1999). *Desarrollo, redes e innovación.* Madrid: Pirámide.

Wilson P. (1995). Reconociendo la localidad en el desarrollo local. In: *Revista Interamericana de Planificación.* n.112, *9-18*.

In: Argentina: Economic, Political and Social Issues
Editor: Jeanne B. Haverland
ISBN 978-1-60456-469-3

Chapter 8

THE FINANCIAL CRISIS IN ARGENTINA

J.F. Hornbeck

SUMMARY

Since 1991, Argentina has had a rigid meontary system bazsed on as currency board. Althought this policy tamed the country's hyperinflation, a prolonged recession, external economic shocks, and growing fiscal deficit have exposed its limitations as a policy tool, leading to a seemingly intractable debt problem. Argentina has rescheduled its financial obligation and reportedly sought assistance from the International Monetary Fund (IMF), including the $21.5 billion stand-by agreement of March 10, 2000. Speculation in the world markets over Argentina's now limited and painful options further undermines its credibility to orchestrate a smooth outcome, increasing fears of another round of regional or global financial turmoil that could adversely affect a variety of U.S. trade and financial interests.

Because of prolonged economic problems, Argentina's President Fernanado de la Rua called for his country to begin a "voluntary debt swap" in November 2001, exchanging $60 billion of government bonds for lower interest rate debt to free up some $4 billion in interest payments. To encourage bondholders to participate, new debt payments are to be guaranteed by future tax revenues. Argentina argues that this will reduce risk levels sufficiently to warrant the lower interest rate and to consider the exchange voluntary. Bondholders, however, argue that, between the lower value of the new debt and the implication that failure to restructure will result in nonpayment, the swap is a "distressed exchange" and hence, effectively a default; The IMF, after augmenting Argentina's standby credit twice during 2001, has remained silent this time. Argentina is straggling to maintain its currency board, enact some type of economic stimulus plan, achieve a zero deficit, and make payments on debt. The debt restructuring is the latest, and perhaps last, attempt to strike this difficult balance.

ECONOMIC STABILIZATION AND THE CURRENCY BOARD

Argentina's limited options to deal with its economic malaise are related directly to the decision to adopt a currency board in 1991, a strategy conceived to fight hyperinflation by putting in place a system that would curtail long-term undisciplined monetary and fiscal governance. Prior to 1991, Argentina had a history of economic and political turmoil that was accentuated in the 1980s by the Latin American debt crisis and repeated failed attempts to establish a credible and effective stabilization program. Policies changed dramatically in 1990 when voters elected the reform-minded Peronist candidate, Carlos Menem. This was no small feat. As one observer wrote, "President Alfonsín handed over the reins of government to Carlos Menem, in the first peaceful transfer of power in Argentina since 1928.[1] The Menem government brought a new era that had many believing Argentina had found a solution to its longstanding economic problems.

President Carlos Menem took an atypically anti-populist approach to governing for a Peronist, pushing major structural adjustment with deep tax reform, broad privatization, and reduced regulation and subsidies.[2] To combat inflation, in March 1991, Menem and his Minister of Economy, Domingo Cavallo, proposed a currency board. The congress approved it with passage of the Convertibility Law, which guaranteed government support for the convertibility of pesos to dollars at a one-to-one fixed rate and for printing pesos only in an amount necessary to purchase dollars in the foreign exchange market. Effectively, each peso in circulation was backed by a U.S. dollar and monetary policy was forcibly constrained to uphold that promise. By tying its currency and monetary policy to the United States, Argentina was able to achieve a similarly low inflation rate.

Equally important, the currency board also required a strong fiscal constraint because the restriction on monetary policy meant that a government deficit would have to be covered by debt rather than by printing money (monetized).[3] Therefore, the currency board raised hopes for a credible economic stabilization based on a compulsory monetary policy and implied new-found fiscal responsibility, both long absent in Argentina. The currency board operated well in the early 1990s. Stabilization brought lower inflation and interest rates, attracted new investment, and spurred economic growth. But its success hinged on continuing strong economic growth and disciplined macroeconomic policies, particularly if it were to weather the inevitable external shock. Three major "areas of vulnerability" were identified from the outset: the fiscal deficit, which was initially held at bay with privatization revenues; a real appreciation of the peso, making exports relatively more expensive and increasing the current account deficit; and the high cost of external debt, which deepened the deficit and dependence on capital inflows.[4]

---

[1] de Pablo, Juan Carlos. Three Major Debtors: Argentina. In Williamson, John, ed. *Latin American Adjustment: How Much Has Happened?* Institute for International Economics. Washington, D.C. 1990. p. 124.

[2] More on the reforms of this time can be found in Wise, Carol. Argentina's Currency Board: The Ties That Bind? In: Wise, Carol and Riordan Roett, eds. *Exchange Rate Politics in Latin America.* Washington, D.C. The Brookings Institution. 2000. pp. 96-99.

[3] See: CRS Report RL31169, *Argentina: Economic Problems and Solutions,* by Gall Maldnen.

[4] Dombusch, Rudiger. Progress Report on Argentina. In: Dombusch, Rudiger and Sebastian Edwards. *Reform, Recovery, and Growth: Latin America and the Middle East.* Chicago, -University of Chicago Press. 1995. pp. 224-29.

ECONOMIC CHALLENGES

One key to Argentina's economic problems in the late 1990s can be seen in the fmcal accounts in table 1. Although the consolidated primary fiscal deficit, which excludes interest payments, was often positive in the 1990s, the overall balance was consistently in deficit. This is one indication of how the interest payments on Argentina's high debt eroded efforts to balance the budget. Another indicator, the external debt service ratio, rose from 30.2% in 1995 to 84.4% in 2001. Only with the assumption of very high economic growth could Argentina (and its creditors) anticipate sufficient exports and public revenue collection to cover its obligations. The excessive optimism of this assumption became increasingly clear as Argentina entered in 1999 a recession, now in its fourth year, generating predictable shortfalls in both.

Table 1. Argentina: Selected Economic and Financial Indicators

GDP Growth (%)	**1995** -2.8	**1996** 5.5	**1997** 8.1	**1998** 3.8	**1999** -3.4	**2000** -0.5	**2001*** -1.4
Inflation - CPi (%)	3.4	0.0	0.6	0.9	-1.2	-0.9	-0.6
Unemployment Rate (%)	16.4	17.2	13.1	14.3	14.2	15.0	16.4
Consolidated Overall Fiscal Balance (GDP)**	-2.3	-3.2	-2.1	-2.1	-4.2	-3.6	-3.7
Consolidated Primary Fiscal Balance (% GDP)***	-0.4	-1.1	0.3	0.5	-0.8	0.5	1.5
Current Acct. Bal. (% GDP)	-2.0	-2.4	-4.2	-4.8	-4.2	-3.2	-2.9
Debt Service ratio (%)#	30.2	39.3	50.0	57.5	75.8	76.6	84.4
Terms of Trade Change	0.3	7.8	-1.2	-5.5	-5.9	10.4	-0.6

* = estimate. Sources: IMF web site http://www.imf.org

** Consolidated budget includes federal and provincial government budgets, trust funds, and capitalization of interest.

*** Primary balance does not include interest payments.

Interest and principal repayments on external debt as a percent of exports of goods and services.

Because much of Argentina's fiscal deficit was financed abroad, its foreign debt and debt service mounted, exacerbating fiscal and current account deficits. This precarious arrangement began to fall apart in the late 1990s when consecutive financial crises in Mexico, East Asia, Russia, and Brazil caused capital to flee emerging markets. Although it survived the Mexican, Asian, and Russian turmoil, the Argentine economy was devastated by spillover from the Brazilian devaluation in January 1999, raising for the first time concerns over the currency board's future.[5] Other factors worsened Argentina's situation. The cost of debt rose with interest rates in part because of rising rates in the United States, but also to cover the perceived added risk. Export revenue needed for debt service fell when the peso appreciated with the strengthening dollar and Argentina's terms of trade declined with lower commodity prices. In short, by the late 1990s, Argentina's current account, budget deficit, and debt position had all degenerated (see table 1).

[5] Wise, *Argentina's Currency Board: The Ties That Bind?*, pp. 101-06.

Two factors bear elaboration. First, the consolidated fiscal deficit captures both national and provincial government spending, suggesting that and fiscal excess has permeated all levels of government.[6] Although the national government has attempted to correct its deficit with tax reform and reduced spending, it has faced a major political battle with provinces over cutting their budgets and reducing federal transfers. Until local budgets are balanced, confidence in Argentina's fiscal policy will likely remain elusive. President de la Rua reached an accord on November 15, 2001 with a majority of governors that will allow for a 13% reduction in federal transfer payments in 2002, but it may fall short of both the budgetary savings and broad political support needed to resolve Argentina's problems. Second, Argentine exports became extremely dependent on the Brazilian market after creation of Mercosur (Mercado Comun del Sur-Southern Common Market) in 1991. From 1991 to 1998, Argentine exports to Brazil grew nearly four times as fast as to the rest of the world, with Brazil eventually having 30% of the Argentine export market. Brazil's financial crisis and sudden abandonment of its pegged exchange rate in early 1999 caused Argentine export revenues from Brazil to plunge by 28%, compromising its ability to service its debt, balance its budget, and meet the macroeconomic constraints needed to support the currency board.

At the heart of Argentina's policy conundrum lies the constraints inherent in having a currency board. The constraints are particularly apparent when faced with a hostile economic environment. For example, in countries with flexible exchange rates, a persistent current account deficit that is not financed by capital inflows would force the exchange rate lower until balance was restored. Given Argentina's fixed exchange rate, it can only address such a situation by allowing dollars to leave the country, thereby reducing the money supply, and causing domestic prices to fall (a de facto policy of deflation).[7] There is a hefty social cost to such a policy, Argentina's continuing recession and high unemployment. Under the constraints of the currency board, however, traditional fiscal and monetary policy responses are not available.

Given limited policy options, the de la Rua administration, again under the guidance of Minister of Economy Domingo Cavallo, opted for increasingly novel and desperate measures. In June 2001, some $29.5 billion of short-term debt was exchanged for new debt with longer maturities and higher interest rates. It was assumed that the return of strong economic growth would allow Argentina to cover the higher debt service. Argentina then altered the currency board by linking the peso exchange rate to both the Euro and the dollar for exports and imports only. This change effectively allowed for a 7% devaluation of the peso for foreign trading, improving Argentina's competitiveness in hopes of sparking the economy, presumably without compromising the fundamental monetary arrangement, which many observers question. Finally, both the federal and provincial governments have begun using their bonds as a form of script to pay public salaries and to circulate as currency in the economy. Currently, 15 provinces have some $1.5 billion of such script in calculation, which if printed without discipline, could serious erode confidence in the convertibility regime.

[6] See: Wise, Carol and Manuel Pastor. From Poster Child to Basket Case. *Foreign Affairs,* November/December 2001, p. 6.

[7] Makinen, Argentina: Economic Problems and Solutions, p. 3.

Debt Management and the IMF

As Argentina attempted to make internal adjustments, it was also forced to seek IMF assistance. As table 2 suggests, Argentina is no stranger to the IMF. Since the Latin American debt crisis in the 1980s, Argentina has tapped the IMF on average every two years and, in general, for increasingly large amounts of money. Argentina's current IMF stand-by arrangement was requested shortly after the President de la Rua took office in December 1999. The IMF approved a three-year agreement on March 10, 2000 for $7.2 billion (SDR 5.4 billion), replacing the extended arrangement in place since February 4, 1998. The credit was conditioned on a strict adjustment in fiscal balance based on the Fiscal Responsibility Law passed by the Argentine Congress in September 1999. Included was a reduction in transfers to provincial governments and their commitment to engage in budget cutting with the federal government as part of a broader revenue sharing reform effort. The arrangement also assumed that Argentina's economy would grow by 3.5% in 2000, and 4% in later years, which clearly did not happen.

Table 2. Argentina: History of IMF Lending (in millions of SDRs*)

Date of Arrangement	Date of Expiration	Facility	Amount Agreed	Amount Drawn	Amount** Outstanding
Dec. 28, 1984	June 30, 1986	Stand-by	1,182.5	1,182.5	0
July 23, 1987	Sept. 30, 1988	Stand-by	947.5	616.5	0
Nov. 10, 1989	March 31, 1991	Stand-by	736.0	506.0	0
July 29, 1991	March 30, 1992	Extended	780.0	438.8	0
March 31, 1992	March 30, 1996	Stand-by	4,020.3	4,020.3	1,318.1
April 12, *1996*	Jan. 11, 1998	Stand-by	720.0	613.0	133.8
Feb. 4, 1998	March 10, 2000	Extended	2,080.0	0	0
March 10, 2000	March 9, 2003	Stand-by	16,936.8	9,756.3	9,756.3
Jan. 12, 2001	Jan. 11, 2002	(of which			
Sept 7,2001	March 9, 2003	SRF#)	6,086.6	5,875.0	5,875.0
Total			27,403.1	17,133.4	11,208.2

Source: IMF website: http://www.imf.org.

* The Special Drawing Right (SDR) is the unit of account at the IMF, its value is based on a basket of currencies and fluctuates over time. As of October 2001 it was equal to approximately $1.30.

** Outstanding balance or mount to be repaid as of October 31 2001.

\# Supplemental Reserve Facility provides funds at higher rates and shorter maturities to countries that have experienced a sudden loss of market confidence, but have corrective reform measures in place.

Argentina's continued poor economic performance prompted the IMF to augment the original agreement on January 12, 2001 by $7.0 billion (SDR 5.2 billion). This was part of a larger package that included $5 billion in loan commitments from the Inter-American Development Bank (IDB) and the World Bank, $I billion from Spain, and voluntary refinancing from the private sector of $20 billion. The IMF advanced these funds with an expectation that the Argentine economy would grow by 2.5% in 2001, which also proved unattainable, leading to a third augmentation of $7.4 billion (SDR 5.6 billion) on September

7, 2001. This increase was also based on promises of strong fiscal reform as passed by the "Zero Deficit Law" on July 29, 2001, and continued efforts at revenue sharing reform with the provinces. Despite IMF funding, it became increasingly clear that the high cost of debt combined with recession and doubt over Argentina' s ability to make needed adjustments placed the country at the brink of default.

OUTLOOK

The prospect for a strong near term recovery in Argentina is poor. Argentina's hopes currently rest with the latest debt swap announced in November 2001. Although the plan is conceptually feasible, it raises significant questions and may have difficulty gaining credibility. The Argentine federal government has some $132 billion dollars in debt, $95 billion in bonds. The current proposal calls for $60 billion of bonds to be refinanced as a tax-receipt guaranteed loan. The swap would lower the average interest rate from between 11-12% to 7% and extend the maturity of the notes by three years. The expected savings is $4 billion, which would be used to finance a fiscal stimulus in the form of reduced pension fund contributions, lower taxes, and higher unemployment compensation. With offsetting lower interest costs, Argentina expects to have its fiscal stimulus and meet short-term fiscal targets, while keeping its currency board in tact.

Both sides of this plan have problems. First, the bond restructuring is offered as a "voluntary swap," but there is an implied understanding that failure to accommodate the Argentine government would lead to an outright default. The international bond rating agencies have designated it a "distressed exchange" and are treating it effectively as a default. The swap targets domestic bondholders first, with the expectation that they have little leverage to resist. The alternative, an outright default, risks bankruptcy for banks, pension funds, and insurance companies that hold large amounts of public debt. If successful, international bondholders are expected to cooperate in kind, which may be difficult without a stronger (IMF) guarantee of repayment. Second, a $4 billion fiscal stimulus would equal 1.3% of Argentina's GDP, but most of the net economic stimulus effect will likely come from the portion saved on foreign rather than domestic debt payments. Whether this is sufficient to pull Argentina out of recession is also unclear. What is clear is that without economic growth and a return to more reasonable lending rates, it is only a matter of months before Argentina again faces an intractable debt situation. It is in this context that confidence is lacking.

Ultimately, Argentina may still face the three difficult policy challenges: default (outright); devalue; and/or fully dollarize. Default would be costly, but debt rescheduling now seems unavoidable. Devaluing would allow for monetary policy to inject liquidity, but at the risk of collapsing the financial system given the high percentage of dollar denominated debt and deposits. Dollarizing the economy seems like the next and least painful step given that the dollar dominates already. This solution would probably lend an element of stability and confidence to the economy, but would not remove the monetary constraint on Argentina's ability to address its deflationary-recession spiral.

U.S. interests involve investment and trade relationships in Argentina and the region, as well as concern over broader political stability. To the extent that Argentina's economy collapses entirely, it could disrupt current efforts to push ahead with the Free Trade Area of the Americas (FTAA) and risk some retrenchment in political relations both with the region and the United States. Chile and Brazil, the other major Southern Cone economies, are watching Argentina closely, cautiously evaluating the potential for significant spillover effects should Argentina default or devalue. Chile is in sound financial and economic shape and Brazil has taken measures to strengthen its financial reserves and adopt more conservative fiscal and monetary policies. Currently, the United States has been verbally supportive of Argentina's plan, but has not offered any concrete policy response. Support for large financial bailouts does not appear to exist and market responses have factored in possible future losses to U.S. businesses. In any case, short of a massive bailout from abroad, it appears that Argentina is the master of its own fate, which currently points to future political as well as economic uncertainty.

INDEX

A

B

C

D

E

F

I

S

T

U

V

W

Y